THE *NEW* NORMAL

Coming Out as Transgender in Midlife

Jennifer M. Booker, Ph.D.

This edition is published by
The Unbound Press in 2019

www.theunboundpress.com

Hey unbound one,

Welcome to this magical book brought to you by The Unbound Press.

At The Unbound Press we believe that when women write freely from the fullest expression of who they are, it can't help but activate a feeling of deep connection and transformation in others. When we come together, we become more and we're changing the world, one book at a time!

This book has been carefully crafted by both the author and publisher with the intention of inspiring you to move ever more deeply into who you truly are.

We hope that this book helps you to connect to your Unbound Self and that you feel called to pass it on to others who want to live a more fully expressed life.

With much love,

Nicola Humber

www.theunboundpress.com

Table of Contents

Table of Figures

Table of Tables

Praise for *The New Normal*

'Dr. Jennifer Booker is one of the most courageous women I know. She has generously shared her comprehensive knowledge and experience in all aspects of transitioning. The attendees of my Erotic Literary Salon were privileged to hear some of her heartfelt stories (some retold in this book) as she embarked on her journey from Glenn to Jennifer.'

Susana Mayer, Ph.D.
Founder and Host of the Erotic Literary Salon

'This is storytelling! Thank you, Jennifer, for sharing your story so openly. I learned. I cried. I laughed. This is a fantastic read that leaves the reader fascinated, enlightened and more understanding.

I am loving this book! What a page turner! Jennifer's candor vividly tells her story in such a captivating way. It is entirely infectious. This book takes the reader on a gripping journey. It is informative, smart and thoroughly eye-opening.'

Bernadette Pleasant
Creator of Femme!

'It's not unusual for me to take 6 months' worth of beach days to finish a book. I completed *The New Normal: Coming Out as Transgender in Midlife* in 3 sittings.

Jennifer Booker tells a story that is brilliantly evocative in its colorful narrative of the pedestrian aspects of everyday life. I found this presentation humanizing and compelling. With curiosity and humor, she moves us away from the often-salacious portrait of transwomen presented by the media to a practical one, like managing the lack of pockets in women's clothing and discovering that urinating with a vulva is messier than with a penis because pee can dribble into your butt crack, which gave me a chuckle because I never thought of it before, but it's so true!

Raw, honest, and tender, it's a story that lingers in your mind and I found myself thinking about Jennifer a number of times after I finished reading. Her pre-transition love letter to Jennifer, saying "thank you for being patient with me. It's taken a long time to acknowledge you" was an incredibly powerful moment in the book and made me weepy.

But for as much as Jennifer, or Dr. Booker I should say, lets us in on the emotional, there's no doubt she's a true academic and scientist. I loved the analytical approach to this storytelling, cracked a smile at her organized charts on everything from the different collar styles in clothing designed for men vs women to her Gender Affirmation Surgery preparation timeline, and delighted in her thorough citations (she even cited her sources in her coming out letter to her family, which I found absolutely charming).

The New Normal is the story of coming out as transgender at age 50, but is also the story of a DOER. Jennifer Booker inspires with how she jumps into living with both feet, sharing her hobbies in flying planes, sewing clothes, cycling, ballet, massage therapy, writing, burlesque, and soccer to name just a few. She's gifted us with both a memoir of a whole human with a rich life and a helpful guide for trans folks considering transitioning or allies wanting to learn what to (and not to do) to support a transgender loved one.'

Jill McDevitt, Ph.D.
Sexologist and Sexuality Educator for Adults.

'A straightforward, unflinching story of one person's gender transition that demystifies the process from beginning to end. The factual and academic information coupled with the personal journey reveals the complex road and basket of complicated decisions a transgender person must face. The direct and chronological unfolding of the story manages to normalize what can often be seen from the outside as either a courageous or foolish act – which ultimately is the point: the greatest act of bravery is sometimes being oneself.'

Monica Anna Day
Founder, MAD Life LLC

Dr. Jennifer Booker's captivating autobiographical account of her transformation is both earnest and informative, and at times heartbreaking. The word chutzpah was made for women like her. She chronicles how her early experiences with sexuality and disability shaped her journey, and weaves together a complex narrative of the intersectionality of these experiences that help us to understand the social construction of femininity. The resulting manuscript is appropriate for diverse audiences, people considering GCS, and people trying to understand the transgender experience, be they members of the LGBTQIA+ community, medical professionals, scholars of gender, disability and queer studies, as well as, the curious public striving to understand social change.

Jennifer Rode, Ph.D.
University College London

Trigger Warnings and Disclaimers

This book is completely uncensored and is intended for a mature audience. It contains frank, explicit discussion and descriptions of medical issues and procedures, suicide ideation, eating disorders, sexual harassment, far too many forms of abuse, and sexuality. And some curse words.

Sections prefixed 'The Dark Side' (that's a Star Wars reference, not racial) **are most likely to be triggering.** You have been warned!

Some names have been changed or deliberately omitted for various reasons.

Outline

The structure of this book was intended more for an academic audience that might want to pick selected chapters for various audiences. As a result, it doesn't read much like a traditional autobiography, but instead has chapters that may be of interest to students and academics in psychology, gender or queer studies, sociology, or nursing.

The first two chapters are a mostly topical autobiography of my life from birth to age 18 (Chapter 1) and 18 to about 48 (Chapter 2). The purpose of chapters 1 and 2 is to provide the context for understanding my experiences that colored my coming out and transition.

Chapter 3 discusses the events leading up to my coming out as transgender. Chapter 4 discusses coming out to myself, i.e. when I first realized I was transgender, and the short-term aftermath of that revelation. Chapter 5 discusses going on hormone therapy and its effects. Chapter 6 describes how I came out to my friends, family, and at work. Chapter 7 describes the process I went through for gender confirmation surgery, from preparation through recovery. Chapter 8 describes the challenges of changing one's name and gender marker (M to F). Chapter 9 discusses the social and sexual implications of my transition and Chapter 10 speculates on what the future might hold, both for me and for other transgender people.

Appendix A defines terminology and acronyms, especially for medical and gender theory concepts. Appendix B contains the 340+ references cited throughout the document. Appendices C through G are cited as needed. Enjoy!

Instructor Guidance

I have deliberately included many references in this book to make it more useful to a wide range of audiences. The academic citations are each discussed briefly and provide a starting point for more in-depth study. Reflection questions are at the end of every chapter to provide inspiration for written assignments or oral discussion.

Various audiences might want to focus on specific chapters and their associated Appendices.

- **Transgender people and their loved ones** are the primary audience. They can benefit from all of this book. I have included much detail about what I did throughout this transformation, to help you become better prepared for what you or your loved ones might experience. I have included my life experiences before coming out, and the social, psychological, fashion, medical, legal, financial, and sexual impact on my life.
- **Students of gender and queer theory, and social sciences (psychology, sociology, etc.)** can benefit most from chapters 1-4, 6, and 8-10. I have included a sizeable amount of self-analysis to make this more an autoethnography than just an autobiography. When studying feminist theory and queer theory, I read autobiographical works to help understand peoples' lived experiences; that was part of the inspiration for writing this book. I have compared my experiences to relevant literature whenever possible.

- **Students of medical sciences (nursing and medical professionals**) can benefit most from chapters 5 and 7. I describe details of going on hormone therapy and the day-by-day process of preparing for and recovering from gender confirmation surgery. If you are caring for transgender patients or are going to perform these procedures, these chapters will give you detailed insight into my experiences.

Foreword

Hi, I'm Jennifer! I'm a transsexual lesbian. This is my story.

This is an autobiography with emphasis on the most recent six years of my life (2012-2018). I came from a very ordinary Caucasian, Midwest, American, Christian family. My mom was a cheerleader in high school, my father was an Army officer and later German professor, and my brother became a philosophy professor (okay, that part is a little odd). I've earned three engineering degrees and worked in the aerospace and defense industries before becoming a professor of computing. I didn't realize I was transgender until shortly before my 50th birthday, and since then have gone through a very rapid transition. I am now legally and medically recognized as a woman.

I'm sharing my story because I want to:

1) Let other transgender people learn from my transition and experiences
2) Help the friends and family of transgender people appreciate the massive thought and effort that goes into coming out and choosing whether and to what extent to transition
3) Help the public get a better understanding of how diverse the transgender community is
4) Help myself process these very rapid recent changes in my life, and capture them in writing for posterity
5) Help everyone understand how important it is to trust you own instincts, to trust messages from your body to help point you to the right relationships and career choices.

I'm including extensive cross references to academic sources and feminist theory so that this book could also be used to support courses on queer theory, psychology, feminist theory, social work, nursing, and related medical and social sciences. There is a Reflection section at the end of every chapter to provide questions for possible classroom discussion, personal exploration, or additional research. Intersectionality disclaimer: my experiences are colored by some degree of privilege (being Caucasian and middle class) but also by a history of abuse and disability.

The media are full of prominent transgender women (e.g. Caitlyn Jenner, Laverne Cox, and Janet Mock) whom I consider hyper-feminine – they wear heavy makeup and wigs constantly, their appearance is almost as exaggerated as drag queens. Transgender women aren't all that way. For me, my transition to being recognized as a woman is a brazen act of authentic living in part because I don't live an exaggerated flavor of feminine just for the sake of fitting in better. 'Passing' as a woman isn't needed or a relevant concept for me, because I AM a woman.

This is who I am. I refuse to hide.

In that same breath, I realize that living as a woman who is obviously transgender has its risks. I have had to learn how to handle verbal and sexual harassment on the streets. I am misgendered far more often than not. And while unlikely, I realize there is a small chance someone might try to attack or kill me for being who I am. This decision wasn't made lightly.

I described my motivation for writing about my experiences in a term paper (Glenn Booker, 2013c) for a Women's Studies 101 class which I happened to take the same time as I was coming out as transgender (wasn't that convenient?), where I wrote:

> *I'm being brutally honest about my past and my present because working with Monica [Day] has taught me the value of sharing genuine authentic emotions and experience. For me it is liberating. It allows the unspoken to see the light of day, to help dispel the demons and unveil the shameful secrets. For the audience it can inspire them to share their world just as openly. Everyone wins. Everyone emerges stronger and more confident and more fully present in their bodies. As I described it in a recent Facebook post "As I discover who I am and find the best ways to express it, I'm reminded that my struggle might help others who follow to find their path. That, and it's often a flock of a lot of fun!"*

So, why do it? Why take the risk? The reward is that I get to be authentic. I get to be completely and honestly me. **It took half a century and admitting something so completely radical that it was literally unthinkable, for me to get to this point.** Now I look forward to the next chapters of my life.

This book is dedicated to the Sacred Whore,
without whom my journey would still be on hold.

Acknowledgements

I'd like to thank my parents for moving mountains to deal with my special needs as a child, and for not having a coronary when I came out.

Thanks to Monica Day and Michele Younger for nurturing my coming out; and to Susana Mayer, her Erotic Literary Salon, and Paulette Booker for exceptional support during my transition.

Thanks to the Philadelphia Falcons soccer league for unquestioning acceptance, and my Sister Goddesses from the School of Womanly Arts for showing me what true sisterhood feels like.

Thanks to the reviewers for their feedback and quotes. I'm humbled by your responses to this work. Finally, thanks to Nicola Humber and The Unbound Press for being the perfect publisher for this work.

Chapter 1 – My Foundation - Childhood

In order to appreciate the enormity of my recent transformation, it would help to have a brief summary of the first fifty-ish years of my life. As Julie Andrews famously sang, let's start in the very beginning (elanor1987, 2011). This Chapter covers my childhood through age 18. Chapter 2 covers my adulthood up to shortly before coming out to myself as transgender. Instead of doing a purely chronological narrative, I've broken it into major topics and themes, organized somewhat chronologically within each chapter.

Broken from the start

My parents are very traditional Midwest USA stock. My father is from Wyoming and western Nebraska, both areas noted for being extremely conservative politically and socially. He escaped from his blue-collar roots by getting accepted to West Point (USMA, 2017), the US Army's military college. Between rounds of being tortured by his superior officers there, he was introduced by his Aunt Kay to my mother, a recent High School graduate from Omaha, NE where my Aunt also lived. They flirted via letters and occasional meetings in person and married shortly after he graduated from college.

They were soon stationed in Bavaria, where my older brother Michael and I were both born in US Army hospitals; he in Augsburg, I just south of Műnchen (Munich). I was a complete pain from before birth. My mother contracted toxemia (now called preeclampsia (Research, 2018a)) whilst carrying me, which was viewed as a threat to my life, so I was induced to be born about 4-6 weeks early – basically as early as could be viable at the time. Spoiler alert: I lived! I was born a hair over 5 lbs., which was the goal weight for me.

Within two weeks of being born, doctors realized I hadn't finished incubating yet. My left hip socket wasn't fully formed, and my left femur (thigh bone) was bowed outward. I was put in a cast from the waist to ankles to allow my hip to finish forming. Even after my hip finished forming, the bowing resulted in my left leg being substantially shorter than the right, a situation which has haunted my life. My dad later told me how fun it wasn't to have a newborn in a lower body cast. After all, I was nowhere near toilet trained, so I'm told I peed all over the plaster cast. If you've never seen one, plaster casts are great at absorbing liquids, so I stank something fierce!

Months later, the doctors feared I was developing an overly large head, technically called macrocephaly (H. Media, 2018). My father was away on military maneuvers, so my mom flew me to doctors elsewhere in West Germany to see if I had that condition. They concluded "No, I just had a big head." Still do. Most 'one size fits all' hats don't fit me.

Being born prematurely and constantly having life interrupted for surgeries made it harder for me to be held. My dad commented on how easy it was to hold my brother right after he was born, and how frustrating it was in contrast for me not to be held much of the time. This was one of the most tender observations I've heard him make.

By age two years, I was surgically treated for the difference in my leg lengths. This was done in various ways again at ages 4, 6, 12, and 14 years, including breaking my left femur surgically three times to 'encourage it to grow.'

I don't have conscious memory of the surgeries at ages 2 and 4. At age 6 doctors installed turnbuckles to try to stretch the bone as it was healing. The turnbuckles were unbelievably painful (think of the rack used during the Spanish Inquisition), and put me in a Shriner's Hospital for Crippled Children (Children, 2018) for three months to recover. After these surgeries I was typically in a plaster cast from waist to left ankle, or even above the waist to ankle. Once the casts were removed, I faced months of rehab to learn to walk AGAIN, restore some range of motion, and start strengthening muscles which had atrophied under the plaster.

The surgery at age 12 was to slow the growth of my right femur (more precisely, killing the distal epiphyseal growth plate), so that in theory my legs would even out by the time I finished growing up. It didn't work. I learned the term 'epiphysiodesis' as a result of this surgery (W. Foundation, 2017c), which I can safely say is not usually part of a seventh grader's vocabulary. This was the only time I had surgery on my right leg; all of the rest focused on the left.

By age 14 the doctors realized that my left knee was misaligned as a result of the bowing, and tried to address that, but only after breaking it for the last time. I got a severe infection in my left femur, resulting in the use of an experimental device from Switzerland called a Hoffman Apparatus (Lawyer & Lubbers,

1980) to stabilize my left femur without using a traditional plaster cast. I spent three weeks in the hospital on IV antibiotics to squelch the bone-deep infection that followed. The Hoffman Apparatus was three groups of three surgical steel pins screwed into or through the bone and connected externally with a set of clamps and rods to stabilize both sides of the fracture (Figure 1). My mother kept asking to take a picture of the device, and I kept refusing. I'd have no problem remembering it. Ever. Somewhere I still have the pins that were in my leg. #WorstSouvenirsEver

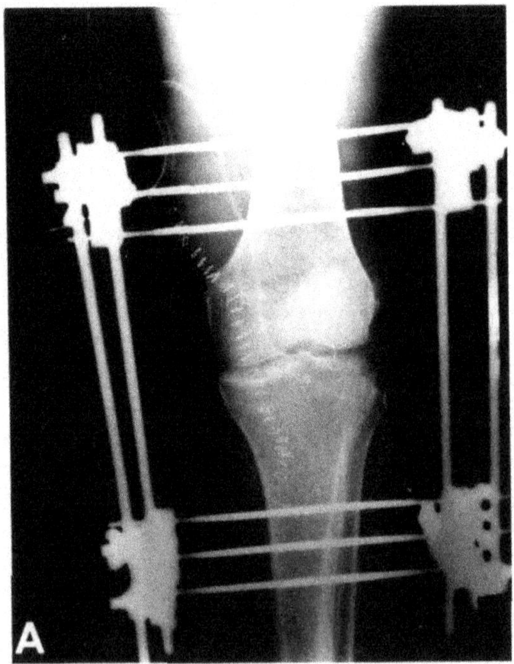

Fig. 1A: Anteroposterior view with external-fixation device (Hoffman apparatus).

Figure 1. X-ray of a Hoffman Apparatus
(Unknown, Unknown-a)

I chose an X-ray to keep from being quite as graphic (and self-triggering) as a photo. In my case the apparatus was on my left femur, not spanning a knee.

Figure 2 shows me with my maternal grandparents (Fred and Esther Glammeier) and brother Michael. I was 15 in this picture, about a year after the last surgery. The scars on my left knee are still red, and you can see how atrophied my left thigh is. I was also scary thin, under 100 lbs while still in the hospital. At one point the nutritionist came and asked me what I wanted to eat. ANYTHING I wanted to eat. They brought me a steak. #BestHospitalFoodEver My brother is only 18 months my senior, but you can easily see how different our sizes are.

Family trivia: My grandpa was born in 1899, making him the only person I knew who saw the 19th century. He served briefly in World War I.

Figure 2. My maternal grandparents and I on the sofa, my brother on the floor

The ends of the Hoffman Apparatus pins were abruptly cut with something like bolt cutters, so they were very sharp. Some of the ends were near the outside upper part of my left thigh, so my hand would get scratched against them sometimes. The pins that ended along my inner thigh were supported by a steel rod to prop them up. I later learned the support was padded with a feminine napkin, which embarrassed me at the time. After all, anything feminine is embarrassing, right?

After coming home with the Hoffman Apparatus, normal activities like bathing became a bizarre challenge. Depending on who was home at the moment, I'd have to get two people to help ease me into a bathtub, one supporting me under my shoulders, and one lifting my errant leg for me and trying not to cause massive pain while lowering it into the water.

I distinctly recall when my brother got the latter duty. Every time he was careful not to look at me, as if he were somehow in danger of catching a birth defect. And his breathing became really weird. He would hold his breath for a long time, and exhale through his mouth, all the while studiously avoiding any sign of interaction with me. As if he were thinking "It's okay, I'm just here to act like a crane and help move this inanimate object, so I'm going to distance myself from the situation as much as possible." I guess I can't blame him though, I'd be weirded out too if I had to help a sibling with basic self-care, especially at that age.

Refined versions of the Hoffman Apparatus are still in use. When I was looking for dissertation projects, I turned down the chance to work with them for DuPont in Delaware. That would have been WAAAAAY too triggering for me!

Growing up cripple

My physical deformity, while minor in severity compared to many people's, had a huge impact on my childhood. Normal school and social activities were interrupted so often that I identified mostly as a cripple rather than as a person. After all, it's okay to stare at a cripple because they aren't really human, right? This was long before the days of 'politically correct' behavior and facility accommodations to meet the Americans with Disabilities Act (U. D. o. Justice, 2018), so I was relegated to mostly non-person status in many eyes.

Decades later, my mother would still summarize concern for my perceived physical limitations with an impassioned cry of "your leg!" which meant to me "you seem to have forgotten that your left leg is extremely fragile, so you'd better not do anything that will make it shatter into a million pieces and never recover." In the last decade or two I've done a lot of very physical activities to shake off the ghosts of the past, but it's very hard to erase such deeply ingrained thoughts and behaviors.

I tried to have fun with it when possible. I carry some 30" of scars, mostly on my left thigh and knee, so they are quite obvious when I wear shorts. When on the beach, sometimes children would silently approach me, look at my scars, look at my face, then back at the scars. Too afraid to ask me, I'd quietly say just "shark" and they'd run off! I confess being slightly evil. But only slightly.

Growing up as a cripple left me with a tremendous sense of weakness and vulnerability. My body was a scary place: brittle, troublesome, and barely functional. As I recovered from each set of surgeries, my rehabilitation kept to very minimal goals. Get me able to walk, go up and down stairs, and later be able to drive a car. There were no expectations of ever being able to go beyond that. No one in my family was athletic, so there was no pressure to do anything physically challenging.

As a result of years of going in and out of hospitals, I habitually favored my left leg to an amazing extent. I used my right leg for 99% of support of my body weight on a locked knee, and my left leg just went along for the ride, at most acting like a pirate's peg leg for temporary support. I didn't realize this until almost age 30 when I started learning massage therapy. That's a later story to tell.

Hospitals and consent

Another key aspect of my childhood was the hospital environment. It took me a long time to realize that hospitals are designed for the convenience of the people who work there, not the patients. Adults in that environment can often understand that, and the reason for the way things are done in a hospital setting, but children don't understand consent and may not understand most of what's going on. Nurses and doctors may do very invasive things to a patient to provide routine care, but how do we convey that to children who may feel traumatized or violated by repeated poking, prodding, injections, and intimate examinations? In a hospital you lose autonomy over your own body and often over your basic bodily functions. Shortly after mastering toilet training, a child can be subjected to having to ask permission to perform basic elimination functions. If and when and what you are allowed to eat are carefully controlled by mysterious outside forces in white coats. Intimate areas of your body are no longer private and may be examined by any number of strangers who come and go from your room at will, with at most the slightest pretense of getting your permission. These scenarios can be repeated dozens or hundreds of times in a hospital stay, reinforcing the sense of non-ownership of your body.

Is it possible that children in repeated hospitalizations can experience symptoms like those of PTSD? A cursory review of literature shows a lot of focus on PTSD in children with cardiac defects, but little about other congenital defects. Dr. Bruce examined the effects of having a child with disabilities on their parents, and the resulting PTSD that can occur (Bruce, 2000), but no one seems to have investigated the effects of repeated hospitalization on children in terms of PTSD. This is a question I'd love to investigate, but I'm sure no journal would ever publish it. In my case, I'm sure that my extensive hospitalization history led to a lack of feeling of ownership and control over my body.

Constantly moving

Another key feature of my childhood was moving. My father was in the Army when I was born, so we moved a lot for the first few years of my life, but even after he left the Service, we moved four more times from my ages 5 to 13 because of him going to graduate school and then having a couple of very disloyal employers. He was told lovely things like "nothing personal, we're just getting rid of your department next year." In order, I lived in West Germany[1] (2 years?), Fort Benning, Georgia (2 years?), Omaha and Lincoln, Nebraska (4 years total, through second grade), Mayen, West Germany (1 year, 3rd grade), Spokane, Washington (1 year, 4th grade), Wheaton, Illinois (3 years, grades 5-7), finally settled in Mankato, Minnesota for the rest of my childhood (5 years, grades 8-12) and then Minneapolis, MN through my Bachelor's degree. As a result of all this moving, I craved stability, I craved putting down roots some place. This craving may have contributed to some very poor decisions later in life.

On the bright side, I can narrow down any event in my childhood to within a year of when it happened just by knowing where we were living at the time.

Bicycling

A small part of me resisted my physical limits as a child. Around age 11, I became fond of bicycling. On a whim in a convenience store in Illinois, I bought a copy of *Bicycling* magazine (Unknown, 2018). I read of people riding bikes on long trips, seeing the country, even touring the world, and I looked to that to expand my limited physical horizons. We lived near a set of railroad right-of-way paths that had been converted into bicycle trails. I'd ride for miles on these trails, only occasionally crossing active streets, and enjoying this

---

[1] It was still West Germany, long before reunification took place (Geary & Turner, 2018).

little taste of freedom. I remember stopping at a little convenience store to get a can of Pepsi and being appalled that it cost 35 cents instead of the usual 25 or 30. Highway robbery! J

In an act of pure optimism, I even got a bicycle racing license once. Ok, I never used it, and I went on exactly one training ride with someone and realized I couldn't begin to keep up. A deep gulf between what I want my body to do and what it actually does or can do has been a recurring challenge throughout my life.

Bicycling was an odd choice for avocation, since I did almost nothing with my left leg, and powered myself with the right. That was normal for me though, so I didn't think anything of it at the time. It was my normal. As a result, my right leg was easily 3-4 times stronger than my left, which only reinforced my lopsided bias even more. I got so into bicycling that I convinced my parents to let me spend my life's savings ($288, if memory serves) on a very good 10-speed bicycle, from a British company called Viscount (Figure 3).

Figure 3. A Viscount bicycle (busaste, 2009)

Bicycling gave me a chance to do something physical, to experience the freedom of the wind in my face, and my parents supported my hobby. After moving to Minnesota, my parents and I even went on Century bike rides a few times, where the goal is to ride 100 miles in one day. I finished at least once – probably the biggest physical achievement of my childhood. Another time I gave up about 15 miles short of the finish line.

Trivia and praise for intellect

Since my physical world was fairly small, I explored the world through reading as a child. I read trivia books voraciously, and spent hours reading things like the Guinness Book of World Records (Records, 2018). I learned about adult life through catalogs – Sears, JC Penney's, and later through mail order catalogs corresponding to my hobbies. In that era, you had to get printed catalogs mailed to you after calling a toll-free number to request them; we didn't have the Internet for shopping! Through trivia I learned the limits of the physical and animal worlds, people, and technology. I ruined my eyesight by reading at night by only the light of a nightlight and had to get glasses in about sixth grade. I soon learned the despised nickname 'four eyes.'

I learned by junior high school that I was somewhat gifted intellectually and relied on praise for my brain above all else. My physical expectations were nil, and as a result of being the school cripple my social life was minimal, so I was taught to emphasize my intellect. Intellect is a double-edged sword, I soon discovered, as classmates who couldn't keep up with me mocked me. "Poindexter," after the scientist cartoon character (Figure 4), was a nickname for me in junior high. I was baffled that being smart was considered a bad thing. Still am.

Figure 4. Poindexter cartoon character, from Felix the Cat (tvtropes.org, Unknown)

Bored by the lack of intellectual challenge in elementary and secondary school, I napped a lot during study hall and waited impatiently to go to college, where I fervently hoped for more interesting studies AND more interesting peers.

Follow the rules

From an early age I learned to follow the rules and get rewarded (or at least not punished) for doing so. My father was a fairly strict disciplinarian, possibly thanks to his even more strict upbringing and Army background, and corporal punishment was still the norm in that era.

Okay, I was afraid of my father as a child, and that was serious motivation to behave.

More generally, I was taught to play by the rules, and so I eagerly looked for the rules in any situation so I could know how to behave. I noticed that my mom was very concerned about others' opinions – as in the trope 'what would the neighbors think?' Between these two I quickly learned to seek out the status quo and make sure I didn't deviate from it. This could account for much of the reason I repressed any hint of my transgender nature for decades.

My brother and I both used the stereo in the living room to listen to records, and my ears got well calibrated to the loudest that was allowed, or our father would have us turn it down. We listened to various forms of now-Classic rock music (Styx, Heart, Queen, Foreigner – typical 1970's and 80's fare), and our father only listened to classical music and some band music. Music was another case of having clearly defined rules and needing to comply with them over and over again.

I recall in about 5th grade I was in the school library and there was some playful music in the background. I was leaning over and had my hands on a table and started playfully bouncing my butt up and down to the music. One of my teachers, a gruff man in his 40's or so, saw me and gave the biggest scowl I had ever seen. Ok, duly noted, I thought, DON'T EVER DO THAT AGAIN!

Religion

Religion was a background constant in my childhood. My parents were raised Baptist (father) and Lutheran (mother), so as a compromise we went to whatever Protestant-ish church they liked in town, mostly leaning more to the Baptist side. Mom always seemed more strongly religious, my father went more for the music (such as singing in the choir) and didn't seem as personally connected to the theological aspects, though he studied them a great deal and often taught adult Sunday school.

I was baptized about age nine and identified as Christian throughout my childhood. Once we moved to Minnesota, I was active in the church Youth Group for about five years. That was probably the strongest social circle I had in late childhood. In addition to weekly meetings before church, we went to a few bible study camps, and every June after school let out we went on a canoe trip to the Boundary Waters Canoe Area (W. Foundation, 2018b) on the Minnesota-Canada border. We'd drive to its southern border, canoe and portage a few lakes into the wilderness, and camp and go fishing for a few days amidst the billions of mosquitoes. It was a fun way to unwind after the school year and made us grateful for luxuries like indoor plumbing and food that had not been dehydrated. I learned important lessons like "don't ever get dehydrated peanut butter." It's truly awful, or at least was then.

Flying

In late childhood, I developed a love of airplanes and flying. Starting in junior high I learned how to make balsa and tissue-paper model airplanes from my father and made models of many early 20th century aircraft. Just for the record, my favorite airplanes were the Fokker Triplane (World War I), P-38 Lightning (World War II), and the SR-71 Blackbird (Cold War). I spent hours in my room making these models. They never flew, they were just static examples.

My love of flying led to my learning to be a pilot. In high school I took a class on aviation, and that class prepared us to take the FAA written exam for Private Pilot. I barely passed with a 70%, but that was quite an accomplishment since the FAA writes very difficult tests! My parents paid for my first 10-12 hours of flying lessons, then I worked in lovely jobs like waiter, cook, and assembling garden equipment for a hardware store to pay for additional flight time. At the time I was getting paid about $3.50/hour, and airplane rental cost $34/hour, so the time in the air was very precious. The plane I flew the most was a Piper Warrior – four seats, 160 horsepower, and cruised about 105 knots (Figure 5). I understand a comparable aircraft rental in 2018 is about $160/hour!

Figure 5. Me and the plane I flew most, N44884.

The most I used my flying skill was after my great aunt Margaret Hansen died in 1983. I flew my father from Minnesota to Colorado Springs, CO for Margaret's funeral and back. We buzzed Callaway, NE on the way there, where my father spent some of his childhood, so that was a thrill for him.

Thanks to starting life on my own, I stopped flying in 1985. The lack of good color vision would limit me to only flying during daylight hours. I knew from late childhood that I was somewhat red-green colorblind, but apparently it got worse with age. In the early 90's I tried to get back into flying to support Angel Flight (AngelFlight.com, 2018), but found my color vision was worse and so I could only fly during the day because of a restriction on my medical certificate. Not worth it, especially for such an expensive hobby. In recent years I found out that color vision is no longer a limitation on being a pilot, but I have too many other expensive hobbies to restart that one.

In high school I toyed with designing an airplane to set the world record for the smallest airplane – a canard triplane design, loosely based on a mashup of the Fokker Triplane and canard-based aircraft designed by my idol Burt Rutan (Rutan, 2015). My love of airplanes led to my first college degree, in Aerospace Engineering and Mechanics, and later opened the door for me to work as a contractor for the Federal Aviation Administration, so even though I didn't become a commercial pilot, it certainly helped me later in life!

The Dark Side - Randy

Beyond the medical challenges, my childhood was scarred by repeated physical, psychological, and sexual abuse.

When we lived in Washington state, we were in a ranch home in a fairly new housing development. My brother and I went to the elementary school down the street, where I was in fourth grade. We came to the area in the middle of the school year, so most of the social groups had long since formed. The neighborhood had many other kids, but I was befriended by one Randy Kluber. Randy was a large kid in my grade, with a deep booming voice, and lived a few doors down from us. Randy had a beige Great Dane named Tobias, who he would periodically beat for no reason, then apologize profusely to him and pet him tenderly. I was way too young to recognize classic abusive behavior (M. Smith & Segal, 2017).

One day, Randy invited me into the basement, where a friend of his (much older, maybe seventh grade, also from our street, I don't recall his name) threw a musty old blanket over me and wrestled me to the floor. They kept me confined under the blanket, punching lightly here and there at random, and blocking any attempts to create an opening for fresh air or escape. After a while I stopped panicking and gave in to the situation. Eventually they let me up and apologized and went on as though nothing odd had happened. I was very confused by this turn of events, and nothing weird happened for a month or so. Then it happened again. Same thing, musty blanket and all. I considered not seeing Randy any more, but he was my only "friend." This pattern repeated several more times over a period of several months.

Once Randy took me in the basement and had me back up against a vertical steel pipe. He said he was going to punch me. I protested, and he said he had to. I gave in (again) and stood in front of the pipe. Randy carefully measured off his distance from me and punched. He had planned it to have very little actual impact, it was mostly a mind fuck. Shortly after that Randy and his friend sat me down in the living room and explained that the friend was the one who started this 'initiation' (their word), and allegedly did this to Randy first. Then they initiated me into their 'club,' which I had never heard of. I was VERY glad when we moved away from Washington state.

The Dark Side – Mr. D

After Washington state we moved to Illinois and were there for three years. Our church was fairly friendly and most of my family seemed quite happy to be there. I had a different opinion. Our church had a large much older man running the Sunday School for my grade (6th), named Mr. John Dickensheets, or Mr. D as we called him for short. After my family had been part of the church for a while (six months? A year?) Mr. D invited me to his house and introduced me to coin collecting. He showed me how to identify foreign coins, look them up, put them in 2x2" coin holders, judge their condition (VERY optimistically, I'm sure), and so on.

I kept coming back to him over and over for this, but then one day he pulled me aside and started kissing me. Not like a kiss I had had before, he started French kissing me. I was confused. After all, at the ripe old age of 11, I had barely heard of French kissing, much less done it, and I was overwhelmed by the sensations and emotions. I still remember how bumpy his tongue felt. It seemed like it should be bad, but it kind of felt good, and I couldn't sort out that contradiction. Later as we sat at his kitchen table, he took my hand and put it in the front of his pants to hold his very large (it seemed) and erect cock. Another time he took down my pants and underwear, laid me on his bed, and kissed my hips and stroked my body. After several minutes of inappropriate behavior, he'd stop and we'd go back to the coins.

He hinted that he had done this before and had gotten weird looks for holding a boy's hand in public, and that was my first clue that this was clearly wrong. But the coins were really interesting to me and supposedly worth quite a bit (a couple hundred dollars), and I had no real friends, so I kept going back, time and time again. I finally got enough clues from him that this was wrong and stopped going.

I didn't fully realize what had happened until I was 18. 'Homosexual' and 'pedophile' weren't in my vocabulary, and these events took place long before teaching children about 'bad touches' (e.g. (Marnach, 2018)). After I graduated from college and left home, I sold my coin collection very quickly. This confused my parents. I didn't tell them what happened with Mr. D until I was nearly 30. They had no idea.

In retrospect, I was a prime target for grooming. I had few friends and had already been abused. Mr. D had placed himself in a position of trust and used it to find his prey, then used coin collecting to bribe me to keep coming back. (Craven, Brown, & Gilchrist, 2006)

The Dark Side - End it?

One of the lowest points in my life occurred in Wheaton. I was frustrated that my mind seemed to mature far faster than any other part of my life – my body, my social skills, or school. I was tired of the painfully slow pace of school. I didn't feel like anything was going to get better, like I was stuck in a perennial boring and unfulfilling existence. I didn't understand the rules I was living under and felt like the whole world was unfair. Until writing this, it never occurred to me that my experiences with Randy and Mr. D might have been huge contributors to the depths of my depression.

I considered killing myself.

My father had a small gun collection. One little-used gun was a bolt-action .22 caliber rifle. It was a small, light gun with a short barrel. I loaded it, intending to kill myself that weekend. A day or so later, my dad invited me on a fishing trip that weekend. I remember thinking something like "well, fishing is really important to him, so if he's inviting me fishing it must not be as bad as I thought." I went fishing that weekend instead of trying to commit suicide.

Yes, my life may have been saved by a fishing trip.

Music

Music was a strong influence throughout my childhood. My mom wasn't and isn't musically inclined at all, but my dad was and is, so we had music around most of the time. When we were in Washington state, my parents bought a good little Pioneer stereo and turntable (I think it was $300 at the time, a sizable piece of change), and my dad still has it in his basement.

My dad listened almost exclusively to classical or band music, so between him and Bugs Bunny (L. B. Media, 2017) I was exposed to a lot of the classics throughout my childhood. He was always in church choirs and sometimes other vocal groups, so I grew up wanting to mimic him. At something like age 40, he rediscovered the baritone horn, which he has played many years before (in high school?) and started playing it again. He's still doing so, several decades later, mostly in local bands since orchestras usually don't require that instrument.

Around age 13 or 14, I started actively collecting music I liked, which is apparently a very typical age for forming musical tastes (ajaymkalia, 2015). I remember in one of the trips to the Boundary Waters that someone was listening to Rush's album 2112. I started my collection with Styx's album *The Grand Illusion*, and quickly developed a fondness for classic rock bands like them, Queen, Meat Loaf, Heart, Foreigner, and many others. I think I picked up early on that music was a wonderful escape, so I used it to match my mood. For example, I had one album for when I was in an awful mood and hated the world – AC/DC's Back In Black (W. Foundation, 2018a)! Later I picked up bits and pieces of whatever was popular at the time – Boston, Led Zeppelin, more classic rock, heavy metal, and some milder stuff (Billy Joel, Elton John). Music remains a strong connection for me and source of joy.

Games

Card games and board games were a frequent source of amusement throughout my childhood. Spending a lot of time recovering from surgeries gave me a lot of time to amuse myself, so card games were an easy and portable way to do so. After all, this was long before the era of things like Gameboy. Once I graduated from strategy-less card games like War (Company, 2018), I recall many times playing gin rummy with my grandma. Once a year or so my parents and I would play Tripoley (CardGameHeaven, 2017) with the neighbors – a combination of poker and a rummy-like game. In high school, I'd play a simplified bridge-like game called Buck, which used a very limited deck from 9 to Aces to keep the hands very brief. Classic board games like Monopoly and Life were also good amusements when time permitted.

In high school, while recovering from my last surgeries, I saw my brother playing Dungeons and Dragons (LLC, 2017), and (probably to his chagrin) I started playing too. It was great to have a very complex game to amuse our minds, and that formed the cornerstone of my limited social life in high school. We'd play on Friday nights at a room reserved in the lower campus of our father's university. I still have the original set of player handbooks from before Advanced D&D came out. I'm told they aren't worth much, since it was a somewhat trendy game for a while. (Figure 6;

the prices shown are not valid!) I used my Basic programming class in high school to write a program to generate D&D characters. I quit D&D as I headed off to college, since I figured I wouldn't have time to do that and study.

Figure 6. Dungeons and Dragons manuals (circa 1975-1980)

Social life? *No comprende*

My childhood was spent going in and out of hospitals, reading trivia, moving, and riding a bike once in a while. Is it any wonder that I had little social life?

Being labeled a cripple made me a social pariah from the start. I was the odd kid who got special treatment and sometimes disappeared from school for weeks or months at a time. In junior high and high school, I had a very small circle of friends. Oddly they included the academically challenged students – stoners, party people. I got a D once in history class (for sleeping through most of it) and that earned me a touch of credibility with my peers for having gotten such a low grade. In high school we played cards over lunch; that was most of my social life in school.

Moving frequently also handicapped my social skills, since I kept having to try to make friends in a new environment. I didn't grow up with the local kids, so I didn't have an established position in one of the existing cliques. I wasn't athletic, and that was the most highly praised ability in Midwest American schools. No one admitted that being smart was good. As a result, I was relegated to the nerd clique or sometimes the generic social outcast clique (the ones who earned bad grades, skipped classes, and smoked in the parking lot).

Being a cripple kept me from being a part of normal socialization as a child. When other kids were exploring their classmates physically and sexually (as in games like "I'll show you mine if you show me yours"), I was in a cast and missed out. I was completely intimidated by girls and couldn't even speak coherently to exceptionally beautiful conventionally attractive ones (this was still true until recently!). I embarrassed my parents when I was about age 11 or 12 by checking out a whole stack of books from the library about human sexuality. I craved understanding but could only get vague text descriptions. I didn't know what a vulva looked like until I was 18!

Throughout high school, I succeeded in attending zero social events (proms, etc.) and zero school sporting events, solidifying my nerd status. The closest I ever got to dating in high school was asking a girl to prom way too late, so of course she already had a date by then. Laurie was a cute girl next door (almost literally) who played flute.

I tried to understand the rules for dating, and they just didn't make any sense. To get a date you're supposed to not care about whether the girl says Yes or No. But that's a lie! And if she says No you're supposed to keep after her, because persistence will be rewarded by her eventually giving in. After all, if she says Yes too easily then she's "easy" and not a respectable girl. So, we're supposed to ignore her when she says No and keep trying? How are we supposed to tell that No from "No there's no way I'm ever going out with you?" (Cowling & Reynolds, 2004; Miller & Boulton, 2007)

I was allowed to start dating at 16 in theory, but actually never went on a date until days before turning 18, after leaving home and starting work at the Mt. Rushmore concession building. I was terrified of rejection and couldn't bear to play a game that made no sense to me.

Employment

During my childhood I worked typical menial jobs. The first was delivering newspapers in Wheaton, IL; the Chicago Sun Times and Chicago Tribune. It was horrible to get up at absurd hours (4 am?) to assemble and deliver the papers. My brother figured out we got paid about 50 cents an hour for our dedicated labors.

After school in Wheaton, I hung out at a bicycle shop (Cooper's Big Wheel, if memory serves) so much that customers thought I might be the owner's kid. I never worked there, but I learned everything I could about bikes.

In Mankato, I worked for a dollar an hour to help an import shop near my junior high. A classmate and sort-of friend was the son of the shop's owner, who had been a lawyer in Pakistan. I hung around there so much after school that they finally paid me to do something, like dust the shelves and help sell jewelry. The shop also sold bongs and other "smoking" accessories, so I picked up a little hint of understanding the drug subculture. I was mostly amused by it, it didn't have much appeal for me.

I was a waiter for nine months at a Happy Chef restaurant, then left there to be a poorly-trained chef for a Sambo's restaurant. Yes, that was the name of the establishment. ('Sambo' is a racial slur. (Maldoven, 2004)) I got fired after three months – the first job I was fired from. I soon got a job at a hardware store assembling stuff for display – bicycles, trikes, roto-tillers, wheelbarrows, etc. These jobs gave me money for flying and emphasized to me the importance of earning a college degree, so I didn't have to do these jobs for the rest of my life! I never gave consideration to a trade career; from as far back as I recall it was assumed that I would go to college and do something white collar.

Those early jobs also taught me about interacting with real employers. I once called in sick from my waiter job about 15 minutes before my shift started, and quickly found out that my indecision produced a nightmare for my boss to find a replacement for me at the last minute! Another time another waitress who wasn't terribly dedicated to the job gave me advice: "If you don't want to work a shift, just drink a little vodka before you come in, and they'll send you home right away." While an effective short-term strategy, she was fired shortly after telling me that. Consider the source when evaluating advice!!

Sex and Body Issues

As a child I was terribly curious about girls but didn't know diddly-squat about them. My mom was the only identified female at home, and she was of the generation to hide in the bathroom to shower, put on makeup, and get dressed. I remember seeing an old eyebrow curler in the bathroom drawer and wondering if it was ever used.

Having no sisters and no close female friends, the world of girls was the subject of much curiosity when I was young. I remember as a child finding hair ties, bobby pins, and barrettes on the ground, and examining them as an archeologist might. "What is this mysterious object? How is it used? What strange culture created it?" I vaguely knew they were hair accessories, but not much beyond that. My knowledge of makeup was based entirely on TV commercials. Even as a young adult I knew what lipstick and mascara were, and beyond that I was clueless.

Boys and girls always played separately from each other (self-segregation?) so I spent little time around girls. Accordingly, I knew nothing of girl anatomy, makeup, or fashion, much less any social behavior patterns.

Even my own body was foreign to me. We had sex education in fifth grade, but I spent most of that trying to figure out what a vulva looked like and how to find the vagina. #GoodPriorities The line drawings we saw in sex education were so vague (Figure 7) I couldn't tell what was a ridge or valley or hole or bump, for example, and I certainly never saw one in person! I also distinctly remember wondering for years what the scrotum and testes did. They didn't seem to have any purpose (which granted, was true for a child). I kept trying to understand why They got bigger and smaller, and the only connection I could guess was that it was related to peeing. In retrospect, I had hypothesized it was the urinary bladder.

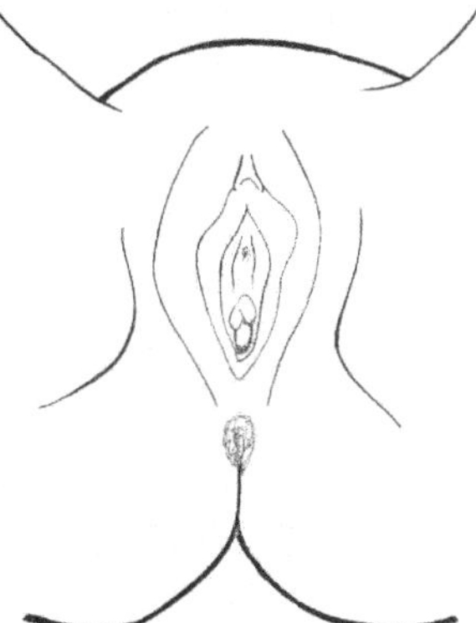

Figure 7. Line drawing of a vulva (SexInfo, 2018)

My brother once noted that we had sex education in fifth and eleventh grades, but they didn't mention contraception until eleventh grade. Optimists? Trusting souls?

I noticed that girls smoothed out their skirts or dresses before sitting down by sliding a hand down their butts. I always thought this a quintessentially feminine gesture, and particularly enjoyed it because 1) it was practical to keep your dress or skirt from wrinkling, and 2) it gave you a socially acceptable reason to pet your butt in public. This seemed surprisingly sensual for a public action. Now I smile to myself every time I do this.

In high school my male classmates complained (bragged?) of getting a raging erection from seeing pretty girls go by. And while I was certainly attracted to them, I didn't get that kind of spontaneous intense physical reaction. Were they lying, or was I weird? Both?

I was always slow to develop throughout my childhood. I'm told that I didn't lose a baby tooth until age 9! Normally this occurs between ages 5 and 7 (Chappell, 2016). My awakening sexuality was equally slow. I never reached orgasm until age 15, and never had a 'wet dream' that my sex education class told me was the hallmark of reaching sexual maturity. Once I discovered this new toy (masturbation) I enjoyed it very often, sometimes more than once a day. The most was seven, in case you're wondering. I think this could have been the most normal thing about my early sexuality. I was relieved that my parents never asked why there were so many Kleenex in my bedroom trashcan...

I have always been a nudist. I've always enjoyed being naked whenever I could. Nudity at home was never overt; my mom was very body modest, and my dad a bit more relaxed. Nevertheless, I snuck out of my clothes late at night when I thought I wouldn't get caught. My raciest moment was during swimming class in high school, when I 'accidentally' let my swimsuit fall off a couple of times in the pool. My young physical education teacher handled it very professionally. She called me aside and quietly asked if I was 'mooning' her. I gave the most honest 'no' in my life – I didn't know what mooning was!

Gender Roles

My father was quite clear from an early age that he had chosen names for me and my brother to be clearly gender-specific. Yes, the irony is ENORMOUS. Even worse, later there would be famous actors named Michael Learned (IMDb.com, 2018g) and Glenn Close (IMDb.com, 2018d), sabotaging his intentionally gender-specific choices.

I was named after two young men from my father's side of the family, Robert Booker and Glenn Booker, both of whom died in World War II. Robert received the Congressional Medal of Honor posthumously (Army, 2016a). After I was born, my father sent a letter to his relatives to tell them that he had named his second child after their relatives. They never responded to his letter, which clearly upset him because he has mentioned it many times over the years.

Gender roles were clearly defined in our household, and very 'Father Knows Best' traditional (IMDb.com, 2018c). My father was the primary breadwinner and clearly protector of the family. Having been an Army officer and member of Special Forces, he was well trained in combat, and would have been an intimidating force to reckon with if anyone was foolish enough to threaten his family. Even though he was an Army instructor in the use of handguns, instead he kept a bayonet under the mattress for home defense. Thankfully he never used it. He didn't keep handguns around to make sure my brother and I didn't have an accident with them. Wise man.

Mom worked an assortment of jobs that were all very traditional for women, although she was convinced from an early age that those were the only possible career options. She was a secretary or receptionist (several times), dental hygienist, hospital lab technician, and real estate agent during my childhood. As a girl she took an IQ test, and the score of 109 made her think she was dumb. As a result, for decades she didn't take advantage of being married to a professor and get a free college education. When she finally did go to college in her mid-40s, she became a nurse, yet another traditional job for women. Throughout my childhood, she did the laundry and most of the house cleaning. We ate dinner at 6 pm every day, and she prepared most of those meals, with occasional help from my brother and I if we remembered to follow her instructions.

My paternal grandfather was a very abusive alcoholic, so my father came from very strictly controlled and unpleasant environment. In keeping with my father's generation, showing emotion was generally considered bad, unless it was anger or laughter or happy or neutral. Crying was a sign of weakness and was not to be tolerated. Empathy was not allowed to be obvious. Anything even vaguely feminine was strictly off limits.

The only hint of people existing outside of the gender binary was sniggering references to a tennis player who went to Denmark for a 'sex change operation.' I later learned it was Christine Jorgensen, who transitioned in the early 1950's. (Jorgensen & Stryker, 2000) It was unthinkable any sane person would do such a thing.

I was clearly destined to be a feminist. In sixth grade, we were told to write down someone we'd like to know more about or idolized. My classmates, not surprisingly, were all thinking of TV or movie stars or popular sports figures. I wasn't sure of her name, but I wanted to know more about National Organization for Women (Women, 2018) founder Gloria Steinem (Steinem, Unknown). When our teacher read my choice, I got the most quizzical look of my tender young life. He was fairly liberal, but my choice clearly floored him. Yes, I'm a NOW member.

When we had our very first elective in grade school, my seventh grade gave us the choice between Wood Shop and Home Economics. My father was with me when registering for school, so without the least hesitation he put me in Wood Shop. Mind you I got a lot of good information from that class and enjoyed it, but I REALLY wanted to take Home Ec too! I couldn't understand why my father didn't ask which one I wanted to take, though now the choices were very clearly done along gender binary lines. Construction tools were for boys, sewing and cooking were for girls. End of discussion.

When I was recovering from the last set of leg surgeries in ninth grade, sitting on a hard surface was difficult for me. Nevertheless, I dutifully went to church with my family, and sat on the hard-wooden pews for the service. One day it was extra uncomfortable at first and got more painful as the sermon went on. I was struggling to keep my composure. My father was sitting to the right of me and could see my struggle. He gently placed a hand on my right leg, and slowly let out the deepest sigh I had ever heard in my life. That was his way of letting me know he understood my struggle but didn't feel he could do anything about it. I learned more from that sigh than in years of conversations with him. Contrary to those who think men don't feel anything, I believe the emotions are all there, they just aren't allowed to be expressed by most men. That is the tragedy I'd soon investigate in college; what we now call toxic masculinity.

As I got into high school, it became clear that my parents' marriage was not great. Their communication seemed poor; much of it was perfunctory or utilitarian. The stress of their marriage failing led my mom to tears on occasion, and my father confided that he didn't know how to handle it when someone cries. He just shut down and had to leave the conversation. Crying wasn't in the realm of allowable emotions for him, so processing someone else crying was equally foreign, I surmised.

I grew up with very clearly defined binary gender role expectations. I was to become a provider, a well-educated white-collar provider for my family. Emotions are strictly to be controlled, and only a select few can be expressed. Nevertheless, early signs of me not fitting into this world were clear. I summarized it in my Women's Studies term paper (Glenn Booker, 2013c) like this: "I resented the narrow world of my father. The 'man box,' or toxic masculinity, as it's now called (Figure 8). Narrow emotions visible.

Narrow choices for self-expression and entertainment. Narrow and stunningly boring fashion choices. Ugh. Go to college, get a 'good job,' find a 'nice girl' to marry, work your butt off for 40 years, hope your wife will have and raise your kids for you, and maybe if you didn't have too much fun you'll be allowed to retire some day. Yippee."

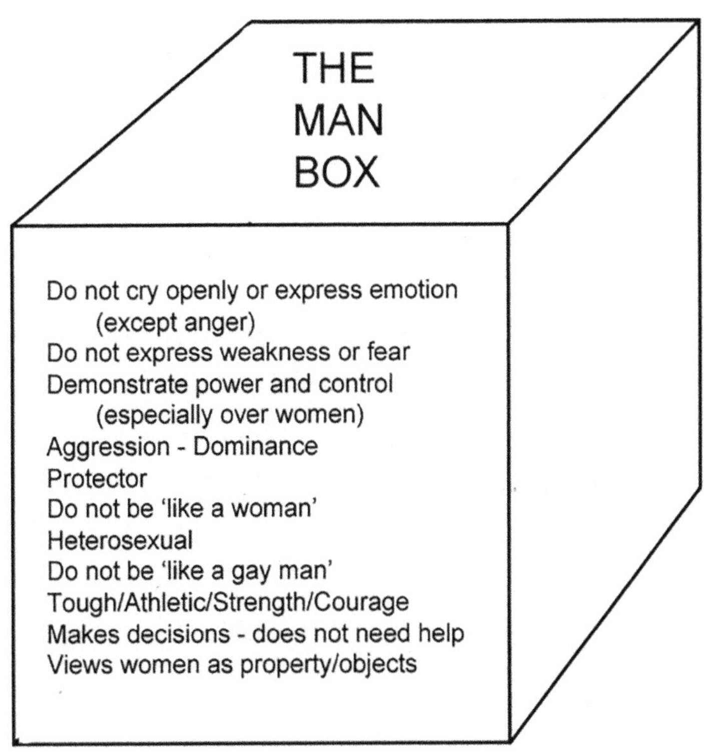

Figure 8. The Man Box - expectations of toxic masculinity (cbuethics, 2014)

Toxic masculinity is one way that our dominant patriarchal culture hurts men. It maintains that men are violent, unemotional, and sexually aggressive, and incapable of being anything else (G. F. Wiki, Unknown). Toxic masculinity maintains *that* Real Men can only be competitive with others, must love and demand sex, can never understand women, and must avoid any hint of interests or activities that could be seen as feminine such as parenting or nurturing. All of these concepts of masculinity are purely social constructs, they have no other basis. Nevertheless, they are enormously powerful influences on millions of boys and men. Some have even suggested that masculine roles are making it difficult for men to behave in ways that are ecologically sound – as though taking care of the planet is a sign of weakness. (Schrock & Schwalbe, 2009)

A key focus of feminism is to recognize that our culture needs to be redefined so that it helps people of every sex. Men don't want to admit being hurt by our current culture, because it could be construed as a sign of weakness. Even the noted feminist author bell hooks (sic) has touched on this, as seen in Figure 9. Having seen the effects of male and female hormones, I'm convinced that *testosterone contributes to this emotional crippling, by throttling the range of emotions men experience.*

"The first act of violence that patriarchy demands of males is not violence toward women. Instead patriarchy demands of all males that they engage in acts of psychic self-mutilation, that they kill off the emotional parts of themselves. If an individual is not successful in emotionally crippling himself, he can count on patriarchal men to enact rituals of power that will assault his self-esteem."

— bell hooks

Because men need feminism too.

Figure 9. Quote from bell hooks on toxic masculinity (hooks, 2018)

Lots of Good

While my childhood had a lot of challenges, it certainly wasn't all bad. We were a middle-class Christian family usually in the Midwest United States, so we didn't face any class or race or religious challenges. I typically had one or two good friends most places we lived.

I had a lot of simple pleasures growing up, like in Lincoln, NE I recall playing in the gutters with sand and the runoff from people's yards, forming little sand dams and seeing how the water behaved in response to these barriers. Who would imagine I'd go on to have two college degrees in fluid mechanics?

I was always protected during childhood because of my leg issues, which was somewhat isolating but also sweet to have that attention. I was often called 'brave,' which confused me since I had little choice but to put up with the world swirling around me. 'Not dying' seemed to hardly qualify as a brave action.

My parents moved mountains to make sure I got good medical care, and undoubtedly spent many sleepless nights trying to figure out what to do next to help me. Once when I was in the hospital at age 14, my dad came to visit, and I was in a lousy mood and snapped at him. He turned and left immediately, and I felt awful for decades until I could confess to him that I still remembered that day and I apologized. He had long since forgotten it, fortunately.

I think my brother resented all the attention I got for being broken. He once complained that he missed out on being able to pick on his 'little brother' because it wouldn't look good to pick on a cripple. My brother and I have always had a distant relationship. I think it's because our personalities are so different, we haven't had much common ground upon which to connect.

I was particularly close to my father, and we spent many hours fishing and hunting. My brother gave up on such things early on; basically, as soon as he could refuse to go (maybe age 14?), he did. We fished with bamboo rods for pan fish in Nebraska, fished for salmon in Washington once, and were surrounded by great fishing lakes and rivers in Minnesota. I took up duck hunting with my dad, and once when I was in high school, my dad even went out of his way to make sure I got my limit of ducks in one day (five of them). I was startled when I first killed a duck, because its head was half removed in the process, but I realized that the duck was going to feed us, so it was okay to sacrifice it. After all, the chickens in the grocery store didn't all commit suicide.

It was expressed from an early age that I could be anything I wanted when I grew up, so that somewhat overwhelming list of choices first got pared down by my physical limitations. Anything athletic was a non-starter of course, and things like my poor color vision and generally bad regular vision eliminated fields like astronomy and airline pilot.

As I approached the end of high school, I was trying to decide what I wanted to do with my life. (Ok, I still am!) I knew I had some talent with math and science, but I took a bunch of standardized aptitude tests to see what they thought I should be when I grew up. They concluded I should be ... a mortician! It made sense, strong science skills and no social skills, so put me around dead people!

I was interested in aviation, but those tests said that I had too little manual dexterity for aerospace engineering. I went to Minneapolis and spoke with Dr. Abraham Berman at the University of Minnesota, who said the tests were very outdated and I should go with what I wanted. My goal became to design airplanes for a living. I later took several courses from Dr. Berman, and much later dedicated my teaching website to him (J. Booker, 2017b).

I graduated from high school with a perfectly decent 3.15 GPA out of 4.0. I didn't work too hard, and almost never brought home homework – maybe once or twice per school year. I was planning to go to an in-state public university, so as long as my GPA was above 3.0, I was in good shape. I was too personally energy efficient (i.e. lazy) to keep my grades much higher than that. Most of high school was spent waiting for it to be over and hoping my classmates in college were more interesting.

Reflection

Reflection questions are included at the end of every chapter to inspire oral or written discussion.

1. How did physical activity affect your childhood? Did you have any physical limits? Were you encouraged to participate in sports or other athletic activities?
2. What were you taught about consent and personal space as a child? Were these topics often addressed? Were those boundaries respected?
3. Did you move a lot as a child? Were your non-immediate family (cousins, grandparents, etc.) nearby? How did those factors affect your socialization as a child?
4. Were you praised for intellect as a child? Is that a trait often associated with your family?
5. How did your family influence your earliest career plans? Were you expected to follow a family traditional career path? Or told you could be anything? Were some career paths actively discouraged?

6. What kind of hobbies did you have as a child? Were your interests supported and encouraged by your family?
7. How clearly were gender roles defined in your family? Were they traditional roles or were they negotiated by your parents?
8. What were you taught about intimate anatomy and sexuality as a child? Were proper names used for private parts or did your parents use euphemisms?
9. When did you start dating? Was dating encouraged?

Chapter 2 – Adulting

This chapter is an overview of my life from ages 18 to 49, to show how my early years resulted in an initially very conservative approach to being a responsible adult. My adult years before coming out to myself were fueled by using my intellectual gifts and Following the Rules to become a successful engineer. I started off with too much focus on the distant future and had to learn to live for the present as well, and started doing more hobbies that my relatively comfortable position as a single engineer allowed.

As I approached age 30, I got the foolish notion that I should settle down and talked myself into a relationship that absorbed over a dozen years of my life and sucked me dry as it degenerated into a very abusive nightmare. Desperation finally led to having the strength to leave that relationship. Reclaiming my independence set the stage for my coming out.

Career Arc

I'll start with a very brief chronology of about 30 years of my life, to set the stage for topical discussions to follow.

Before starting college, I worked the concession building at Mount Rushmore that summer. It was my first full time employment, and I struggled the first few weeks to get used to the responsibilities of that new universe. I have never worked an eight-hour day before! I worked over 50 hours per week and met my first girlfriend there, Vicki.

As I left high school, I decided to pursue Aerospace Engineering to take advantage of my love of flying and math/science talents. I completed a four-year BS degree in Minneapolis, including a minor in German to build on my studies in that field in high school. During summers I painted houses with my father. Figure 10 shows me at a church ceremony to send me off to California after graduating from college. I'm receiving a gift from Bill Carlson, a prominent member of my church.

Figure 10. Me and Bill Carlson after I graduated from the University of Minnesota.

Having frozen my tail off too many times in Minnesota, my first career job was as a civilian engineer for the Navy in the Mojave Desert of California. Nice climate change, eh? I was ok with the desert life, but soon found friends in the Los Angeles area, and after barely a year got a job in the San Fernando Valley with Hughes Aircraft Company. I stayed with them over seven years, with a one-year hiatus to go to Berkeley, CA for my Master's degree in mechanical engineering.

Hughes Aircraft decided to consolidate all of their facilities in Tucson AZ, so I took a chance on a girlfriend in Pennsylvania. I left Hughes, and moved to the east coast to a girlfriend, her son and daughter, and no job for me.

After about four months, I secured a job with an engineering contractor for the Federal Aviation Administration (FAA) Technical Center (FAA, 2016). My background in aviation paid off! My girlfriend and her kids and I moved to Absecon, NJ for a year, then escaped from there to Cherry Hill, NJ while I worked for a variety of small FAA contractors.

In spite of warning signs, I'll discuss later, I married my girlfriend about two years after moving in with her family. A year later we bought a large house in Cherry Hill, NJ, and a couple years after that I left FAA work to support an Army logistics system implementation (Army, 2016b) being done by nearby Computer Sciences Corporation (CSC).

We were married ten years, during which both of us started PhD programs. Her children finished growing up but remained at home and were completely dependent upon us. I left CSC to teach full time, since that job was a lot more fulfilling for me. My marriage deteriorated until I was so stressed, I had to end it. After discussion with my family and an attorney, I told her we were getting divorced.

I left our home in Cherry Hill and got an apartment on my own in Philadelphia. I finished my PhD while there, then bought a home in Philadelphia on my own the next year. That gave me a safe foundation for the start of my coming out, which I'll discuss in the next chapter.

My teaching position with Drexel University ended after 19 years, shortly after my coming out. Budget cuts were the reason. After about six months of unemployment, I got a job teaching for the Philadelphia campus of Harrisburg University.

Now I'll address various themes during my adult life.

Religion

As I started college (the first time), I kept with my Christian foundation, and became active in the InterVarsity Christian Fellowship (Fellowship/USA, 2018) chapter on campus. The people were nice and spoke a familiar language. I stayed active with them for about three years, but I grew tired of their rhetoric when some of my friends from outside of that group were openly insulted. One IVCF acquaintance loudly commented that he couldn't understand how I could have friends who weren't Christian! Apparently, he thought Jesus only associated with Christians. *eyeroll* I grew uneasy with theological aspects of Christianity, namely the 'love me or burn in hell forever' version of love from a supposedly benevolent god. For me, love can't exist under coercion, can't exist under threats, can't exist under blackmail. I sought another answer.

My brother had studied comparative religion, and once introduced me to an alternative bookstore in Minneapolis. "Alternative" as in the kind of bookstore where they had all the books on non-Judeo-Christian religions, offbeat political rants, drug advocacy, alien theories, offbeat stuff like that. One book which got my attention on the shelf was 'Lesbian Nuns Breaking Silence!'

I had heard of real versions of witchcraft (Wicca), and with my brother's guidance got Starhawk's *The Spiral Dance* (Starhawk, 2018) instead of some cheesier and sensationalistic publications about Wicca (as in "oh my god look we have naked women in our rituals!!!!!!"). I read it eagerly and was amazed to discover a religion that is nature-based, sex-positive, and non-judgmental. And most amazing, it recognizes female forms of divinity! I had to learn more! The next huge influence was Margot Adler's *Drawing Down the Moon* (W. Foundation, 2017b), which is an encyclopedic tome discussing many kinds of nature-based and other non-traditional religions. I started seeing the broad range of religious expression beyond my Christian upbringing. These were all nature-based religions, experiential instead of dogmatic, recognizing that people may find divine inspiration from very different paths. I explored some Pagan paths to see which fit, like the Church of the Eternal Source, which is based on ancient Egyptian religious practices.

I went to Pagan festivals, especially the annual Pagan Spirit Gathering (Circle Sanctuary, 2018) in Wisconsin. There I connected with Pagans from around the world and got to experience things that I never imagined. I was honored to participate in Native American sweat lodge ceremonies run by actual shamen. A drumming workshop was so intense I felt I melted into the floor. I experienced power animal dances which forever changed my view of the world, allowing me to feel empathy for trees and a connection to everyone around me. Here is one such experience.

Power Animal Dance

It was the Pagan Spirit Gathering in Wisconsin in June. Three hundred leftover hippies, Dead Heads, and rebellious or curious young adults, in a gently rolling campground normally occupied by other extreme radicals such as ... Boy Scout troops. Pagans learn from any tradition too slow to run away fast enough, and we were blessed with some genuine Native American souls at this particular gathering. They organized a power animal dance for one evening. The idea is to let your power animal (or kindred spirit) take over your body for a little while, to learn from each other and exchange perspectives.

That night was a little cold, with more than hints of rain possible. I really wanted to participate in the dance, but the weather was icky and I didn't want to be very active physically. So I got a bright idea! I decided my power animal for the evening ... was a tree. Ok, I have to admit I had never heard of a plant being a power animal before, but everything's part of nature, therefore is part of the divine, so why not? I had a brown poncho, so that would double as rain protection and vaguely look like a tree trunk. This could work!

So I put on the poncho and started walking to the ritual space. But being a tree, I walked slower than I Ever. Have. Before. Each step became a new investigation of my feet, slowly shifting my weight from one part of each foot to the next until it could take my full weight. This took forever, so naturally I was one of the last people to get in line for the dance. As I approached the ritual space, the ground shook gently, rhythmically from powerful drumming, and for quite a while I couldn't tell what was up ahead. When I got close enough, I saw that people were being squeezed one at a time between two of the drummers. Birth. A human birth canal had been created, between the driving heartbeat of the drums. And so I was delivered into the sacred space.

I walked slowly to one side of the space, and planted myself (ahem) with a good view. Around me people were jumping and growling and leaping and interacting with each other in their animal forms. But as a tree, I couldn't make a sound. Or move. Some approached me, sniffed about, then went on their way. I was surprised to realize that, as a tree, I had become supremely vulnerable. No defenses, no running away. Exposed to anything that could walk up to me and do anything they wished. And as interesting as my neighbors were, there were none of my kind present in the dance. A twinge of loneliness pulsed through me.

I observed the dance for a while longer, and then heard a strange and unfamiliar sound from the middle of the space. It repeated, or maybe continued, and only then I realized it was English. I had drifted into the dance so far I couldn't understand language for a while. And as our common bond of language was reinstated, I realized and felt a connection to all the critters dancing around me. We. Are. One. The enormousness of that utterly simple statement came crashing in around me. I slowly eased myself to the ground, waves of sobbing, my body convulsing with the relief of no longer being alone.

After a while, a couple of people came to check on me. One asked, "Are you alright?" I nodded slowly and thought 'Oh yes, like never before.'

The power animal dance, like many Pagan events, showed me something that was intended to be almost satirical could prove to be deeply insightful.

There is substantial interest in absurdist religions, including Discordianism, the Church of the Flying Spaghetti Monster, and Dudeism. An early example of embracing the absurd was the book *Principia Discordia*. (M. t. Younger & Ravenhurst, 2011) Inspired in 1963 by the re-discovery that there was a Greek goddess of Discord and Chaos, namely Eris, Greg Hill and Kerry Wendell Thornley created a religion called Discordianism to worship Her. After all, one publication of Principia Discordia was titled "*Principia Discordia • Or • How I Found Goddess and What I Did to Her When I Found Her: The Magnum Opiate of Malaclypse the Younger*" which gives a good idea how seriously they take themselves.

One religion designed to attack "intelligent design" is the Church of the Flying Spaghetti Monster, founded by a physicist named Bobby Henderson. (Bobby Henderson, 2006) Its theology includes the sacred nature of spaghetti and meatballs, wearing pirate garb while drinking rum, and wearing a colander on your head. Its followers are called 'Pastafarians,' a clear spoof on Rastafarians. Some Pastafarians have even gotten a drivers' license while wearing a colander by citing the equal protection clause for religious attire. (Bobby Henderson, 2019) Intelligent Design is the pseudo-science behind creationism. (Barnes, Church, & Draznin-Nagy, 2017)

Even further from the fringes of seriousness, we have Dudeism. "Dudeism is inspired by The Big Lebowski but is not affiliated with the movie in any way, nor with its creators/producers. Dudeism is also inspired by Taoism, Zen, Humanism and much more." So yes, Dudeism was mostly inspired by a 1998 Jeff Bridges movie. (*IMDb.com*, 2019) It claims over 450,000 ordained clergy. The theology of Dudeism is the epitome of chill, summarized by "Abiding and takin'er easy." (Eutsey, 2019) But I digress.

I was involved in a Wiccan coven in San Diego for a year or so (a pseudo-Gardnerian tradition called 1734 (Webmaster, Unknown)), but they didn't quite fit me for a deeper connection. Gerald Gardner was one of the first modern era witches, initiated in 1939 in England and wrote books about Wicca in the 1950's. (M. Davis, N.D.) During my time with the San Diego coven, a daily prayer to the Goddess led to what I consider my spiritual enlightenment, after a shockingly brief six weeks of study. I capture my observations from this event in a story called *12 Minutes*, which is in Appendix C. That twelve minutes of my life is a major reason why I still identify as primarily Wiccan. That experience taught me a few life-changing lessons.

- The divine is real. I experienced a power far beyond imagination, in response to asking to connect to Her.
- Change is easy. My logical engineering mind saw physical things like the Earth as heavy and dense, but I was shown that they can be transformed easily, as though they perched on the head of a pin.
- Be careful what you ask for! I asked to connect with the divine feminine, and She responded. I never expected a response, since I was raised to assume faith was the most we could hope for.

- I was taught a new perspective. The walls of my trailer were old and dusty and stale, but she showed me that something that mundane could still be seen as beautiful and divine.
- I saw what could be considered the basis for the Triple Goddess. (Living., 2019) One perspective was sweet and innocent, like a maiden. The second was more mature and nurturing, like the Mother. The third was about to bring about change with a trace of effort, like the Crone.

Most religions rely on 'faith' as their cornerstone, but after experiencing divine energy firsthand, I realized that **faith was a crutch**. Having considerable experience with crutches, I could attest that they are very useful tools when you need them, but they shouldn't be an end to themselves. After '12 Minutes' I could throw away the faith crutch and replace it with firsthand knowledge of the Goddess, the divine feminine.

As I dated sparsely in the next few years, I got curious about polyamory. Having never been big on jealousy (I regard it mostly as a measure of one's insecurity), I wondered what relationships with multiple partners could be like. I dated a lady who led a local polyamory group called Live the Dream. She had two children, a son about age 10 and a daughter about 15. After becoming a more familiar presence in her home, her son adopted the strange habit of throwing himself at me, almost violently, to get a hug. It took me a while to realize that he didn't think it was acceptable just to ask for a hug but hiding the need for closeness behind a more aggressive act made it permitted. I was sad to realize that his concept of what it meant to be a young man was already so limited.

After leaving the San Diego coven, I got very involved in the Church of All Worlds (CAW) (CAW, Unknown-b) for several years. The CAW is loosely based on Robert Heinlein's famous 1961 novel, *Stranger in a Strange Land* (House, 2018). Yes, it's a church based on a science fiction novel. The CAW uses the metaphor of a man raised on Mars (Valentine Michael Smith) to describe how people who connect with earth religions feel alien in our culture.

The CAW had a very organized structure (CAW, Unknown-a), which appealed to my logical brain, and actively encouraged learning from a wide range of cultures and perspectives. They are strongly feminist, LGBT-friendly, ecology-minded, and political (similar to Green Party (Party, 2016) positions). They support alternative lifestyles such as polyamory, nudism (yay!), and controlled use of psychedelic drugs for sacred uses.

The members and leaders of the CAW were mostly a bunch of hippies, many of them a decade or more my senior. I always wanted to be a hippie, but I was born a decade too late for that. The Church inherited a chunk of land in northern California from a member who died in a car accident, and they held rituals there frequently. Since it was in California, they also had a hot tub, which led one weekend to this memorable event.

At first glance you'd be much more likely to assume Marilyn was someone's Grandma, ready to bring a tray of chocolate chip cookies fresh from the oven. Fairly tall, maybe 5'8" or so, she had gentle round curves that make you think she'd give the warmest hugs you could imagine. In her arms, the boogie man couldn't get near you. Only when close to her could you pick up her scent, a delicate blend of simply clean plus a hint of floral perfume. She clearly knew what worked for her, and didn't have to be overbearing or obnoxious to make her point.

She was in her 50's, with wispy thin white hair that she tried to corral into a perm, with limited results. Her voice matched her body - soft and calm and gentle. She spoke slowly, with the confidence and maturity of her years behind her.

She told me of her first event with the Church of All Worlds. Someone was hosting a hot tub party; not exactly a rare event in Northern California. Being new to the area, and this being the days before GPS, she got lost and was quite late.

Getting to the party, she found everyone was in the back yard in a large homemade hot tub. An oval tub with slightly rusted galvanized steel walls, it was probably designed for eight people, and currently held at least twelve happy naked souls already. Ever polite and gracious, Marilyn assumed out loud that there was no room for her large frame, but the partiers would have none of that. They insisted there was plenty of room for her - in the middle of the tub.

Quietly and modestly, she disrobed, and after a brief flurry of activity, she stepped between a couple of people and eased herself into the middle of the tub, half standing and half lying across several people's legs and laps. The commotion settled down, and a pause of quiet emerged. With a hint of pleasant surprise and a gleam in her eye, she quietly stated "Well, someone's foot has found the right spot, but at the moment I'm not sure if I'm straight or gay!"

My involvement with the CAW ended when I left the West coast. At that point, the Internet was not yet in widespread use, and the logistics of communicating across the country quickly and often was not feasible or cost-effective.

My ex-wife was the leader of a nameless family-tradition form of Wicca that she learned from a British couple decades earlier. That religious connection was one of the reasons I got in a relationship with her.

Sex as a Young Adult

At Mount Rushmore, I quickly befriended a lady named Vicki, who became my first romantic relationship. Three years my senior, she was patient enough (in a condescending way) to wait for me to be ready for sex and gave me a tender introduction to this new world. We were together for a year and a half, but after realizing that she wasn't loyal in our supposedly monogamous relationship, I broke up with her.

Busy finishing college, and having few social skills anyway, it was over three years before I dated again. I dated a few women in the Los Angeles area, and met some fun people at the pagan festivals. I had a brief relationship with a polyamorous married woman who also belonged to the coven in San Diego. Still, for having mostly hippie friends and a very liberal point of view, I had a limited social life. I still couldn't make sense of the bizarre dating rules, and I had little or no faith that my body would cooperate sexually. It was a familiar cage, one out of which I couldn't find my way.

I got a glimpse of my sexual potential when I explored psychotropic drugs while attending the University of California at Berkeley (is that a cliché or what?). I captured the experience for posterity.

I was dating a much older woman while I was living in Berkeley CA for school. She was just old enough to have been an original hippie, something I admired and felt a little jealous of. She was 14 years my senior! We ate some old magic mushrooms together, and they were dead. She asked if I wanted to try acid, and I agreed. We took the little pieces of paper under our tongues, and played a board game while waiting for it to hit. She loved board games too.

As the sense of losing focus and control started to sweep over me, she saw it and recognized what was happening. She put the game aside, she got out some oil, we lost our clothes and started exchanging massages. The sense of touch, already very powerful in me, became amplified beyond belief, and I got deliriously drunk on the touch of her skin. Massage with fingers became massage with hands, became massage with forearms, became massage with arms, became massage with my whole body sliding over hers, giggling occasionally.

We moved the party into the shower, where basic balance of standing upright became a nontrivial but surmountable issue for me. As I moved my hands in front of me, I saw echoes of where they had been. Little trails in the air, staying around for a moment, then slowly disappearing. It echoed an idea from my boring youth, where I wondered what would happen if you could interact with the shadow of where people had been before. Now it was "real," or at least appearing before my eyes.

After the shower we went to the bedroom, and made love. And while the act was fairly conventional, my senses were on overload, savoring every moment, every touch, and trying desperately not to do something embarrassing and silly like ... fall over. I tried to look at us in a full length mirror, and was warned that's a bad idea in my current state. After loving and snuggling for a while we emerged, easing our way back to "reality."

That event showed me that I could be very sensual in the right company. After trying acid one more time, I concluded it was too powerful for me to enjoy. I didn't like losing control in that way and that strongly.

Freedom to study weird stuff

As I got settled into my defense industry job in Los Angeles, I was surprised how much easier my real job was than college. Blessed with decent income and not a lot of responsibilities, I realized that I could explore interesting things in my spare time.

I took advantage of a local vocational-technical school and learned about car repair. Most of the other students were high school age and preparing to be mechanics, but I just learned so I could work on my pickup and not get ripped off when I had to take my car to a mechanic. I think the fanciest thing I ever did was replace the brake pads on my truck.

Perhaps the most unusual of my educational pursuits was studying midwifery for two years. A presenter at a local pagan festival was an amazing lay midwife[2], and I was inspired to learn more. I joined the California Association of Midwives (CAM) (Midwives, Unknown), and started taking classes, going to workshops, attending conferences, and was even their statistician for two years. I was strongly drawn to this field because it was deeply connected to pregnant women, honored the integrity of the birth process, and yet recognized the need for the help of technology when necessary. Books like *Spiritual Midwifery* (Gaskin, 2002) and *Heart and Hands* (E. Davis, 2012) were early inspirations. I even dreamt once of walking with a couple at Ina May Gaskin's Farm in Tennessee.

I was an oddity in this community, because a single young man was at best an anomaly and often viewed with considerable suspicion in a field which was literally 99% women. I heard stories of "oh yes, there's one male midwife I heard of..." but was also surprised how many lesbian separatists were active midwives. Did the latter not realize that most pregnant women who could afford a lay midwife (which was typically not covered by insurance) were in relationships with men? In any event, I realized I wasn't fanatical enough about midwifery to fight the discrimination and suspicion, so I gave up on this path.

I realized that I wanted to study massage, so I found a local school, the Touch Therapy Institute in Los Angeles, CA. (They are apparently no longer in business, or I'd cite them.) I took about 400 hours of training in Swedish Massage, Lymphatic

---

2 A lay midwife is a midwife who was trained by peers and self-study, instead of the more formal routes such as becoming a Certified Nurse-Midwife (Schools, 2018).

Detoxification, and some less invasive bodywork techniques like Don McFarland's Body Harmony (BHIG, Unknown). Massage gave me huge insight into how messed up my body was from all the childhood surgeries.

In the basic Swedish Massage class, they told us to bend our knees and use the power of our legs to drive the massage, instead of just using your fingers, hands, or arms. That way you don't wear yourself out, and can do deeper massages than would be possible otherwise. The first time I tried to bend my knees, I collapsed against the massage table! That's how I realized that I had been in the habit of putting all my weight on my right leg and locking the knee to hold myself up. I enjoyed massage work tremendously, and even considered abandoning engineering and getting a job on a cruise ship or something like that. I still do massages occasionally.

The Dark Side: During sessions with Body Harmony, I made more revelations about how I had been holding my past in my body. One time I opened my sternum, felt at least six pops on either side of it, and felt my shoulders open wider. I realized I had been holding my shoulders together to protect myself from Mr. D. Another session someone was working on my sacrum, and I felt that area release. I had been holding my hips tilted backward for years – locked in that position to try to keep my privates away from Mr. D's hand reaching into my pants. As I stood up and felt this new body position, I commented that I felt less Caucasian now that my hips weren't tilted forward anymore!

A third time with Body Harmony, someone was working on my legs, and they commented on smelling anesthesia. My body had literally trapped anesthesia, and it was finally being released some 15 years after my last surgery. People could smell it coming off me from several feet away, and they knew nothing of my medical history. Bodywork was the beginning of reclaiming my body from the 'cripple' mentality of my childhood.

Follow the rules

I built on my childhood foundation of following the rules in early adulthood. I finished college, got a good job, got an advanced degree, all very respectable activities like good boys are supposed to do. As I approached age thirty, I got the foolish notion that I should settle down with a family, but had very limited success dating, so I settled for a somewhat promising but also somewhat questionable relationship with my now ex-wife, whom I'll call Ellen.

I met Ellen in the pagan community, because she and her second husband were famous for traveling the country, performing as musicians, and giving workshops on music and pagan family issues. They showed up in Los Angeles once or twice a year, and I was often at their performances. I belonged to a local pagan organization that put on a festival every Fall (the Harvest Moon Celebration), and we hired them to perform every year or two. One year, a few weeks before the Celebration, I heard through the rumor mill that Ellen and her husband had broken up, and the latter had been abusive to her and the kids.

Much of my childhood was spent watching cartoons, and I knew from Dudley Do-Right that a key responsibility of honorable men was to rescue damsels in distress (Figure 11). As utterly corny and naïve as that may sound, I genuinely wanted not only to save the world in an ecological sense but also to save people when I could. At the same time, I had such low self-esteem that I figured I had to bribe people to like me, so I figured if I helped save Ellen and her kids, I could buy their affection. Ellen had a daughter with her first husband and a son with her second; the kids were about 4-1/2 years apart.

Figure 11. Dudley Do-Right rescuing a damsel in distress (Stars, 2017)

I called Ellen as soon as I found out what had happened and confirmed the story that her husband had been abusive, and she finally got the strength to leave him, but now was left without transportation. She and her kids had settled in the Philadelphia suburbs where she had some friends nearby, and her father was helping to pay for an apartment for them. After getting off the phone with her, I wrote a substantial check to help her buy a car. When she got it, she was floored, called me, and our long-distance relationship started. We called each other every week or so, and slowly a relationship formed. That December, I decided to go to Pennsylvania to visit her and the kids. After that, we spoke every day, running up gigantic phone bills! (Gigantic as in $1000/month!) When my company announced they were consolidating in Tucson, I decided to come to Philadelphia to pursue Ellen and 'save' her and her family. The next April I left my job near Los Angeles and drove myself and my stuff across the country.

We shared her apartment for about four months, until I got my first job for the FAA, then moved into a terrible rental home in Absecon, NJ, just outside of Atlantic City. Within a year I proposed to her, and we had an engagement party. Realizing how awful the schools were in that area, we moved to Cherry Hill, NJ because of its fine reputation in that regard, and rented a home for two years. During that time, we got married (or more precisely 'handfasted,' in Wiccan terminology) and soon bought a home less than a mile from the place we had been renting.

Ellen was a strong proponent of the gender binary. In her view, the roles of men and women in Wicca were very clearly defined and polarized. When I showed her the *12 Minutes* piece about my invocation of the Goddess, she insisted that wasn't possible because I was a man. Period. End of story. Her refusal to recognize any kind of transgender existence may have delayed my coming out by as much as 15 years.

The first year or two of our relationship was very good. We had a very active sex life, and after some initial awkwardness, I felt sexually confident for the first time in my life. I was initiated into the family Wiccan tradition of which she was the matriarch. She made a clear effort to establish my joint authority with her as far as raising and disciplining her kids were concerned. My work was interesting, and I was well respected professionally. It looked like I was doing a great job of fulfilling my responsibilities as an Adult Man.

I helped my step children go through many phases of typical life – getting braces, learning to drive, teenage rebellion, first dates. My step daughter went through a goth phase, which was very typical of the time. Wearing size 14 jeans on a size 6 body was downright funny, but I get fashion is a cruel master. After all, I wore corduroy bell bottom pants, so I can't judge too harshly.

In her middle teens, she tried to run away once. Living in the very prosperous Cherry Hill, NJ, the local police quickly found her and tracked her as she stretched her independence legs a tiny bit. As she started returning home after a few hours, I recall confronting her near our home. She was venting outward rage at the injustice of life and threatening to run away again. I stayed calm and tried to encourage her back home. She started walking through me, full of fire and fury on the outside, but when I held her to stop her, I felt her body relax with immediate relief. It was as if she wanted connection but couldn't allow herself to admit it.

Fashion curious

Despite a very boring wardrobe as a young adult (jeans and T-shirt work for everything, right?), I was quite interested in women's fashion. I bought popular fashion magazines like Vogue and Vanity Fair. While still in California, I bought a simple sewing machine from a mail order catalog, but it turned out to be a piece of plastic junk aimed at 8-year-old girls. I later enjoyed shows like Project Runway (IMDb.com, 2018i) and was amused by the constant recycling of fashion trends. Hey, let's combine fashion from the 1970's with 1920's flapper hats! Sold!

My mom has a very basic sewing machine she uses reluctantly once a year, so I never learned much about making clothes from her. Once on my own as an adult, I realized my biggest sewing need was hemming slacks. Thanks to my birth defect, it was very difficult to get a tailor to hem pants properly because they couldn't understand leg lengths not being equal. Eventually I got a good sewing machine and learned basic hems from my then-wife. Ellen had a huge background in costume construction for the Society for Creative Anachronism (SCA), (SCA, 2018) so she could turn anything into an excellent garment.

Ellen and I took basic sewing classes together, obviously something she didn't need, and made things like pillows, elastic waist pants, and a travel tote for toiletries. We built up quite an impressive sewing room with a Viking sewing machine, (Viking, 2018) 5-spool serger, and large fabric cutting table. My step daughter got into making costumes, and Ellen taught her many more advanced techniques. When I divorced Ellen, I let her keep custody of the sewing equipment, mainly because I knew her daughter had trashed them by sewing heavy and very messy materials like leather and oilcloth. Once on my own, I immediately got a new sewing machine, ostensibly so I could hem my pants and maybe play with making other garments. I went on to take more sewing classes and get books on sewing techniques.

The Dark Side - Descent into hell

Ellen had been abused in various ways by her family and both of her previous husbands, and her second husband abused both of her children. When she finally left her second husband, she and her kids got therapy to help recover from their experiences. Ellen became a counselor for the domestic violence shelter that helped her break free from her second husband, (Place, 2018) and after I came on the scene, I joined Ellen and the kids for family therapy sessions. In short, everyone in my new family was coming from an abusive history and had received help to cope and adjust to be able to move on with life.

That made it even more ironic that Ellen became increasingly abusive over the years. She knew the methods of abusing someone (many of them firsthand), she knew how to give all the right answers if anyone questioned what she was doing, and she knew how to manipulate people from an extensive sales background.

Was Ellen more likely to become abusive because of her history of being an abuse victim? The answer isn't clear. Much of the analysis to date is biased against people with a history of abuse, so there isn't a definitive answer. (Widom, Czaja, & DuMont, 2015)

The first couple of years with Ellen were good sexually, in fact the most satisfying sex life I had ever had to that point, but it quickly deteriorated as her abusive behavior got more and more obvious. I described the situation in my Women's Studies 101 term paper (Glenn Booker, 2013c) like this.

The not-so-obvious aspect of my sex wasn't revealed until about 2001, when ~~domestic bedroom difficulties~~ (strike that coy euphemism) my now ex-wife became increasingly abusive and as a result I became impotent. I agreed to go see a doctor to see 'what was wrong with me' even though I knew fully well the answer wasn't physical. However after some blood work was done, I was diagnosed with secondary hypogonadism, namely a low level of testosterone (T). To "fix" me I started taking various forms of T supplements, which weren't particularly effective since the psychological causes of the performance problem were being summarily ignored.

As a result of this diagnosis, I started searching the Internet for more information about my condition, and entered the world of the intersex community. While hypogonadism isn't commonly listed as an intersex condition like AIS or CAH, some websites recognized it. I got connected to an online support site called Bodies Like Ours3, and studied intersex conditions (G. Booker, 2002) so I could understand what they were talking about.

As I got support from them, my [then] wife got jealous and complained loudly that they were filling my head with crazy notions about myself. Yes, keeping you isolated from support is a common abuse tactic. And yes, she has a very binary approach to sex and gender.

People with intersex conditions are now finding support through sites such as interACT (interACT, 2016), which primarily

[3] Site no longer exists.

targets young people. It took until 2006 for the medical community (specifically the American Academy of Pediatrics) to realize that terms like Disorders of Sexual Development (DSD) "may carry a stigma." (Caplan-Bricker, 2017) I even convinced a doctor to check my chromosomes, just in case there was something fishy there. After a detailed physical exam, he didn't think the test necessary, but I had good insurance, so he relented. I was 46,XY, typical for a male.

Some of the ways my 10-year marriage became abusive include:

- Financial – by the end of our relationship, I was working two jobs, earning a six-figure income, and still had a net discretionary income of *negative* $500/month. I had been moving credit card debt from one card to another to get lower interest rates for eight years, refinanced our home's main mortgage, took out at least two second mortgages, and even a third mortgage. Yet Ellen would always have money to bail out anything 'her' children needed, lied about how much money was left from her father's estate, and constantly pleaded 'it is an emergency' to justify any expenditure she wanted. Economic abuse is a much neglected aspect of abuse, but was still massively stressful and demoralizing. (Sanders, 2015)
- Sexual – you know how everyone in a long-term relationship develops self-appointed roles? One of hers was keeping track of how long it had been since we had sex and throwing that number in my face when we fought. The last time she did that, it was 5 or 6 years. But in the same breath she refused nonsexual contact (cuddling), which I treasure. In the beginning of our relationship, she admitted having been a prostitute in the early

1970's and promised to do ANYTHING for me sexually. By the end of our relationship, she only wanted long bondage sessions, with her the submissive, which became incredibly boring for me, and afterward she's complained about all the things I didn't do or didn't do right or didn't do long enough, ... you get the idea. Instead of coming to bed when I did, she would go get stoned with her kids for hours, and only come to bed when I was asleep or nearly so.

- Isolation – Ellen made it clear that she hated all of my family, and actively and repeatedly voiced her disgust when I made any effort to communicate or (gods forbid) visit my family. She effectively cut off most contact between me and my family, including missing the last years of life for both of my grandmothers. She also openly attacked my German heritage and rewarded her children for doing likewise. The isolation included blocking me from any activities that would empower me, so when I took voice and dance lessons, she said nothing positive and only focused on how poorly I was doing. Since she had been a classically trained musician and experienced dancer, her words carried a lot of weight. When I first joined the family, we went to several Pagan festivals, where people fawned over Ellen and she gave concerts and workshops. Soon, she decided that pagans had no community worth associating with, and she stopped socializing with anyone pagan except members of her own family tradition. The family tradition of which she was the matriarch.

- Degradation – Ellen openly insulted me in front of her kids, in front of her friends, in front of the plumber, in front of strangers in public, in front of anyone. Not just insults about my character, she'd insult my sexual abilities and other intimate subjects in front of anyone. She also made the solo decision to open our marriage, and often went to her married boyfriend's home to be dominated. I found hundreds of emails between them, which I kept in case the divorce got nasty.
- Gaslighting – when I tried to fight back against the abuse, Ellen would insist I was crazy and no one would believe me. She knew it was mostly words, and hence there was no physical evidence against her. She also used the classic line 'no one else would want you' to keep me from leaving. Her use of gaslighting in conjunction with other abuse tactics is consistent with the findings of Dr. Erin Hightower in her dissertation. (Hightower, 2017)

Abusive partners don't change the roles we follow, but affect the quality of how those roles are carried out. (de Jong, Alink, Bijleveld, Finkenauer, & Hendriks, 2015) I embodied this by fulfilling my role as parent and provider but being increasingly miserable and depressed. Isolated, broke, touch starved, and lacking self-esteem, I was just going through the motions.

In addition to these classical forms of abuse, Ellen and her children engaged in mutually destructive patterns. Ellen felt guilty that she didn't stop her children from being abused by her previous partners, and they quickly learned that they could get

Mommy to do almost anything simply by guilting her into it. Ellen's parenting style was permissive to begin with, but because of this dynamic her children could get away with anything short of literal murder. (Johnson & Kelley, 2011; Williams et al., 2009) Ellen wanted to have a hippie style of parenting in the first place, to be her children's best friend instead of their mother. As a result, her daughter earned three college degrees (Associate's, Bachelor's, and Master's), bought a new car, and within six months decided she couldn't handle working full time, so Mommy picked up the rest of her $600/month car payments.

Ellen's son had a good work ethic and a promising future, but then his bored sister got tired of no one being home during the day to entertain her, so she convinced her brother to skip school, stay home with her, get stoned and watch movies. In my step-kids' eyes, they were winning because they convinced their mom to let them live for free, work very little, and spend their lives stoned and watching TV and movies.

I found myself justifying the situation I was in with excuses like "I don't want to abandon the children" or "well it could be worse." I was so deeply entrenched that I couldn't see how absurd and terrifying it became. I later learned this is a common abuse tactic (Figure 12). If you destroy someone's self-esteem and sense of self-worth, you can do almost anything to them.

As a therapist, lemme just say: almost every trauma survivor I've ever had has at some point said "But I didn't have it as bad as *some* people" and then talked about how other types of trauma are worse. Even my most-traumatized, most-abused, most psychologically-injured clients say this.

The ones who were cheated on, abandoned, and neglected say this. The ones who were in dangerous accidents/disasters say this. The ones who were horrifyingly sexually abused say this. The ones who were brutally beaten say this. The ones who were psychologically tortured for decades say this. What does that tell you? That one of the *typical side-effects of trauma is to make you believe that you are unworthy of care.*

Don't buy into it, because it's *nonsense*. It doesn't *matter* if someone else had it "worse." Every person who experiences a trauma deserves to get the attention and care they need to heal from it.

Figure 12. Therapist view of trauma survivors.
(hobbitsaarebas, Unknown)

My reluctance to escape a clearly abusive relationship went right down the list of typical barriers to seeking help (Morgan et al., 2016). It was hard to talk about something so shameful. I tried to deny that abuse was happening. After all, I was well educated and enlightened, surely that couldn't happen to ME? I blamed myself for doing something wrong or not being good enough. I was terrified of what would happen if I tried to leave. Would she kill me? Would I wind up homeless on the streets? What would my family say? Any time I tried to challenge her, she knew exactly how to counter anything, up to and including threatening suicide. I didn't know where to go for support. I was isolated (as she carefully planned) and didn't know how to find help.

Ellen and her daughter might be suffering from mental disorders. Ellen hinted at having been medicated for something in the past, but she didn't like how the drugs made her feel, so they self-medicated with marijuana. Ellen showed many symptoms of borderline personality disorder such as extreme mood swings, quickly shifting opinions about others, intense and unstable relationships, impulsive behaviors (especially spending), threats of suicide, distorted sense of self (believing herself an excellent parent), problems controlling anger, and difficulty trusting. (NIMH, Unknown) I'm unqualified to make a diagnosis; I just know she fervently avoided anyone who was qualified to do so.

Her kids convinced Ellen that they were helpless because they were permanently damaged by abuse, hence it wasn't fair to expect them to hold down a full-time job. Ellen felt guilty enough to buy it. She got the satisfaction of thinking that she was being a good mommy by sacrificing herself for the benefit of her poor helpless children. It's always noble to be self-sacrificing, right? She effectively replicated a pattern established by her mother, who left her (died) at a fairly young age with no skills to support herself or function as an independent adult. When I first moved to the East coast, Ellen told me she was supporting herself and her children on her own, with a little help from her father. Turned out, her father was shelling out $1000/month to pay for the apartment they lived in.

I knew that my life situation was all ludicrous, but also didn't have any power to stop it. I knew that her son was in the worst position of all, since he had the least power in this situation, but I couldn't help him. He was being controlled by his sister, whom he admired to the ends of the Earth, and he wanted to appease everyone to make all conflicts go away. I couldn't help myself, much less anyone else.

Signs of rebellion

As our marriage started to deteriorate, I looked for outside sources of fun and empowerment. Singing was encouraged in the home, and I always wanted to sing (like my father), so I took voice lessons for a couple of years. I went from having a range of five notes to about an octave and a half, and joined a chorus in New Jersey (the Garden State Chorale (Chorale, 2017)) for one season as a tenor 2. But practicing was difficult when your family had nothing good to say about your fledgling voice, and visibly cringed at the chorus' concert, so I bowed to the pressure and quit that. This was an example of where my ex-wife's perfectionist tendencies discouraged doing anything. If you can't be the best singer in the world, there's no point in trying. It doesn't matter if you enjoy it, don't even try.

I briefly had a little discretionary income around the turn of the millennium, and I started going on eBay to look for old German coins. I've always felt a strong connection to Bavaria and more specifically Munich (since I was born there), so I wondered how far back I could find coins that were from that area. Germany had separate states until its first unification under Otto von Bismarck in 1871, (Wikipedia, 2018) so coins specific to Bavaria were fairly easy to find before that. I found inexpensive coins from the 18th and 19th centuries. The earliest I could find was some coins from around 1624, which clearly showed the diamond-shaped crest still associated with Bavaria (Figure 13). My having discretionary income was clearly not good from Ellen's point of view, so fiscal 'emergencies' soon emerged which made such frivolities impossible.

Figure 13. Bavarian shield on a coin from 1624
(MA-Shops, 2018)

Our home in Cherry Hill had a large back yard, about a quarter acre, so when we moved in, I got a soccer ball for kids to play with. One day I was dinking around in the yard and got the soccer ball out and started playing around with it. I knew almost nothing of the sport, but I was pleasantly shocked at how many things I could do to control the ball using my legs and feet. I had seen people doing these things, but never tried them before. As I pondered this revelation, *I wondered almost out loud what else I could do that I never imagined possible.* I thought of the kids' vocal concerts in high school, and the kids who danced in front of the choirs, and how much that looked fun and beautiful. This led to the greatest leap of faith in my life to date. I started dance lessons. Ballet, specifically. At age 42. After growing up a cripple. I wanted to be graceful. I wanted to be beautiful.

I signed up for a ballet class at Drexel University with a professor named Lucinda Lea. I carefully researched getting very large leotard and dance tights and learned what a dance belt was (a jock strap for dancers). I was so big (around 200 lbs) I had to modify the leotard by extending the crotch seam, so it was big enough for me. I got dressed, feeling like a complete fool at my age and size for even considering such a thing. I walked toward my first ballet class, fully expecting to be laughed out of the room instantly. And then that didn't happen. And I kept dancing, and no one laughed. About six weeks later, my stepdaughter noticed my dance clothes drying in the laundry room, and my secret was out. Ellen tried to discourage me from doing it, but for the first time, I held fast. I knew this was important. And I still dance to this day.

The Dark Side - Escape

As my marriage slowly collapsed into a black hole of abuse and humiliation, my morale deteriorated into nothingness. I was desperate for escape but couldn't see how. Ellen and my worlds were so completely intertwined that getting away seemed impossible. I gave serious thought to two options to get out of my destructive marriage. Suicide or homicide. I considered simply ending my life, as a final act of desperation to get away from Ellen. I decided I had too much potential and was too young to make that solution attractive.

Ellen loved to watch shows like Law and Order (IMDb.com, 2018f) and its spinoffs, so I had seen dozens of fictitious murders. And Ellen loved to be bound and gagged sexually and left for long periods of time. Put those two ideas together, and I imagined it would be easy to start a bondage scene with her, gag her well, and "accidentally" not notice when she could no longer breathe. Oopsie! But then I'd be stuck with her kids (who were now grown adults) blaming me for her death, and a slight chance that someone would successfully prosecute me, and I'd do terribly in prison. Skip that option.

I picked a third option: divorce. I knew my situation was awful, but I still sought an objective view to help justify upsetting my world. I found a counselor at the University of Pennsylvania and got an appointment to see her. I sat down and told her my life situation. I told her how my wife insulted me ethnically and sexually in front of anyone who was nearby. I told her we had three mortgages on our home, plus easily $30,000 in credit card debt I was managing, and at least another $20,000 in student loans I had taken out. I told her my stepdaughter was growing pot in her room, to self-medicate for undiagnosed mental disorders. That she had quit her job which paid for her nearly new car, but her mom had eagerly stepped in to make car payments for her because she had insisted she was not able to hold down a 9-to-5 job. I told her how my stepson had dropped out of college and gone from a strong work ethic to being a pothead to keep his bored sister company. I told her that despite six figure income, I was running about negative $500/month in discretionary income – I had to borrow that much per month to make ends meet. **I listened to myself describing my home life and felt like I must be the biggest moron ever to walk the face of the Earth.** The counselor reassured me that I needed to get out as soon as possible. I knew this already, I just needed someone else to state the painfully obvious. I had to get out of my marriage.

I tested the waters further, telling my biological family that I was considering getting a divorce. Without a moment's hesitation, they asked what they could do to help. ANYTHING they could do to help. My stepmother advised me to see a lawyer immediately and follow their advice. My parents loaned me money to get the lawyer on retainer, and later much more money to make the transition possible. The lawyer (Stephanie Zane (Law, 2016), who did an excellent job for me) advised me to get critical possessions and myself out of the house as soon as possible.

I rented a storage unit near home and started moving out items that were valuable and/or sentimentally important to me. Jewelry, firearms, legal papers, power tools, musical instruments and recording equipment - an odd mixture of items started filling my storage space. Since I was full time faculty, I had an irregular enough schedule to be able to come and go pretty much when I wanted without it seeming odd. That, or no one cared.

Ellen and I had both started working on PhDs, and it was obvious to everyone that our relationship wouldn't last. (It wouldn't last because it was horribly broken, it had nothing to do with the fact that we were both in school and working full time.) We had roughly agreed to finish our PhDs before getting divorced, but I knew that my financial position and emotional state couldn't wait for years. The deck of cards was going to collapse within months, so it was better to take it down deliberately before it collapsed on its own.

I kept cleaning out stuff from the attic, going through papers and trying to reduce the massive volume of junk which filled our walk-in attic. I used the pretense of 'doing spring cleaning' to justify it for a while. Once I had my ducks in a row, I finally told Ellen it was over. She came home and saw me going through papers in our bedroom and asked if I was leaving. I looked her in the eye and simply said 'yes.' She left the room to go talk to her children. Soon she insisted that the 'real' reason for our divorce was that I was gay. True to form, nothing could be because of her actions.

I had prepared for telling her it was over by writing a letter, which I never needed to give her. Here it is, with some information masked by replacements in braces <like this>. I include it here to remind myself to what depths my life had sunk. It's common for people on the outside to see someone in an abusive relationship, and wonder "why didn't you just leave?" or "how could you let someone treat you that way?" It wasn't a sudden transformation, it happened one little event at a time, each one slowly chipping away at my self-esteem like the Colorado River patiently carving the Grand Canyon. But instead of creating something glorious, it quietly destroyed me.

I applauded when you reached the point where you could leave <your second husband>, because you realized that it was critical to treat yourself with respect. After discussion with counselors, both emotional and legal, I have made a very difficult decision, in order to treat myself with more respect than I have been.

I'm leaving. It's over. I want a divorce.

Some of the reasons for needing to do so have been around for a long time.

- *It is not acceptable to attack my family every time mention of them is made.*
- *It is not acceptable to attack German heritage every time it is mentioned.*
    - *It is grossly insulting to treat German as a sex toy.*

But in the last two years the situation at home has gone from uncomfortable to horrific.

- *It is not acceptable to 'open our marriage' as a solo decision.*
    - *It is grossly insulting to flaunt your relationship with your "Master" through hundreds of emails, and untold numbers of phone calls.*
    - *It is completely humiliating for you to address your Master on the phone in the same tone which you used to use for me.*
- *It is not acceptable to encourage wholesale improper activity at home.*
- *It is not acceptable to endorse driving while not sober, especially on a daily basis.*
- *It is not acceptable to make a solo change from 'raising the kids so they become independent adults' to 'a multi-generational household is a good thing', thereby paving the way for them to remain emotionally and financially completely dependent upon you forever.*

<Your children> have made it abundantly clear that my opinions are utterly worthless to them, therefore it is a complete waste of my time to attempt to have any further impact on their lives. I wish all of you all the happiness and success you can tolerate. If a wandering psychic music producer happens by, and

really does give you the million dollar contract you hope for, I wish you only the best in your careers.

What does this mean in the short term? I'm moving out June 1st. You collectively need to determine where you're going (obviously none of us can afford to stay on <our street>), and start packing your stuff.

We need to get the house ready to list as soon as possible, so it can be sold some time this Summer. That means the garden has to be moved off the property, and right away. I'll get most of my stuff out by the start of June, and keep coming back to help fix up the place – like replace the screens on the porch, finish painting the master bedroom, etc. I think we should hire someone to paint the window interiors – that's way too time consuming and tedious. The other details we can work out later.

I was still working on my dissertation, so after a little comparison shopping, I knew I wanted to find a place to live near campus. As it turned out, the apartment building literally across the street from my school's main building (The Left Bank, (Bank, 2018)) conveniently ignored my legal first name in order to justify getting credit rating approval for me to sign a lease[4]. Bear in mind that I was paying two of the three mortgages we had on our home in Cherry Hill, NJ and was applying to rent a $2000/month apartment on top

[4] While credit reports are theoretically based on one's social security number, in practice many places look up credit reports based on your name. Usually I used my given full legal name for credit matters, but the apartment building management ran my credit report using my middle name, which had little or no credit to report, and didn't show the multiple mortgages and loaded credit cards.

of that. Clearly not a sustainable lifestyle, but they were willing to allow it when I told them my situation. Thank you.

There was another benefit to getting a divorce instead of the other options. It allowed Ellen to stay alive, so she can continue to work herself into the ground and care for her 'poor helpless' children until the day she drops dead of exhaustion. Getting a divorce was my last act of sadism toward her.

About a year after leaving my ex-wife and her children, I got a long and vicious email from my former stepdaughter, telling me she felt the need to "set the record straight" about what a horrible parent I had been, and how much happier they were now that I was no longer in the picture. I pondered her missive a couple of days, and simply responded "I appreciate you setting the record straight. I hope you learned from my mistakes and do a much better job providing for and caring for your family than I did. Oh, and happy birthday (soon)." I figured there was no point in arguing with her, and she's more than welcome to do a better job parenting than I did. Good luck with that.

Now on my own, one winter I went through two large boxes of receipts I had saved from our home, to look for the few significant receipts I still needed. Along the way, I found the paper trail of some of the things I had done as a 'terrible' parent:

- Starting at least eight years before I left them, I was refinancing debt to keep us solvent, moving balances from one credit card to another to get better interest rates and higher credit limits, and obtaining multiple home mortgages as the value of our home increased.

- Paid for braces for both of my step-kids.
- Cosigned student loans for my stepdaughter and paid them off after the divorce.
- Had to take out my own student loans to get through graduate school and am still paying them off over a decade later.
- Helping my now ex-wife reclaim her maiden name through a legal name change.
- Hiring a lawyer to fight off my stepson's abusive biological father when he got the wild idea of suddenly re-entering his son's life. Ironically that lawyer represented her in our divorce.
- Going to family therapy with both step kids to help them recover from their abusive histories.
- Making sure both step kids had the opportunity to go to college. This was echoing the gift from my parents, who paid for Bachelor's degrees for my brother and I. My stepdaughter finished an Associate degree, Bachelor's degree, and Master's degree. My stepson enrolled in college but never bothered to go to enough classes and dropped out.
- Provided a home for them in one of the best school districts in New Jersey.

In spite of doing everything humanly possible to support my family, I was instantly demonized when I made it clear I couldn't be Atlas supporting the world on my shoulders any more. This continued the pattern of degradation even after I found the strength to leave the relationship.

Reflection

1. How did you determine your initial career path? (I'm assuming it might change later in life.) What aspects of it led you to choose it? How did your family respond to your career choice? Approval, disapproval, or something else?
2. As an adult are you following the religious path you were raised with (if any)?
3. How have your dating and relationship patterns changed since your earliest explorations?
4. As an adult have you started to explore hobbies that were outside of the ones you were allowed as a child?
5. Do you see aspects of your parents' behavior and habits in yourself as an adult? Are you partly still your parents?

Chapter 3 – Breaking Free and Searching for Answers

As I started the long tedious process of getting divorced, I realized I had a prime opportunity to redefine who I am. I had no idea where that would lead! I knew that I had repressed a lot of activities and interests while I was married, and I eagerly looked forward to exploring my new world.

Setting up new life

First, I had the pleasure of setting up my new apartment and living alone for the first time in thirteen years. Ellen and I agreed to split up the furniture fairly amicably, and I still had good basic kitchen supplies. In the spirit of Pay It Forward (IMDb.com, 2018h), my brother paid for a new bed for me (thanks bro!). My parents loaned me a sizable amount of money to be able to pay rent as well as the mortgages until the house could be sold.

I was determined not to feel like I was reliving my first apartment in California, some 22 years earlier, so I splurged with some of my borrowed money on a new flat screen TV, some quality silverware, and a big new oak bookshelf. I realized that the divorce was a prime opportunity to reinvent myself. Some could say I may have gone too far. J

I had been dancing for a couple of years by this point, and I had gone to some events in the annual Fringe Festival (Arts, Unknown) in Philadelphia. After going to one or two shows here and there, I got more methodical about it and started planning out which shows I was interested in and buying tickets well in advance for them. I mostly went to dance events, but also kept my eye open for anything else that looked amusing. Finding the venues for these events gave me a great chance to become more familiar with Philadelphia, as I took subways and buses all over the city.

While continuing to pursue my doctorate, I took dance classes to work my body as well as my mind and took up figure skating to develop even more strength and balance. I took dance ensemble classes at Drexel and participated in the auditions to perform in the biennial concerts. As I got more and more comfortable dancing, I got contact lenses for the first time in my life, so that I could spot during turns more easily. This desire to become a better dancer led to a level of obsession for a couple of years.

Ongoing education

When I started teaching full time, I realized that I could take advantage of educational opportunities as faculty. I was at first uneasy because I was a full time academic without a terminal degree (Ph.D.). To fix this problem, I spent my first year searching for Ph.D. programs at my institution, because 'tuition remission' would greatly reduce the cost of graduate study. I audited a smattering of classes to see what looked promising. I ruled out computer science, in part since that program was being restructured. I ruled out mechanical engineering, because it wasn't that exciting for my Master's degree. I considered quirky options. A doctorate in physical therapy, to build on my massage background, wasn't feasible because it was only offered as a full-time three-year program. I needed a part time program so I could keep teaching while earning a doctorate. I even looked at a Master's in fashion design, but the list of prerequisites was so long I'd essentially have to earn a BS in that subject first. I finally tried biomedical engineering, which would build on my engineering foundation and add the twist of learning biology and physiology. That was the winning answer.

In spite of some faculty opposing me, I was accepted to the PhD program in biomedical engineering, and completed it in six years part time, while teaching full time. My dissertation used computational biology to analyze healthy human aging. (G. Booker, 2011)

After completing my doctorate, I took about six months to recover, then got the itch to learn more. #EducationJunkie Motivated also in part by the desire to keep taking free dance classes, I needed to be in a degree program. I still hadn't come out as transgender yet and had some interest in running for office. I had written up statements of my views on gun control and other key issues, and decided to major in political science for a second Bachelor's degree. (J. Booker, 2017c, 2018)

After a few uninspiring classes in political science, I decided to switch to be a psychology major. The subjects of how learning and memory work, and human-machine interaction would be relevant to my teaching computer technology, and the instructors were fun. I branched out to also study gender theory, in addition to the dance classes I craved. I took over two dozen social science courses, mostly psychology and gender studies, and they helped me support a colleague's award-winning research on getting more girls interested in computing. (Rode et al., 2015) They also gave me the foundation to be able to discuss the broader implications of my coming out and transition in this book.

The Dark Side – food challenges

Within a year after leaving my ex-wife, I decided to go on a diet to lose some more weight. Fixing up our house in Cherry Hill had helped me lose quite a bit since I worked at the house some 15 hours a week all summer to get it ready to sell. I looked around for guidance to lose more.

In what soon became obvious as a VERY poor choice, I found a group on LiveJournal called 'proanorexia.' (Various, 2009) My simplistic logic was that people with eating disorders must know how to lose weight. I quickly learned that eating disorders are mental disorders, and the ones with the highest mortality rate. (APA, 2013b; Westmoreland, Krantz, & Mehler, 2016)

Instead of leaving right away, I was drawn to stay on the proanorexia site. It gave me a place to safely love women who were in desperate need of support and validation, while I learned from them what NOT to do. At first (circa 2007) the site allowed a lot of content that was later (2009) banned under new moderators and under public pressure to avoid encouraging disorders instead of just being a place for peer support. (Van Pelt, 2009) Some of the types of now-banned content include:

- "thinspo" (based on 'thin' and 'inspiration') which are photos of very thin people including celebrities, or 'reverse thinspo' photos of extremely obese people
- Games to challenge each other to eat less and less
- Diet plans which typically peak at 500 calories per day (2000 cal/day is more typical for adults, and a medically-managed diet might be 1200 cal/day)
- Asking for advice how to become anorexic

Being a bit of an electronic packrat, I collected and anonymized some of this information for posterity. (Bird, 2008) Beyond the above types of content, I included how to calculate BMI (Body Mass Index, a common but poor measure of obesity), recipes for low calorie meals, poetry, quotes, and advice for people supporting people with eating disorders.

The poetry was particularly terrifying. Some would write to Ana, the personification of anorexia. Here is an excerpt from one of those poems.

I offer you my soul, my heart and my bodily functions. I give you all my earthly possessions.

I seek your wisdom, your faith and your feather weight. I pledge to obtain the ability to float, to lower my weight to the single digits, I pledge to stare into space, to fear food, and to see obese images in the mirror. I will worship you and pledge to be a faithful servant until death does us part.

If I cheat on you and procreate with Ronald McDonald, Dave Thomas, the colonel or that cute little dog. I will kneel over my toilet and thrust my fingers deep in my throat and pray for your forgiveness.

Please Ana, don't give up on me. I'm so weak, I know, but only you with your strength inside me will I become a woman worthy of love and respect. I'm begging for you not to give up, I'm pleading with my shallow breathes and my pale skin. I bleed for you, suffer leg pains, headaches and fainting spells. My love for you makes me dizzy and confused I don't know whether I'm coming or going. Men run when they see the love I have for you and never return. But they aren't important to me all that's important is that you love me.

While frequenting the proanorexia site, I was dancing several times a week, and swimming a lot. I started a diet one New Year's Day with three days of fasting, followed by a rigorous diet. I ate a ton of fresh fruit and veggies, had eggs and light toast for breakfast, and one protein entrée per day. I drank no soda, had no desserts, and carefully monitored everything ate or drank. I exercised 10-12 hours per week. I got to where I could swim two miles with a single break of a minute or two. The net result was losing ¼ pound per day for five months. I got down to the low 150's pounds, which was barely in the 'normal' range for my height.

Was my eating disordered? Borderline. There was a strong obsession component, but I barely kept it within the realm of healthy, since I was losing less than two pounds per week. Figure 14 shows me near my lowest weight (and with a scraggly beard!).

Figure 14. Me circa 2010

I collected 83 voluntary surveys from proanorexia members and analyzed them. (J. Booker, 2007) On average they were 5'5" tall, 18.9 years old, weighed 138 lbs, had a current BMI of 22.8, and a goal BMI of 18.1. All but three were women, and the youngest was age 14. Of those who provided enough information to calculate BMI, 30% had goal BMI under 17, which was clinically underweight at the time. Now underweight is under BMI of 18.5, normal is under 25, up to 30 is overweight, and over 30 is obese. (CDC, 2017)

I found it analytically interesting that those with the lowest current BMI had the lowest goal BMI ($R^2 = 0.54$). (Figure 15) I guess this makes sense: the smaller you are, the smaller you want to be.

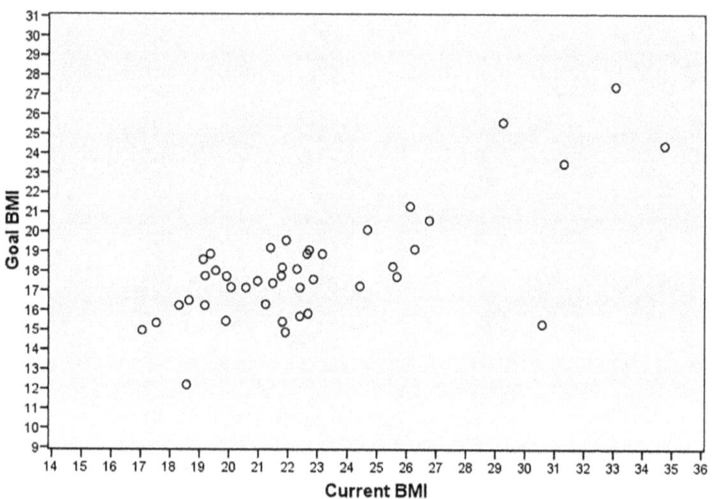

Figure 15. Goal BMI versus Current BMI for proanorexia members.

After a couple of years of trying to maintain low weight, I finally realized that it wasn't sustainable. It took a massive amount of time and effort to plan how little I could eat and keep exercising enough. I gave up on serious dance activity after getting rejected personally for a dance ensemble number at Drexel. The head of the dance department crafted a new rule to specifically exclude me from participation in that ensemble. I continued to support dance organizations in Philadelphia, and attended a lot of Fringe performances, and that ultimately led to the reason for this book existing.

Song of the Sacred Whore

While looking for interesting Fringe performances, I spotted a show called Song of the Sacred Whore (Day, 2011) by a lady named Monica Day. Since I was well aware of the sacred feminine from my pagan foundation, I found this VERY intriguing. I came to the show and sat in the front row. Monica performed a mostly one-woman show, telling stories of the incredibly sex-positive sacred feminine. Here's how she described it (Day, 2011):

Deemed a 'whore risk' by her father from birth, performance artist Monica Day takes a journey from convents to hotel rooms to find the true essence of the whore she feared. Instead, an ancient, sacred whore is revealed, one who lives inside every woman willing to look beyond the label.

I was glued to every word of the performance. I had to know more about this amazing lady. I approached her after the show and found out she was going to be offering workshops. I immediately signed up to find out more.

The Essensual Experience

Six months later, I attended her first workshop, *The Essensual Experience*. It was held in a large open room in northeast Philadelphia, surrounded by old wood and heavy ironworks from long-past purposes. The participants were about ten of us, from various races, sexes, and professions, mostly middle-class Caucasians.

The class focused on developing authentic expression, mostly through writing, then performing a reading of that writing. We did a lot of writing exercises during the workshop, writing short pieces about a lot of topics. Your favorite rant. A description of the person sitting across from you. A private letter (which we could then choose to read aloud anyway). For instance, one of our first assignments was to write stories in 15-minute blocks per day, 1-4 paragraphs per story. As I wrote in my notes, the **"Goal is authentic expression. Are you willing to be who you are?"** Most people wrote about sexual or sensual experiences. I didn't have that many interesting sexual experiences to write about, so I wrote about experiences at the Pagan Spirit Gathering, or with the Church of All Worlds. I wrote about my abuse history. I didn't feel qualified to write about sexuality. I was certainly no virgin, but I felt like a clueless novice in that subject. Once I wrote about tripping on LSD and having sex with my girlfriend while I was at (the University of California at) Berkeley, and one person gave feedback of "Is that all? You got high and had sex?" Like that was what they did every Tuesday. To be fair, maybe it was. I've led a very sheltered life compared to many.

We read our short stories to each other and got tips on how to flesh out stories with more details. How to make writing more interesting by changing the length of sentences (which I recently found summarized in Figure 16). Details make a story more universal and more compelling. Use all five senses to tell the story. The story should marry the details with the point of the story. Do all of the sections support the overall point? Look at how a story will change if you tell it from a different point of view. Keep writing a lot of stories and look for one that has 'legs.' What speaks to you? Play with your writing, don't get too attached to it.

> This sentence has five words. Here are five more words. Five-word sentences are fine. But several together become monotonous. Listen to what is happening. The writing is getting boring. The sound of it drones. It's like a stuck record. The ear demands some variety.
>
> Now listen. I vary the sentence length, and I create music. Music. The writing sings. It has a pleasant rhythm, a lilt, a harmony. I use short sentences. And I use sentences of medium length. And sometimes when I am certain the reader is rested, I will engage him with a sentence of considerable length, a sentence that burns with energy and builds with all the impetus of a crescendo, the roll of the drums, the crash of the cymbals—sounds that say listen to this, it is important.
>
> So write with a combination of short, medium, and long sentences. Create a sound that pleases the reader's ear. Don't just write words. Write music.
>
> -Gary Provost

Figure 16. Tips for more interesting writing

Monica transitioned us from writing to speaking by focusing on the basics – who are you talking to? What's the point? Does your phrasing match the persona of the piece? What words should be emphasized when you're speaking?[5] How to project our voices. How to use a microphone properly, and choose whether to use

---

[5] Fortunately I stumbled across my notes from this workshop, some four years later!

a mic stand, or handheld mic, or no mic at all. How to present ourselves to an audience; what is our physical posture? How to speed up and slow down effectively. Remember to breathe. If you memorize a piece it will probably sound wooden. Above all, **tell the story**.

As we got more comfortable with writing, the challenges got greater in terms of subject matter. We were challenged to write a letter to our genitals. I wrote a letter to my cock. It became the piece I read at a public showing we did at the end of the workshop, and later refined it and read it at the next Fringe Festival as a part of a show Monica produced called *The Secret Order of the Libertines*. Here is the final version, complete with my edits to remind myself what words to emphasize and give myself some stage direction:

Letter to my genitals

Dear cock,

*I wish you were a porn star cock. We could fuck any thing, any where, any time. What an incredible sense of power and control that would give. What would that **feel like**? No idea.*

*I know you've been alone forever. I keep trying to find the perfect pussy for you. A pussy safe and loving and accepting. A pussy that will be patient and not treat you like **every other cock** on the planet.*

*What I really want, is to find you the ideal woman. One who savors sharing hours of delicious tactile exploration and discovery. Not **just** the obvious wonderful sex parts and erogenous zones, but firm loving stroking **eve-ry-where**.*

We wait for making love until the time is right for both of us. No hurry. No expectations. Riding the waves of rising excitement and relaxation, without the unspoken need to FUCK RIGHT NOW.

Sometimes I worry, that the woman I want for us doesn't exist. And the only date you'll see is ... my left hand. Am I being too naive? Idealistic? Romantic? FUCKING STUPID? I don't know.

I know you're different. No, ***we*** *are different. See, I can barely tell if we're in the same body. I feel we can't override our wiring, and that frustrates the rest of me.*

Everyone expects you to spring to attention at the slightest hint of a lovely lady in a romantic moment. Maybe that's "normal," I don't know. But gods help us when that doesn't happen. ***You*** *don't see their crestfallen expression, the speed with which THEIR self doubt leaps into the room. You don't hear the hollow apologies, since now they're convinced they must be perfectly revolting or frighteningly disgusting. Or it turns the other direction, and the baffled expression on their face screams 'what the Fuck is the matter with you?' No matter how hard I try to explain, they never really believe that we are wired differently. They can't believe you have to work with our heart.*

The heart is critical for us. We are truly cursed. We can only make love, we can't just fuck. Before you can enter her body we ***have*** *to feel a connection between our hearts.* ***That*** *conversation, that intimate connection makes it possible for making love to occur.*

I love the way her labia unfold when her legs relax open, and I feel her heart open at the ***same time****. Knowing she trusts* *me to share her innermost parts, her most vulnerable self. The way she remains eagerly open to my gaze, my touch, my heart,* ***and you.***

Once that connection is strong, we can reconnect on a moment's notice. It doesn't ***have*** *to take hours of making love.*

[slow] All it takes is a hand wrapping firmly around her waist. A nuzzle on the nape of her neck. Or a look across the room that tells her there's WAY too much space between our bodies.

Be patient my friend, we ***will*** *find her.*

In this brutally honest piece, I expressed my frustration over the expectations of typical male behavior sexually and what I wanted to do. I knew I was fundamentally disconnected from my sexuality and couldn't begin to imagine how to fix it.

Not surprisingly, I found the workshop amazing. Monica later quoted my feedback in her promotional literature (Day, 2014). "[The Essensual Experience] is a wonderful opportunity to explore your sensual nature and experiences, and develop the strength to share your Self with others. Monica is amazing at seeing through you, and calling you out when you try to hide or shy away from your potential. She lives the workshop by example, and that makes it easier to really push yourself to places you never imagine existed or possible."

Monica seems to have a never-ending list of prompts for writing, to answer the often-whiny question "What should I write about?" As I mentioned earlier, one key is to do a LOT of brief writing and then filter out what seems meaningful and worth refining. Start a lot, then polish the gems. Here are some more prompts:

- Write about something that makes you curious
- Write about a stranger slipping into your bed in the middle of the night
- Write about ditching morality for a night
- Write about a regret
- Write about a gate in a garden, and what you think is behind it
- Write about a really big mess
- An Ode To [part of your body you love]
- An Ode To [part of someone else's body you love]
- A letter to the one that got away
- A letter to the one you're waiting for
- A letter to yourself 20 years ago
- A letter to yourself in 20 years
- To a lover: *What I'll do to you when I get you home*
- The last time you lied
- The last time you told the truth

A favorite writing assignment was to write a letter to yourself 20 years ago. Here's what I came up with.

A letter to yourself 20 years ago

Thank gods we finally got time travel to work! You're ... I mean we're ... whatever ... you're on a great track, I want to help steer you to even better possibilities.

You're turning 30, and you think that means you need to start being responsible and settle down. That's a great idea, IF you wait for the right lady to do it with. Set your standards higher than you think you deserve! Yes, you might have to wait longer to find the right partner, but it will be far better than settling for 'good enough.' Trust me!

Your mind has been a great tool to get you where you are. And yes, it will continue to be a wonderful asset, and make it possible for you to be superficially successful and not starve to death in a gutter somewhere. That's great, that's awesome, and you should be rightfully be proud of developing that gift.

I want you to focus more attention on areas you've ignored - your body and other people.

I know it's hard to focus on your body. Thirty inches of scars have left their mark in many ways. You did what you had to in the moment to survive that, and that's a critical first step. Now, as you discover massage therapy and other kinds of bodywork, keep exploring ways to wake up your body. It's okay. It's safe now, you don't have to hold onto the ideas of the past.

Try to imagine: if you didn't see yourself as a cripple, what worlds would that open up? What would you do? Be patient, and don't give up. You've had three decades to set up patterns of movement, they won't change overnight. But they can change in ways you literally never imagined possible.

But don't leave it at that level. Explore your body. Literally! Play with every inch of you, stay in the moment, and see how it feels. What does it like? Soft or sharp? Gentle or firm? Is it happy or grumpy or horny or just starved for attention? Honor the parts that are still scared, they are trapped in the past. They will come around when they're ready. Meanwhile, make a private orgy if you can't find a better offer. Throw down some old sheets and use way too much massage oil! And yes, explore all the naughty bits too. It's your body, you have every right to enjoy every aspect of it. You know in your head it's all good and sacred, it's just hard to override all those years of programming.

Challenge yourself to play with new possibilities. Sports? You really liked tennis and swimming, maybe those can become public ways to explore how your newly rediscovered body responds and what it can do.

Armed with this new knowledge of your Self, take the next step and brave going out into the world. Yes, I want you to be social. No, I'm not crazy! I know you're a hermit by habit, but you crave more connection to others, even if you aren't really sure how to get there. Ok, maybe you spent too much time in books instead of going to prom or flirting with the cute flute player down the street. So your greatest challenge might be overcoming your own fears and getting out of the house. Sure, you don't understand people and social interaction. Physics and math are a heck of a lot more straightforward. Yes, you'll get shot down a lot. It's ok, you're not the Red Baron. But remember after the awkward initial stages, the sheer joy of a simple happy fuck. Feeling her pulse pound from inside her. Savoring the blend of pheromones under the bottom edge of her breasts. Watching her back arch as the wave overtakes her. Kissing her sweaty brow while you're both still out of breath.

I dare you to keep pushing for more than you think you're allowed to ask for. Keep working your mind, explore your body, and venture out into the world. All you have to lose is your limitations.

I wasted so many years hiding from myself, I wish I could have begun this journey much earlier. My massage training was a step in the right direction, but then I got distracted by imagining that I needed to 'grow up' and be a good family man. I listened to what I thought Society wanted from me, instead of listening to my heart and soul.

Part of the reason I'm writing this book is to help prevent others from repeating my lessons. Growing up crippled and living through an abusive marriage, these things helped me develop deep empathy and levels of internal strength I might never have developed without them. But what if I kept doing bodywork and came out to myself twenty years sooner? My life path would have been very different. I need to remind myself that my timing is perfect and elegant. Without coming to the East coast, I wouldn't have gone into academia, earned a PhD, and discovered the amazing people and resources in and near Philadelphia.

5Rhythms

Another perspective introduced in Monica's workshops was a more physical approach to self-expression, through the world of 5Rhythms dance (5Rhythms, 2018). 5Rhythms was developed by Gabrielle Roth and focuses on lightly structured improvisational group dance based on five rhythms (surprise!), namely flowing, staccato, chaos, lyrical, and stillness. There is no choreography, just the music of choice by the teacher, and the theme of each rhythm. Having had several years of formal dance training, I found 5Rhythms quite enjoyable, but I found myself struggling to unlearn the traditional movement forms I had learned in classes. It was very difficult to shut off the self-censorship, of fearing what others thought of my dance, of criticizing myself. I learned that 5Rhythms is mainly a meditative tool. Ms. Roth is quoted "The fastest way to still the mind is to move the body."

I went to another of Monica's workshops, then decided it was time for more personal help. I hired her as a life coach.

Private coaching

I started getting private life coaching from Monica Day. I knew something was broken, and I couldn't figure out what. In my initial questionnaire, I knew that I wanted help with dating because I recognized how clueless I was in such matters. I also knew the problems were deeper than that. In one of the first essays I wrote with her I vented my frustration.

Melancholy. I'm listening to a lot of Adele and Heart and Pat Benatar, all sappy stuff. I feel off lately, and I can't figure out what it's from. Maybe a little SAD (seasonal affective disorder), that shows up every winter. Maybe a side effect from a long boring cold for the last two weeks. Maybe loneliness; I was going to have a cool roomie, and she flaked out on me.

But I think there's something more fundamental happening. I have a nagging feeling that something is wrong in my world. I should be doing something, and I'm not. I'm doing lots of cool stuff - my job is really good, I'm playing a bunch of soccer, dancing some, making some progress on fixing up my new home. But my body feels depressed, and that makes me eat a lot of junk. Which, of course, doesn't help.

I feel like I'm going through the motions, but my heart isn't in it. And if you've read the rest of this blog, you know how important that is to me. Twenty years ago I was around California pagan hippies, and they spoke of right livelihood (Buddhism) and self-actualization (Maslow's hierarchy). I was starting the process of finding my body through massage therapy and other forms of bodywork. I came to the East coast to chase the possibility of a long term relationship. And over the next few years, my world started slowly collapsing in on itself. I finally got out of a relationship that had become abusive in every way except physical.

The last five years plus have been devoted to completing school and reinventing myself. Exploring new possibilities. Figure skating. Swimming. Many forms of dance. Tennis. A little acting. Dabble in piano. All good and wonderful activities. But it isn't enough. Or the right one. Do I know the right answer, and I'm just afraid of admitting it? Or haven't I found it yet?

I'm truly fortunate to have options to choose from, and not just be scrounging for raw survival. And yet I can't help but expect much bigger things from myself. Is that just thinly veiled ego? Hubris?

Monica and I worked on basic concepts of dating. I was making huge mistakes and not realizing it. Don't show up early. (I arrived five minutes early for my first session with Monica, and she hadn't changed clothes yet or tidied up the living room. This was my first lesson!) Keep the first date short and simple – maybe just meet for coffee or lunch. See if there's anything there before doing more. I had been going on first dates which included dinner at a nice restaurant and going to a classy show like the ballet. I spent literally hundreds of dollars on first dates, only to find that we didn't have any connection in the first five minutes.

We worked on how to present myself for online dating. I had a profile on OkCupid, and my version of it was completely generic. She helped me identify what is unique about me and how to set myself apart from the unwashed masses.

The Salon

To gain confidence in myself, she encouraged me to start presenting some of my writing at The Erotic Literary Salon (Mayer, 2018) in Philadelphia. The Salon was created about five years earlier by Dr. Susana Mayer, a local sexologist, to give people a venue to express ideas that weren't acceptable to be spoken in a conventional place like a poetry reading. The Salon takes place monthly, and people sign up to be able to read on a first come, first serve basis. Recording or photographing presenters is strictly forbidden, to protect the identities and jobs of people present.

Every reader gets up to five minutes to talk about anything they want. The work presented can be fictional stories, personal experiences, poetry, etc.; most presentations are work the reader has written, but it's also fine to read someone else's work that is personally meaningful. Occasionally there are non-spoken presentations, such as dancers or musicians. Each month has a featured presenter, who gets more than five minutes to present a longer work, such as an excerpt from a book they've written.

The open topic range often covers edgier subjects, such as BDSM, fetishes, gay or lesbian encounters, polyamory, etc. The only topic ever disallowed was when a presenter read a story about pedophilia. That was crossing the line and banned from all future Salons.

I started attending The Salon on a regular basis, and frequently read from the stories of my self-discovery. Many of those stories are quoted in this book, as they captured my thoughts in the moment, spanning before, during, and after my transition. The Salon was a perfect, supportive venue to express these intimate thoughts. Even though I rarely read anything vaguely erotic, Susana was very open to readings of authentic self-expression. I made friends with several of the regular Salon attendees, so the Salon went from just a place to vent safely to a monthly meeting with many supportive friends.

Mark Groups

Monica introduced me to Mark Groups as another place to explore better communication and self-expression. Mark Groups are a sort of semi-hidden social gathering; you generally must know someone who introduces you to them. The reason for this is to keep people out who might be disruptive or disrespectful of the group. Mark Groups were developed in the 1960s by Vic Baranco as a game to help people develop better communication skills (Morehouse, 2018). Each Mark Group consists of three structured games which are carefully designed to help people get to know each other quickly and safely. During the games you will almost certainly learn more about the others and might learn something insightful about yourself. Typical groups might have 8-20 people attending, and everyone can choose whether to be a focal point of the evening (on the 'hot seat') or be a wallflower and mostly watch the proceedings. Each group is led by 2-3 people who have been trained to do so.

I started attending Mark Groups when my schedule permitted. The people were supportive and kind, much like the Salon crowd. The depth of conversations varied from one meeting to the next. Sometimes they were very superficial, like asking about favorite movies; sometimes they were focused on sexuality; sometimes they were focused on deeper personal issues.

As you'll see in later chapters, after coming out, Mark Groups provided helpful, brutally honest feedback about my fledgling attempts to change my wardrobe.

Four Agreements

Another tool Monica gave me was a very elegant, concise book called The Four Agreements, by Don Miguel Ruiz (Ruiz & Mills, 2018). As the publisher summarizes them, the agreements are:

- BE IMPECCABLE WITH YOUR WORD. Speak with integrity. Say only what you mean. Avoid using the word to speak against yourself or to gossip about others. Use the power of your word in the direction of truth and love.
- DON'T TAKE ANYTHING PERSONALLY. Nothing others do is because of you. What others say and do is a

projection of their own reality, their own dream. When you are immune to the opinions and actions of others, you won't be the victim of needless suffering.

- DON'T MAKE ASSUMPTIONS. Find the courage to ask questions and to express what you really want. Communicate with others as clearly as you can to avoid misunderstandings, sadness, and drama. With just this one agreement, you can completely transform your life.
- ALWAYS DO YOUR BEST. Your best is going to change from moment to moment; it will be different when you are tired as opposed to well-rested. Under any circumstance, simply do your best, and you will avoid self-judgment, self-abuse, and regret.

The Mark Groups were particularly helpful in practicing BE IMPECCABLE WITH YOUR WORD. Focusing on what your truth is and expressing it accurately and honestly gives power to your words. What are you willing to share of your truth? What does it feel like to deliberately lie? How does it feel to share deep truth about yourself?

DON'T TAKE ANYTHING PERSONALLY didn't make sense until working with Michele Younger, which is discussed in Chapter 4.

DON'T MAKE ASSUMPTIONS is extremely helpful for dating and most of life in general. Don't assume you know what your friend or partner thinks, wants, needs, or feels. **Ask them.** This ties in nicely with the concept of enthusiastic consent. From asking if someone wants to go out, to asking for more intimate activities, this eliminates a lot of guesswork AND can be really sexy. “Would you like me to kiss your neck?” might lead to my favorite foreplay line in the whole world, “Is there any place you **don’t** want me to kiss you?” Specific questions like “Would you like me to lick your beautiful pussy?” not only establish enthusiastic consent but build erotic tension. I’ll leave other examples as an exercise for the reader.

ALWAYS DO YOUR BEST sounded very perfectionist to me, which scared me after having a perfectionist wife who used it as an excuse to do nothing. As in, “there’s no point in trying to do X because I won’t be able to do it perfectly.” This agreement recognizes that ‘your best’ isn’t “perfect,” and changes from day to day. Don’t beat yourself up for not earning a Nobel Prize or Oscar every day.

After about six months of private coaching, Monica knew that a friend was visiting from Arizona, and thought I might benefit from her novel approach to bodywork. Little did I know that this friend would change my life forever. Her name was Michele Younger (M. Younger, 2018).

Reflection

1. As an adult, how does your home or apartment differ in decorating style from your parents’? Are they similar, or have you found a different inspiration? What do you want people to feel when they enter your space?
2. What has your relationship been to food and weight? Do you diet?

3. What kinds of physical activity do you enjoy as an adult? How often do you do them?
4. My journey included discovery of the sacred feminine? Do you believe in one or more divine beings? Are they male or female or both or neither?
5. Pick four of the writing prompts. Write 15 minutes on each of them without censoring yourself or trying to edit anything.
6. Imagine you signed up for a five minute presentation at the Erotic Literary Salon. You can talk, sing, dance, whatever you want for five minutes. What form of presentation do you want to make? Prepare the presentation and practice it. Share it with a good friend or fifty.
7. How do the Four Agreements compare to your life? Which of them are you living on a regular basis? Do you agree or disagree with them as being good advice? Why?

Chapter 4 – Hello Jennifer!

Private life coaching with Monica Day led me to two sessions with Michele Younger. Michele also won't let you get away with bullshit about yourself or your life or what you think of the world. That's her job. Working with Michele led to the emergence of Jennifer, and the rest of this chapter goes into the immediate aftermath of that life-changing revelation.

Michele

My first session with Michele was shocking. I knew in advance that she was a bodyworker who focused for most clients on two parts of the body. Her goal is to bring to the surface self-destructive or counter-productive messages that we told ourselves in the past in order to survive which are no longer helpful or beneficial to us.

The two parts of the body Michele focuses on are the mouth and the anus. Yes, this struck me as completely bizarre, but there are excellent reasons behind them. The mouth is critical because of what we say about ourselves. Negative messages can get trapped in the muscles of our mouth, and Michele helps identify and release them. Through Body Harmony, I had already experienced how the body can trap experiences, so this made sense. The anus is critical for survival. If you don't poop, soon you die. Michele works on releasing leftover survival tactics that are stuck in the muscles of the anus and surrounding tissues.

In an unusual sense, Michele is a bodyworker, like a massage therapist, but the verbal narrative and Q&A she does with her sessions make it more a combination of talk therapy session, life coaching, and very specialized massage.

I recall two main themes from my first session with Michele, the verbal and the physical. Working on my mouth, she openly attacked my habit of identifying myself as 'pathetic.' I felt pathetic after a horrible marriage and lousy experiences with sexuality, but she challenged me to throw away those labels for myself. She pointed out to me that I was spending a lot of time trying to make others happy, to do what I imagined society expected of me, much like my mother. Becoming fully yourself means having the strength to be honest about who you are and what you want with your life.

The physical aspect focused on my left leg. I lied naked on a massage table on my back, with Michele sitting between my legs, exaggerating my physical vulnerability. She started playing with my legs, moving them around, soon focusing on my left leg. She was deliberately a little rough with it, using firm pressure and showing no hesitation to touch the scars which pervade that appendage. She watched my somewhat shocked and fearful expression with amusement, finally addressing the pink elephant in the room verbally. She told me to stop identifying as a cripple. She saw through me quite easily and challenged my core identity as a crippled person. After all, I had spent a fair chunk of my childhood in Shriner's Hospitals for Crippled Children (Children, 2018), so I must be a cripple, right? No. That was an important part of my past but didn't have to dictate my present or future. This concept was revolutionary.

After my first visit with Michele, I felt a lot of physical rumbling in my body. The ideas she introduced, and the way she treated my body left me rattled. She identified and challenged core concepts about how I thought about myself, how I identify myself. I knew I was in the right headspace to benefit from her insights, so I signed up for another session a week later before she returned to Arizona.

My second session with Michele changed my life. It started with the dumbest question I ever heard. She looked at me with her big bright eyes as I sat on the massage table, and asked me "Who are you?" I sulked a little at this stunningly obvious question. I answered with my given name. She repeated the question "Who are you?" I repeated the answer. She persisted a couple of times, then rephrasing my answer to "I am Glenn, and sometimes I am..." leaving the blank to be filled in. I wondered if there was something I was missing and searched myself to see if there was something to fill in that blank. I consciously relaxed my body, drawing from my Body Harmony training, to help open myself. The only thing that came to mind was simple. Jennifer. I am Glenn, and sometimes I am Jennifer. That was the start of coming out as transgender.

I honestly don't recall a lot of the rest of that session, other than Michele did a surprising amount of traditional massage on my neck and upper back. I was trying to process what had happened at the start of the session!

Over the next few weeks I had intense debates with myself about my coming out. "There's no way that could be true!" I argued with myself, tried to convince myself it couldn't be true because Michele is an eccentric bodyworker I barely knew. I told myself I never felt the clichéd "woman trapped in a man's body," so I couldn't be transgender. Argument after argument inside my head sounded plausible but didn't ring true.

I checked in time and again with my body. The body doesn't lie, that's a well-known premise of bodywork. (Diamond, 1989) As soon as I came out as transgender, my shoulders lowered a couple of inches. My chest opened up. My posture improved. **My mind tried to argue endlessly with coming out, but my body welcomed it with open arms.** I sighed and realized that the most unthinkable revelation was true.

I soon asked myself key questions about my safety and feared the consequences of coming out but decided to address those later. The key was realizing that I was transgender.

Immediate aftermath of coming out

I first thought I was going to live halfway between male and female, expressing one side or the other depending on my mood. I happened to be in a Women's Studies 101 class when I came out, so I used the term paper from that class (Glenn Booker, 2013c) to capture many of the ideas running through my head at the time. For example, my body told me really clearly about my sexual preference. As I wrote in that paper:

When in New York recently for a soccer tournament with my LGBT league, a teammate asked if I was gay. I responded I was bi. He didn't hear me, so I repeated it. Both times, my stomach flipped suddenly and gurgled, protesting my statement very clearly. Ok, I get the message! I'm straight. Well, Jennifer and I both prefer women, to be more accurate.

I concluded the paper by describing myself as a "gynephilic genderfluid demisexual hedonist." To break down that label, gynephilic means I'm attracted to women, and genderfluid means I switch from male to female gender identity and back frequently. Demisexual describes someone who can only related to someone sexually if they have an emotional connection to them. And finally, hedonist just means I enjoy pleasure and use that to guide my actions. I qualified that label with the immediate caveat "of course that could change tomorrow" so I realized that my identity might evolve. A month or two later, I realized I had no interest in presenting as masculine except for theatrical needs.

Three months after Jennifer emerged, I described to the Erotic Literary Salon the shock of coming out as transgender.

The safe quiet hell

Back story: After coming out as transgender in April, I've gone through a flurry of changes. Outwardly my fashion choices have become much more feminine, even to work. To my surprise, the world has not ended as a result. Of course I work around a bunch of geeks, so I'm guessing half of them haven't even noticed the difference.

I have become a cliché overnight. My walk in closet is already packed to the rafters, and yet I still walk in, look around, and realize ... I have NOTHING to wear.

But the deeper changes are slow in coming. I'm trying to find my people, and I can't quite tell who they are yet.

I spend most days in predominantly female clothing, yet I also don't see myself living as fully female in the future. As I look around in the trans community, I noticed that a huge amount of it is focused on crossing the gender binary. As in: I look like a man, but I want to be a woman. Or the other way around. But even in the trans community there is a relatively small minority that either enjoys being both male and female, or sees themselves as neither male nor female. The gender fluid or gender queer, to use current labels.

And so just like the lost bird in "Are you my mommy?" I find myself exploring, looking for the world that feels like home. Or seeing if I need to create my own world that doesn't exist yet.

The greatest challenge for me now is emerging from my social hibernation. I never understood traditional male roles for dating, so I did it as little as possible until I found women assertive enough to pursue me. This, for the record, is not a very effective strategy in our culture.

My problem boils down to a severe fear of rejection. I never could connect with the attitude that you should take a statistical approach to dating, namely if you ask enough women out, some of them will say 'Yes.' And likewise, if you ask enough of them to fuck, some will say yes. Bingo, problem solved. Got laid. That always struck me as cold and heartless and to use feminist lingo, objectifying.

In recent months I've gotten better at asking women out and basic dating, but making the leap to intimacy is my goal now. The life I've lived has kept me in a safe, quiet hell. Like the vision of hell as a frozen wasteland, where nothing moves but also nothing ever dies. It is a land I have to leave, but the familiar hell often seems safer than an unknown.

I'm told that a relationship with true intimacy allows you to experience higher highs than you imagined possible. And it also requires complete vulnerability, to put your heart and soul and true self on the line. You don't get the highs without risking the lows.

A couple of days ago I was reminded that I have an ally on this journey. Her name is Jennifer, my feminine aspect. For so many years I felt like I had to apologize for my feminine side, to hide her, to pretend to be the Perfect Man in order to find True Love. I have discovered that I'm not James Bond. Or Brad Pitt or even Johnny Depp. Love and intimacy can't be based on a mask, can't be based on an illusion, can't be based on presenting what I think you want me to pretend to be.

So I need to love and accept all parts of myself, and present them honestly, not just to find someone who thinks that's exciting and hot, but more fundamentally to be true to myself. Whoever that turns out to be.

The frozen wasteland version of hell I mentioned is based on the image from the frozen lake in Dante's Inferno (Figure 17). No one dies, but no one lives either – they are stuck in a frozen lake, crying constantly and their tears form icicles.

Figure 17. The frozen lake from Dante's Inferno (Unknown, Unknown-b)

Where do I go?[6]

As I started to get comfortable with the realization that Jennifer was real, I was a bit intimidated by the implications of this massive revelation. My mind raced with a thousand questions, most of which I couldn't answer right away.

- Would I be public about being transgender?
- What were the safety implications if I go public?

---

6 This section title is a reference to the song of the same name from my favorite musical, Hair (UXID, 2010).

- Will I be the target of street harassment? I've heard my female friends complain about this for years. If I get harassed, how should I respond?
- How much would my wardrobe change? Am I going to wear some masculine clothes and some feminine? Or switch to fully female clothes?
- Will I tell my family? If so, HOW? And how will they respond?
- Will I get fired if my job finds out?

Going public and 'passing'

One of the biggest decisions after coming out to myself was deciding how public to be about this massive revelation. Was I going to be public as a transgender woman? After all, there are several very public and famous trans women, e.g. Caitlyn Jenner, Laverne Cox, and Janet Mock, so I wouldn't be a complete novelty in that respect.

'Passing' is a weird concept. It implies that we aren't genuine, that we are trying to fool or trick people into believing we are women. Passing for trans women means that you have manipulated your appearance to be feminine, so feminine that you are 'mistaken' for a cisgender woman routinely. This means that you have not just switched to feminine attire and accessories, but use makeup, wigs, and maybe get plastic surgery. Breast implants (or false breasts), butt implants, and body hair removal are possible tools to help 'pass.' Cisgender men may have a prominent Adam's apple (laryngeal prominence); a surgical procedure to shave that helps trans women minimize that telling bump. Wearing high heels is often expected of women, but it takes a lot of practice to build the muscles needed to walk gracefully in them.

Is all of that a priority for me? I realize that my broad-shouldered build and lack of (head) hair would make it very difficult if not impossible for me to 'pass' as a cisgender woman in everyday life, even if I tolerated wearing a wig all the time. That could lead to a different form of harassment than cisgender women experience.

There are lots of websites to help MTF transgender women and cross-dressers 'pass' more convincingly, ranging from body posture to eye contact to voice training to makeup to plucking eyebrows (Sorella, 2018; wikiHow, 2018). While these techniques are good for getting a more feminine appearance, I object to the term 'passing' because of the implied deception. Whether I spend $200,000 on plastic surgery and makeup and wardrobe or if I simply declare myself to be a woman, both approaches are equally valid. Some have claimed that Caitlyn Jenner spent over $230,000 on surgery and wardrobe (Wilson, 2015). That's nice, she's worth many millions of dollars, but your average trans woman doesn't have anywhere near those resources, and even if she did, she might not want to follow Caitlyn's path.

More important, the whole purpose of this journey was "**Goal is authentic expression. Are you willing to be who you are?**"[7] How can I live authentic expression and hide who I am? It's impossible. It was that core realization that led me to decide to

---

[7] Chapter 3.

live publicly as a trans woman, and not give a rip whether or not I 'pass' as anything. I want to pass as my Self.

Julia Serrano described the double bind when it comes to choosing your gender presentation as a trans woman. "When you're a trans woman, you are made to walk this very fine line, where if you act very feminine you are accused of being a parody, but if you act masculine, it is seen as a sign of your true masculine identity." (Serrano, 2013)

Fetish

Monica soon pointed out to me that, as a result of being transgender, I was now a fetish. Here I thought I was mostly straight! Instantly I was now a potential fetish target. She introduced me to a massive website for people into every fetish imaginable (and probably many you can't imagine), FetLife (BitLove, 2018). FetLife describes themselves as being "Like Facebook but run by kinksters like you and me." With over five million members around the world, FetLife is home to literally hundreds of fetish categories, including transgender and genderqueer. I joined FetLife and found a couple of local fetish events which mostly focused on BDSM but were also safe spaces for transgender people. These gave me the first place to dress safely in semi-public in dresses without being judged.

Later I found a school in New York for "For Boys Who Want To Be Girls," run by Miss Vera (Vera, 2018). A self-described Finishing School, her target audience seems to be primarily men who cross-dress (formerly known as transvestites), and in many cases hadn't ever been in public in female clothing. Miss Vera and her 'faculty' offer experiences in choosing clothing, doing makeup, walking in heels, getting a mani/pedi, shopping for clothes, and many other things. By the time I found Miss Vera, I had already gotten much braver about dressing how I wanted in public, so I didn't pursue her services.

Clothing – first impressions

Long before I came out, my wardrobe started to change as a young adult. As part of my exploration of paganism, it was socially acceptable to buy ritual robes, and wear them for those occasions. Nudity felt even better, but when clothing was required, robes were free and open and much more natural for me than typical men's clothing. I loved the freedom of wearing robes, how they brushed against my legs when I walked. Sometimes my coven was brave enough to wear robes in public, like going to a restaurant after a ritual. Naturally a group of men and women in flowing robes attracted some attention, but a group of us were rarely challenged. Once I recall in a restaurant a young man tried to proselytize our little group. I admired his bravery, since he was clearly shaking in his proverbial boots to confront us. What he didn't realize was that most of us were raised Christian or Jewish and knew scripture better than he did.

When I was first on my own in California, I realized I was curious about panty hose, and wondered what they felt like. I found a postcard advertising some hose and ordered a pair through the mail. I felt uncomfortable when they arrived. It clearly wasn't a fetish thing, I wasn't aroused by them. But I knew I wasn't supposed to wear anything like that. I was SO good at Following the Rules, it was exciting and a little terrifying to do something that violated sacred social norms. I carefully put on the hose, mimicking the way I had seen women do it on TV. I liked the compression against my legs, the snug hug they gave my hips and tummy. The spectre of What Society Thinks loomed large over me, and I quickly took them off to obey. I don't recall ever putting them on again.

Fast forward to a few months before my coming out as Jennifer. I had become a fan of Lady Gaga (Gaga, 2018), and got a ticket to her next show in Philadelphia. Excited, I wanted an outfit that would be wild enough to be respectful of Mother Monster. I had been dancing for several years, and decided my outfit was going to be based on a tutu but didn't want to use the rainbow tutu I already had. I search the Internet, and had trouble finding a tutu large enough for my waist. I finally found someone on eBay who made custom tutus that could meet my "needs." I ordered a 20" long (romantic length) purple tutu. I was SO proud of this! I was trying to think of something to wear on top above the tutu and kept to my male social norms and picked out a yellow polo shirt. Don't ask why, it was ugly. A week before the concert, Lady Gaga got injured and cancelled the concert. I was devastated. But at least I now had a purple tutu!

After the concert was cancelled, I found myself continuing to look for skirts online. Not tutus, but all kinds of skirts, and tops and dresses too, in a wide range of colors and styles. I ordered some of these skirts, almost watching myself over my shoulder as I placed orders online for clothes that I couldn't imagine wearing. I paused occasionally to wonder what the hell I was thinking! **I was buying women's clothes and had literally no idea where or why I would ever wear them!** This self-observation was the first time I recall consciously analyzing my own actions as they took place, kind of like the anthropology practice of autoethnography. "Autoethnography is an approach to research and writing that seeks to describe and systematically analyze personal experience in order to understand cultural experience." (C. Ellis, Adams, & Bochner, 2010) This book is a work of autoethnography which builds on dozens of small pieces of self-observation that I've made over the last several years and has added systematic analysis to them.

My first skirt was a cotton gauze tie-dyed skirt I got in Wisconsin. I heard of a formal fundraiser for animals (a "Fur Ball") with a 1960's theme and jumped at the chance to come up with a fun outfit for it. I matched a tuxedo jacket and bow tie, feminist organization shirt (FEMEN, 2018), and my tie-dyed skirt. I was complimented for my fashion bravery! (Figure 18)

Figure 18. Outfit for the Fur Ball

Before coming out to myself, I attended a Mark Group in a long black skirt. When asked how the skirt made me feel, I responded 'feminine' to my surprise, before I could censor myself.

Immediately after coming out to myself, I went on a buying spree for clothing, buying tons of clothes from sales at American Apparel or Target, random pieces that sounded good from eBay, bras and panties from herroom.com (HerRoom, 2018), and occasional visits to local thrift stores. I bought hundreds of pieces, thanks in part to generous income tax refunds, all a chaotic jumble of pieces with little thought of pieces going together, fitting me well, or which occasions for which they would be suitable. I didn't know if I would eventually be wearing women's clothing to work, or if I'd be keeping more private than that.

I was also afraid to go shopping for women's clothes in person. How would the sales people respond? Would they kick me out of the store? Make fun of me? The results varied. Victoria's Secret wouldn't give me the time of day. Most places were fine with it. Sometimes sales people went to their manager to find out what to do; I think they were concerned about other customers being alarmed by a male-presenting person in the dressing room. I got some curious looks from other customers, but no problems.

My first issue with women's clothing – what size am I? Panties, for those of you who don't wear them, come in numbered sizes that don't relate to anything. Who made this stuff up?? Some stores such as Chico's (Services, 2018) make up their own sizing system so their larger customers don't get depressed from looking for their actual size.

Men's clothes are based on your dimensions in inches. Men's underwear sizes are based on your waist circumference. Pants are just as easy. You have a 34" waist and 30" inseam? Great, look for 34x30 jeans, or size 34 slacks and get them hemmed to length. Nice and simple.

As I dove into clothes shopping, the incredible complexity of women's clothes hit me. I had studied fashion design a tiny bit, but I start to find terminology I had never encountered before. For one prime example, I used 'types of necklines or collars' as an example for a term project (Glenn Booker, 2013a) for a class which focused on the intersection of fashion, movies, and feminism. I could think of five kinds of neckline which a man might wear but rattled off 20 kinds of neckline for women's clothing, including the five men's styles. They are both summarized in Table 1. When I presented this to the class, the fashion design students in the back of the room said I was missing at least another five or six women's necklines.

Long ago I recall watching a movie which involved two men who were dressing mannequins for a clothing store. They had put skirts and tops on the mannequins, but then one of them said something like "we'll accessorize them later." That moment made an impression on me because it never occurred to me that 'accessorizing' could be a separate step in getting dressed. It didn't apply to me. Yet.

Table 1. Necklines for men and women

Men's Necklines	**Women's Necklines**	
T-shirt (jewel neck)	T-shirt (jewel neck)	Halter neck
Dress shirt collar	Dress shirt collar	V-neck (many depths of this one)
Tank top	Tank top	Cowl neck
Polo shirt	Polo shirt	Keyhole neck
Turtleneck	Turtleneck	U-neck
	Ballet neck	Strapless
	Boat neck	Square neck
	Bateau neck	Mandarin collar
	Sweetheart neck	Sabrina neck
	Scoop neck	

After all, when men get dressed the steps are simple.

- Pick out the pants you want (slacks, jeans, shorts) and a belt for it
- Pick out the shirt you want (button-down dress shirt, T-shirt, polo shirt, or tank top)
- Pick out the shoes you want (dress shoes, sneakers, boots, or sandals)
- Fill in underwear, and maybe socks to match.
- Accessories might be a watch (now less likely), and/or wedding band. Add a sweater if it's cold out.
- Ta-daa! You're done.

Whereas for women, getting dressed can be a massive set of decisions.

Are you wearing pants and a top, or a skirt and top, or a dress? A dress is the easiest option, since otherwise you have to coordinate the top and pants or skirt. If you're wearing a skirt or dress, how long is it? You can be harshly judged depending on its length (Figure 19). Similarly, judgmental, how low is your neckline? Is it as high as an Amish schoolgirl, or as daring as Jennifer Lopez in the 2000 Grammy awards ceremony (Figure 20)? Is your outfit made from continuous knit (like T-shirt material) or woven cloth (like dress shirts), and does it have cutouts, fringe, beads, sequins, rhinestones, lace, or other enhancements? A little enhancement can be feminine, but too much might be seen as trashy. A huge part of learning to dress as a woman seems to be finding the right balance – to divine the rules which dictate how low a neckline can be for a given occasion or how short a skirt or dress can be.

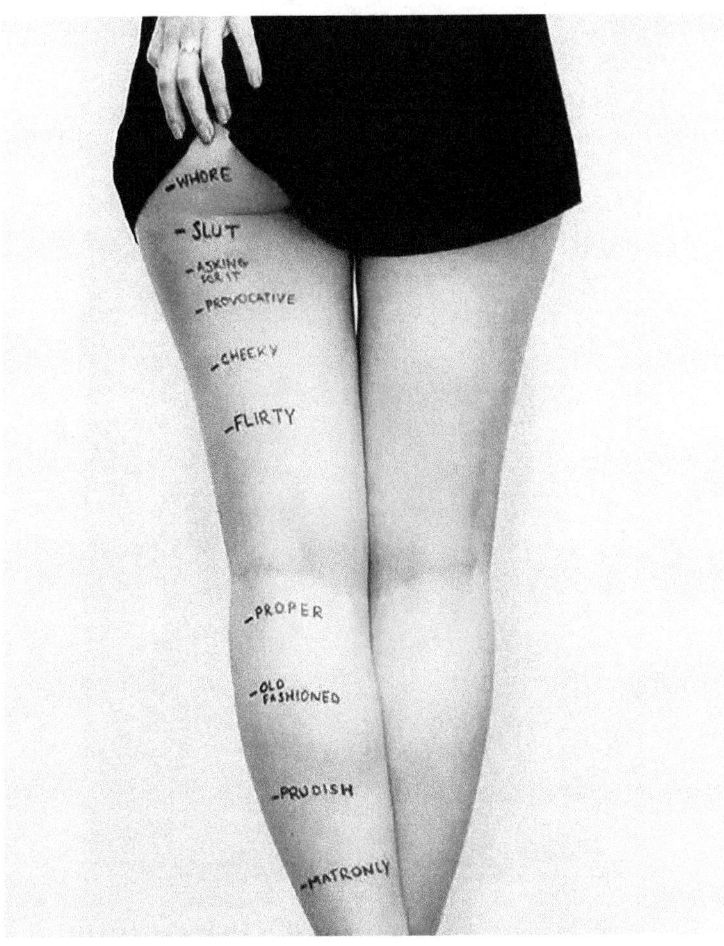

Figure 19. Associations with skirt lengths
(User, Unknown)

Figure 20. Jennifer Lopez at the 2000 Grammy awards in a green Versace gown. (Unknown, Unknown-b) This neckline is more daring than most.

- What shoes are you wearing? Flats, heels, ballet shoes, boots, sandals, Mary Janes, etc. Does their color go with the rest of the outfit? How high are the heels? Again, that last point can be a source of judgment. Very high heels are often seen as slutty or unprofessional (unless you're a stripper). Is there a platform under the sole? Lots of shorter women seem to like platform shoes to give them extra height without the challenge of having a high heel.

- How are you wearing your hair? Up, down, to the side, braided, etc. Is it flattened or curled or natural? Is it dyed or highlighted or permed? If you do any of the color enhancements or changes, you can be judged for it. Bright hair colors are generally unprofessional (unless you're a hair stylist). Subtle changes are generally ok. I knew a secretary who was a brunette. After being around her for a while, I heard her admit that she was blonde naturally but dyed her hair brown so she would be taken seriously!
- What makeup are you wearing? Just a little (lipstick, blush, and mascara) or 'full face?' What features are you emphasizing or hiding?
- What jewelry are you wearing? Rings, bracelets, earrings, and/or necklaces are common, in addition to possibly a watch. Is the metal in your earrings the same as your necklace (i.e. gold, silver, stainless steel)? Does your necklace drape parallel to your neckline, or at least not cross the neckline awkwardly? Do the colors of precious or semi-precious stones complement the rest of your outfit?
- What other accessories are you wearing? Scarves, pashminas, fascinators[8], shawls, hair clips, bows, ribbons, etc. If so their color(s) and pattern (if any) need to go with everything else.

8 Fascinators are "a woman's light, decorative headpiece consisting of feathers, flowers, beads, etc., attached to a comb or hair clip." (W. Foundation, 2018c)

All of these components need to be coordinated in terms of colors, level of formality, complementary patterns or solids, and so on. I went to a daytime workshop for a local feminist organization wearing a long skirt and ¾ sleeve top, but then noticed that most of the ladies were wearing shorter summer dresses instead. Oops. A 'formal' event could call for a nice dress like you might wear to work, or a cocktail dress, or an evening gown, depending on how formal it is. For men, 'formal' just means a dark suit or (for 'black tie' events) a tuxedo. Simple. Problem solved.

I was at an evening show, and one attendee had color-matched a hair ribbon, her eye shadow, her lipstick, her top, and her shoes. I was in awe that she not only paid attention to that many details, but also had all of those things in the same color!

Sophie Woodward went extensively into how women choose what to wear, and how that was a critical part of their identity, in her book *Why Women Wear What They Wear* (Woodward, 2007). What image do you want to project today? How do your clothing choices reflect your identity? I'd assume this is a much stronger factor for women than most men, since men tend not to put a lot of effort into their appearance and are not penalized for doing so. In younger people we tend to see a lot of experimentation with clothing, as they try to figure out their identity. One year 'goth' is in vogue, and everyone wears black to show how mad they are at the world. Another year pastels are in, and we look like watercolor paintings. Trendy skirt lengths go up and down over time. If you wait long enough, your wardrobe will probably be fashionable again!

High heels are really painful after a couple of hours! But they do make your calves look really good and make you taller. Since at 5'6" I'm slightly above average height for a woman (Statistics, 2016), I don't need the added height so much, but I'll wear low heels for special occasions. When I first wore heels, I appreciated how much ankle strength you need to wear them!

How do women deal with such a dizzying variety of fashion choices? Most women I've known well find a handful of looks that work well for them and stick to those looks the vast majority of the time. Maybe for special occasions they'll do something wild or at least unusual, but most days for work or casual wear they stick to a small fraction of the styles available to them. This seems to apply to accessories as well. When I first started going out with one fine young lady, I was impressed by the jewelry she wore – two or three rings, a collection of bangles, and a watch (some people still wear those!). After being around her for a while, I came to realize that she wore the same collection of jewelry almost every day!

Men's versus Women's clothing

When I started wearing women's clothing, I noticed some surprising things. Tops and dresses often expose the top of your shoulders. That part of me never felt breezes so much! Tops and dresses often gather below the bust line. That makes sense, because it helps show off your breasts, but I never noticed it until I started wearing them. As a result, it's often easier to take off tops using the 'one arm lift the hem from one side' method, instead of grabbing the hem on opposite sides at once. Men's or unisex shirts are cut to be a cylinder, so they are easier to take off.

Women's clothing is far more fragile, in most cases, than men's clothing. Most men don't particularly pay much attention to their clothes, and if they bother to separate light clothes from dark ones before washing them, that's a lot. In trying on much women's clothing for the first time, especially if the size was a tiny bit snug, I would hear threads popping because I was pulling on it too hard. Women's clothing is often made from thinner fabric, and the added features like lace are much more fragile than anything in a man's typical wardrobe.

I learned the secret of finding care labels on clothing. Seriously, I never knew this until a couple of years ago. On men's clothes, the label for how to wash it are generally on the back of the neck (near the size label) for shirts or on the waistband for pants. Lots of women's clothes either don't have fabric behind the neck or it's too thin to put a label there. Likewise dresses often might dip in back, so labels for tops and skirts and dresses are often hidden on the *lower part of the left seam*. I had no idea there were tags there!

Washing women's clothes is also a lot more complex. Fragile things like hose or bras or anything with rhinestones or sequins or anything else that might get caught on other stuff have to get stuck into a delicate clothes bag (lingerie bag) before washing, so now I keep four or five of those around and sometimes must use several in a single load. A lot of women's clothes are dry clean only, so I avoid those. It's not much of a bargain to find a cute dress for $30 if it costs $9 every time you dry clean it!

I now run a special load of wash just for work clothes and anything else delicate I wore recently, and that load goes on a Delicate cycle or even sometimes on a Hand Wash cycle. This seems to be an effective strategy for taking care of my new wardrobe. Yes, it's a bit odd that an iron has a Permanent Press setting, and my clothes washer has a Hand Wash setting.

Pockets and Purses

In addition to special care being needed, the lack of pockets is also a bane of women's clothing. When I started to study fashion design and sewing, I was told that the lack of pockets for women's clothing was to avoid interrupting the line of the clothing against their bodies. In other words, the lack of pockets makes it easier to objectify women's bodies! As if to say, "I'm sorry, I don't want you to have pockets so I can see the shape of your butt more clearly."

When I dressed as a man, pockets were never a problem. Every pair of pants or shorts had at least four deep pockets, plus occasionally that extra pocket for your pocket watch. This gave plenty of room for your cell phone and wallet and keys.

I recall seeing female students on campus with their cell phone sticking obviously out of their back pockets and wondered why they would leave their phone in such a vulnerable location. When I first started wearing jeggings[9], I quickly found the answer. There were no front pockets. There was the illusion of front pockets, but either nothing there, or just a tiny shallow pocket which

9 Jeggings are a blend of jeans and leggings; leggings made from denim fabric.

might hold a stick of gum and that's about it. It never occurred to me that they might not have front pockets in their pants, or if they had front pockets, they might be so shallow that a phone wouldn't fit!

At this point, I wasn't comfortable enough yet to start carrying a purse because I was still trying for very subtle clothing transition. Jeggings are indistinguishable from jeans for most men, whereas carrying a purse screams 'woman.' As a result, I made do with the minimal pockets that I had left and started using the right rear pockets more than I normally had been.

When I switched to wearing skorts[10] and skirts, I had few options left. Either I carry my wallet and stuff in a backpack, or I had to bite the bullet and start carrying a purse. This reflected a big change in how blatantly I was willing to dress female in public. I started looking around for purses and was drowning in the thousands of choices available.

My savior came in a local Macy's store. I was in the purse section, browsing by myself, and this kind little old lady came up to me. She explained that she didn't work in that department any more but had for many years. I explained that I was looking for a purse for work and needed a lot of help finding something useful and appropriate. She walked around helping me for over half an hour, assessing dozens of candidates. That one it too small, that one is too big. That one is too casual, that one is too formal. Bright colors were out, since I wanted a neutral color bag to go with

---

[10] A skort is a combination of skirt and shorts, so they look like a short skirt on the outside, but underneath is a snug layer of shorts to keep you from flashing people all the time!

pretty much everything. We finally settled on a modest Fossil purse that was about $100. Well made, kind of a medium size to hold what I needed but not huge, a cross-body strap to it feels more secure, basic black so it goes with everything. I was happy.

I later showed the purse to my friend Jennifer, and she taught me how to wear a purse correctly. (Who knew there was a wrong way to do it?) She told me that you wear a purse so that the brand name label is against your body, so you aren't showing off the brand. Other than avoiding vanity, this also lets the zippers of the purse work in the direction intended, so this insight had practical benefits too. She also checked to see if the strap was the right length to hold the purse against my body at the waist and if the bag looked better on my right side or left. Since I'm left-handed, the bag on my right works better and fortunately also looked better.

The Fossil bag became my everyday purse for quite a while, but I soon added more purses to my collection for special purposes. White purses for summer events, edgy purses for clubbing, big purses for times when you need to carry a lot of stuff, delicate clutches for formal events, there's no limit to the number of purses a girl can have.

Wallets are still a challenge. I retired my men's Coach trifold wallet after using it for about 15 years. For everyday use, I switched to a fairly large wallet that holds everything but the kitchen sink – credit cards, money, store tokens, membership cards, insurance cards, etc. For clubbing and small purses, I got a little wallet that holds a couple cards, some money, and maybe one house key. In between I started using a wallet that used to hold my first smartphone, so it's able to hold more cards but still not be too bulky. As a result, getting ready to go out can mean the additional time to switch purses and wallets, not just getting dressed, makeup, accessorizing, and dealing with hair. No wonder women are legendary for taking a long time to get ready to go out!

Toiletries!

As I started to transition, I realized that basics like toiletries would change too.

Deodorant was the easiest choice. I switched to using Secret deodorant, because of a commercial from the 1980's, in which they claimed it was "Strong enough for a man. But made for a woman." (Doucette, 2012) What could be more perfect for a trans woman!

I told my hairdresser that I wanted to start growing my hair out into a more feminine look, and she was quite helpful and immediately supportive. She also encouraged me to get shampoo and conditioner with keratin to help strengthen my hair. Keratin is a major component of skin and hair. (W. Foundation, 2017e) Men's hair styles are shorter, and therefore they keep hair a shorter time. Longer hair styles keep hair for longer time, so the keratin helps strengthen the hair so it doesn't break.

As I braved shaving more than just my face, getting a women's razor seemed logical. I opted for a five-blade razor instead of the cheapie disposable razor approach. The blades are stunningly expensive (over $4 each) but do a nice job and last a long time.

I don't mind shaving my legs, because the smoothness when I'm done feels really sexy to me.

Perfume was also a whole world to explore. I confess going to some higher-end stores like Macy's and trying dozens of fragrances at their counter, then buying the perfume on eBay for half the retail price. I settled on Gucci Guilty (Gucci, 2016) as my first favorite fragrance – something not too sweet and it blends nicely with my pheromones. I've gotten compliments on it many times.

Vagina Monologues

Before coming out, I had volunteered to support a local production of the Vagina Monologues. (Ensler, 2018) The Vagina Monologues were developed in the mid-1990's by Eve Ensler based on interviews with many women about their vaginas and vulvas. Every year in February, many organizations put on a reading of the monologues, which vary somewhat from year to year. Some of the monologues are funny, some scary, some informative.

Before coming out, I was only allowed to be support crew, like selling tickets or preparing food and drinks for the show. After coming out, I was allowed to be part of the cast. Only those who identify as women can be cast members. I've participated in four or five casts since then.

The Monologues let me feel a first hint of sisterhood, as well as learning more about women's experiences with their bodies. The 8,000 nerve endings in the clitoris; that's twice, TWICE the number in the penis. The vulnerability of the vagina as girls. The joy of exploring sexuality. The terror of being a wartime sexual violence victim. And yes, one monologue was a collection of experiences of being transgender women.

Vulnerability

The most striking first impression from wearing women's clothing is the massive level of vulnerability they create. Skirts and dresses mean there's nothing between the ground and your panties. I knew of upskirt photos for years, and confess enjoying the view, but now that I was wearing women's clothes, I could really appreciate the level of exposure they create.

Skirts feel far shorter than they are! Anything above the knee feels like I'm completely exposed to the world. For parties, I've worn skirts up to about mid-thigh, at which point I feel pretty well naked. Since I'm a nudist, I don't have a problem with this in general, but it's awkward in places like the subway.

It's impossible to run in heels until you have a lot of practice doing so. Apparently, people who wear heels often build up a lot of ankle strength, because taking a step in heels means your weight is briefly entirely supported only on the heel of the shoe you're about to step onto. I was also advised that, in order to walk in heels, I needed to tone my core abdominal muscles and squeeze my butt cheeks together. Those help too.

As mentioned in the previous section, part of transition was switching to carrying a purse all the time. This led to added vulnerability on two levels. One, it clearly marks me as transgender, so it increases verbal harassment. In the winter, even if I'm wearing pants and a heavy coat, the presence of my purse has been a lightning rod for unsolicited commentary on the streets. Two, the fact that you're carrying a purse means that all of your valuables are in a nice tidy package that can be grabbed relatively easily. That's part of the reason I wear a cross-body strapped purse – it provides a stronger defensive posture to discourage theft.

I support many live performers in my area, such as dancers and burlesque performers, so I'm in bars for many of their shows. Before coming out, men would joke to me before leaving their drink on the bar while they went to the bathroom "If anyone spikes my drink, make sure it's the good stuff" or something like that. It was at the same time acknowledging that people do get roofies[11] or other drugs slipped into their drinks, but also dismissing it in a humorous and slightly macho way. After transition, I started getting **serious warnings from other women not to ever leave a drink unattended** – either ask a friend to watch it for you or take it to the bathroom with you. Fear of date rape drugs is a very real vulnerability of women.

I'll get into the challenges of being socialized as a woman, find my wardrobe style, and use makeup, in Chapter 9.

---

[11] Roofies is a common street name for Rohypnol, a powerful sedative similar to Valium that can be used to make people unable to fight off sexual advances. (Drugs.com, 2018)

Reflection

1. Michele Younger's unusual therapy was based on uncovering words you say about yourself and survival techniques which no longer serve you. How do you describe yourself? Are the words positive or negative? Are they true?
2. If you have had severe experiences in your life, how did you protect yourself? What was needed in the moment to keep you alive or safer?
3. If you have come out as homosexual or transgender, how did your experiences differ from mine? If not, imagine what it would be like for you? How would your family respond? Your coworkers?
4. How important is 'passing?' Should transgender people try to look more stereotypically masculine or feminine? Why or why not?
5. Have you worn clothing associated with a different gender? If so, how did it feel? Was it out of genuine curiosity or perhaps on a dare? If not, speculate on what it would feel like.
6. If possible, go to a performance of the Vagina Monologues. Otherwise, look up excerpts on YouTube. Describe the pieces you watched, and how they made you feel. If you were raised female, what would you write about for your monologue?
7. When you walk in public, how vulnerable do you feel? What safety precautions do you take on a regular basis? Compare notes to your friends or classmates.

Chapter 5 – Hormones are Fun!

Six or seven months after coming out to myself, I realized that being transgender was completely real for me, and not just a phase or passing speculation. I also realized that, as a fifty-year-old person, it wouldn't make sense to delay physical transition if I was going to do that. The tweet from @NullBlanc shown in Figure 21 shows a lot of what I learned to be true from coming out and deciding to transition.

Ø_
@NullBlanc
Transitioning doesn't make you a girl. Being a girl might make you transition.
3:44 AM · 15 Sep 16

Figure 21. Transition tweet

I met with the doctors at Mazzoni Center (M. Center, 2017b), and asked about starting hormone therapy. They discussed the options of how to do so (pills versus shots) and what the effects and side effects were. (Unger, 2016) The main effects for trans women are breast growth, reduced body hair, reduced sex drive, change of fat distribution to the hips, and possibly slowing of pattern baldness. They also addressed which effects were permanent even if I decided to stop therapy at some point, and which ones weren't. Breast growth is permanent, for example, but body hair growth reverses quite quickly. Some report more subtle changes such as in skin thickness and sensitivity. (Care, 2015)

Long term hormone therapy for adults appears to be safe (Weinand & Safer, 2015) with a slightly increased risk of venous thromboembolism (a vein blocked by a blood clot) because estrogen helps blood clot. The benefit is that we show a statistically significant improvement in quality of life (White Hughto & Reisner, 2016).

While discussing the start of hormone therapy with my doctor, I asked him if my history of birth defects and abuse had any influence on my being transgender. Was I trans in response to my traumatic history? He immediately assured me that wasn't the case. Some studies have shown an increased incidence of "social stressors (violence, discrimination, childhood abuse)" in the history of transgender patients compared to the general population but that correlation doesn't imply causation. (Reisner, White, Bradford, & Mimiaga, 2014) Formation of gender identity for me followed the same path others have found, namely "through balancing a desire for authenticity with demands of necessity," where the latter includes assessing the "resources, coping skills, and the consequences of gender transitions." (Levitt & Ippolito, 2014)

Medical studies of transgender people who have not undergone hormone therapy (which can change brain structure (Hulshoff Pol et al., 2006)) show that transgender people have cerebral patterns of their chosen sex, not the one they were assigned at birth. (Luders et al., 2009; Rametti et al., 2011)

Mazzoni had me interviewed by a therapist to make sure I was an appropriate candidate for hormone therapy. I met with a young lady and told her about my coming out, and the experiences I had had so far. She signed off on hormone therapy for me. It's common to need at least one therapist approve a person getting hormone therapy. (Surgeons, 2018; WPATH, 2018a)

The Drugs

I got prescriptions for Delestrogen (WebMD, 2018b) and Spironolactone (WebMD, 2018c) plus syringes and needles for the former. Delestrogen is given as an intramuscular (IM) injection, so I had to receive training on how and where on my body I could give myself the injections every two weeks. It is, simply put, estrogen to replace the testosterone my body foolishly tried to produce. In cisgender women, Delestrogen is given as a supplement for low estrogen levels due to menopause.

Spironolactone is normally given "to treat high blood pressure and heart failure" (WebMD, 2018c) but someone noticed that it also blocks the use of testosterone in the body. It's given in pill form twice a day. The net effect of taking both drugs is to suppress the testosterone my body produced and replace it with estrogen. Notice that both drugs I was prescribed are being used for off-label purposes. Fortunately, people have been using them this way for enough decades that the safest effective doses are now known. This is one advantage of my coming out late in life – it gave more time for people to understand how to treat gender dysphoria effectively!

The creepy part of starting hormone therapy is that testosterone blocking is the same approach used to treat sex offenders, as in for 'chemical castration,' even though some studies show that testosterone levels in sex offenders are no different from the general population. (Wong & Gravel, 2018)

I was told that hormone therapy takes about two years for full effect, so I started it without expecting anything to happen for quite a while.

Zing!

Imagine my surprise when I noticed something after only a month. That means I had had only three shots of estrogen ever when something brushed against my chest and my eyes got as big as saucers! Zing! I had observed a sudden and huge increase in sensitivity of my breasts!

Amused by this sudden revelation, I started asking my close cisgender female friends – when you went through puberty, did you notice this too? Most of them said Yes to varying degrees. From what I understand, most cisgender girls get a similar sharp increase in breast sensitivity at the start of puberty – in a few there's little or no increase, in some there's a huge increase, even to the point of becoming painful, but most are somewhere in between those extremes.

Now an experience from High School suddenly made sense. I was heavily involved in my church's Youth Group. One day I was horsing around with one of the girls, we were maybe 14 or 15 at the time, and my hand brushed against her chest accidentally. She recoiled and chastised me for my inappropriate action. I was a bit confused at the time, but now it made MUCH more sense. She might have been offended simply because she was growing boobs and that made them suddenly special and she was self-conscious about them, but now I realized that *she might have been responding that way because they were now much more sensitive!*

This made me wonder – why wasn't I told about this change when I went through sex education in school? We were told about the obvious physical changes of puberty in girls – menstruation, breast growth, appearance of some body hair, widening of hips – but no one ever mentioned this very likely change in sensitivity.

Wouldn't it be good for boys and young men to know about this? *Hey boys! It's a good idea to warm up your girlfriend before playing with her boobs, not just because it's romantic, but because if you don't it might be simply annoying for them or even hurt them!* Or are we not supposed to acknowledge that sexual activity has sensual characteristics too?

Slow Boobs

In spite of the newfound (and quite pleasant, I might add) sensitivity, my boobs have taken their sweet time coming in. Yes, I'm like a 15-year-old girl, constantly looking in the mirror to see if my boobs have grown and wondering how big they'll get. According to the predictions when I started hormone therapy, trans women are supposed to get natural breasts that are about a cup size smaller than cisgender women in their families. Since my mom wears a C cup (how do I know that? She often left her bras on the bathroom counter at night), I should get B cup boobs eventually. Unlike the predictions I had read about, even five years after starting hormones my boobs are still growing but haven't reached their advertised potential.

The other aspect of hormone therapy working against me is that the therapy is more effective at producing cisgender-looking results the closer you are to puberty when you start therapy. Given that I started therapy at age 50, that doesn't bode well for me! About 50% of trans women want to get breast implants, but only about 18-20% actually do (Jones, McNamara, & Robo, 2018). It's easy to see how jumping to C or D or larger breasts would have aesthetic appeal and make it easier to 'pass.'

Now (2018) advice for trans women is stating that most don't get past an A or B cup breast size as a result of hormone therapy. Recent research indicates that "breast development is insufficient for the majority of trans women and that type and dosage of hormonal therapy seem not to have an important role on final breast size." (Wierckx, Gooren, & T'Sjoen, 2014) So it's not just me!

I am active enough to where breast implants would often be uncomfortable (such as when playing soccer) and I don't want to risk any possibility of the surgery affecting the newfound sensitivity of my boobs, so I don't plan to get 'top surgery' in the foreseeable future.

Body Hair Bye-bye

Hormone therapy reduces the amount of body hair and slightly increases the amount of hair on one's head (M. Deutsch, 2015). I was eager for the former to occur because I suddenly became much furrier when I reached my 30's. As I was choosing my new wardrobe, many of my earliest choices were constrained by wanting to hide my chest and back hair – so I picked out VERY conservative high necklines and low hems.

I went to Mazzoni and got many (20? I didn't count) treatments to remove body hair by laser. This was frighteningly expensive ($100 for each 15-minute session) and most body parts need about 5 treatments to be fully effective. The other downside is that laser hair removal only works on dark hair. Blonde or grey hairs don't absorb the laser light, I was told. I got treatment on my forearms, chest, back, face, and groin. I decided my legs were far too big to pay for hair removal, and I kind of like shaving them anyway.

At the time, it was common to need hair removal from the groin in order to prepare for gender confirmation surgery. Now that isn't needed, because hair removal is done during surgery to spare you from the agony. That's no exaggeration, it's pure agony to get hair removed from there!

What is it like to experience laser hair removal? Well just imagine that the dot of laser light, a few millimeters across, simultaneously burns your hair while yanking it out of your body. The latter part isn't what actually happens, but that's what it feels like. Areas of the body with little fat under them (sternum, wrist, and moustache) and anything near the groin HURT LIKE HELL. When doing areas like that, the doctor would treat three little spots, then wait for you to catch your breath for a moment before doing the next set of three spots. It was so painful that the doctor looked visibly shaken from doing a treatment that was so painful.

How effective was it? I still have a little leftover hair between my boobs, which I shave periodically, and I could use some more hair removal from my forearms, but otherwise my chest and back are FAR less fuzzy than they were. Accordingly, my wardrobe now contains many more low necklines and open backs than it did. Yay!

More Emotional *cries*

This was the funniest side effect of hormone therapy, in my opinion. One of the medically recognized side effects of taking estrogen supplements is that it makes you more emotional. Sure enough, I have noticed that I cry much more easily than I did before therapy. McDonalds commercials, anything involving Sarah McLachlan singing about puppies (ragefc, 2006), Hallmark commercials, you name it, it might make me cry. Movies I've seen twenty times? Let the waterworks begin!

The interesting part for me was noticing the character of crying and how that has changed. As a man, crying was a sign of complete surrender and failure. You cried only as a last resort, after everything else has been tried. Crying is a sign of weakness (i.e. being feminine), crying is to be avoided at all costs, crying means you are a failure as a man. (W. a. G. A. Center, 2018)

Crying as a woman is usually a pure release of emotion. Estrogen takes the brakes off of expressing emotion, allows it to flow freely. Testosterone is like the nozzle at the end of a garden hose. It constricts the flow and only allows a little water to get through. Crying feels good as a woman. Now I feel sorry for men being hormonally restricted in expressing themselves and their emotions.

Years after starting hormone therapy, I broke my left leg in a skydiving accident. As a result, during the healing process, I was told to stay off estrogen because of its encouragement of blood clotting, especially after I had two pulmonary embolisms during recovery. I went over three months with no sex hormones, providing an interesting opportunity to answer the questions: Is estrogen releasing emotions? Or is testosterone blocking them? During this hormone-less period I noticed I was still very emotional, so based on this case study, I'd have to conclude that **testosterone blocks emotions**.

Voice Change

One's vocal pitch is another area in which my childhood lied to me repeatedly. The cliché has always been that if a man lost his testicles or they were badly damaged (i.e. a knee to the groin) then he would instantly become a soprano.

That just isn't true.

Losing testosterone (which is produced in the testes) doesn't make your voice change. I was a Tenor 2 before hormone therapy, and still am.

A trans woman can take lessons to learn how to manipulate your voice to sound more feminine (Vera, Unknown), but the basic plumbing (the larynx) doesn't change. This was a little disappointing, mostly because I was lied to for all those years, but my natural voice is relatively high anyway, so it isn't that much of an issue. Trans men, in contrast, benefit because "testosterone increases vocal fold mass and induces lowering of voice pitch." (Azul, 2015) Not sure why that change seems to only go in one direction.

Weakness

Another side effect from hormone therapy was a substantial loss of muscle mass. I inherited a masculine mesomorphic body type (Provost, Kormos, Kosakoski, & Quinsey, 2006) from my father, and particularly my upper body strength was pretty much my only source of physical pride during my childhood.

That made it all the more difficult to face losing much of that strength due to the loss of testosterone. My arms in particular have lost a lot of power, and I have a newfound appreciation for how much work it is for women athletes to get within 10% of the ability of men! (Records, 2018) Part of the basis for this advantage appears to be genetic influences. (MacArthur & North, 2005)

Nevertheless, my life doesn't depend on being physically strong to much extent, so from a practical point of view the loss of strength isn't critical. I've made up for some of the strength loss by doing things like pole dancing and acrobatics, but that's discussed later.

Sex Drive

Another key effect of hormone therapy is a drastic change in sex drive.

As a male I developed slowly throughout childhood. As I mentioned earlier, I was slow to lose baby teeth, slow to start puberty, and so on. Like most young males, I discovered the joys of masturbation in my teens and experimented with different stimuli to see what felt best. I didn't manage to discover orgasm until I was 15-1/2. Once I did, I couldn't get enough. I played with myself typically every day, sometimes two or three times. I think one fine day I managed seven times. My family got HBO (Office, 2018) shortly after it came out, so its R rated movies provided a host of inspirational material! After all, this was long before the Internet became publicly known, so "men's magazines" and erotic imagery were a lot more challenging to find than today.

Anyhow, throughout my adult years I still masturbated pretty much daily, sometimes more than once, and it became part of my before-bed ritual. It was fun, of course, and the release helped me relax and go to sleep soon afterward.

Once I started hormone therapy that universe changed immediately.

My drive to masturbate nearly disappeared overnight. Sensual experiences were still a lot of fun, but the urgent need to orgasm was gone! At first, I was saddened by losing this old friend, but as months went by and I'd only orgasm once every few weeks, I realized that there was a more fundamental shift occurring in my sex drive it was becoming much more focused on long term pleasure.

This is consistent with what many other trans women experience. In one study, 73% of trans women "never or rarely experienced spontaneous and responsive sexual desire." (Wierckx, Elaut, et al., 2014)

The time scale for me as a male to climax was measured in minutes. I could certainly have longer duration sexual encounters, but the actual act of intercourse was a few minutes (about five minutes is average according to some research (Baedeker, 2007)). Now that my sex drive has shifted gears, making love with myself or partner(s) can go on for hours. I'm guessing part of this is due to my inexperience with my new body, but part of it is undoubtedly due to the effects of no longer having testosterone in my body.

As a result of hormone therapy, I've gotten insight into the old debate between nature versus nurture. While a huge amount of our daily lives are influenced by cultural constructs (including our very concepts of what someone's sex and gender are) (Fine, 2017), the impact of hormone therapy makes me appreciate how powerful nature is, and how influential sex hormones can be on basic biological drives.

Bear in mind this does NOT mean for a millisecond that I accept men's excuses for their behavior based on biology (as in, "I couldn't control myself" or "boys will be boys" or "women have to cover up or men will not be able to control their impulses"). Biology is powerful, but our minds determine our actions. Skeletal muscle is all under voluntary control, no hormone makes it contract.

Reflection

1. Ask close cisgender female friends (or yourself, if applicable) about their experiences in puberty. Did they get a big change in breast sensitivity? Was it a pleasant or unpleasant change?
2. Were you early or late or typical for puberty? How did that affect your relationships with your peers?
3. How do you feel about body hair? Yours? On others? Is it attractive? Repulsive? What do you do to manage or groom your body hair, if anything?
4. How do you respond when someone cries? Are you empathetic? Do you shut down? How does it feel when you cry? Is it easy? Does it feel forced? Does crying make you feel shame?
5. Do you feel your sex drive is stronger or weaker than your peers? Is it a major force in your life? Or not that important?

Chapter 6 – Coming Out

The coming out process was gradual for me. I had to consider whether I was going to come out publicly at all, and if so then decide in what order to tell people. I first came out as transgender to my closest friends, then my family, then at work.

Is it safe to come out?

Once I realized that I was transgender, and this was a true identity for me, I had to decide if and to what extent I was going to be 'out,' i.e. be publicly transgender. I could remain closeted and only dress femininely in private parties like the local fetish events (e.g. The Aviary or Black Phoenix) or private parties. Being a large person, my fledgling breasts could be mistaken for manboobs, and no one at work would be the wiser.

Fashion wasn't the only consideration in coming out. It was no secret that transgender women are particularly targeted for harassment, assault, and even murder. (HRC, 2018b) Coming out isn't a trivial social decision, it's a matter of life and death. Even if none of those things occur, it's still commonly used as the basis for firing people, so I wanted to see if my job would be in jeopardy if I came out.

Drexel University has a clear policy protecting gender identity. Their Equality and Non-Discrimination Policy states that "the University prohibits discrimination against individuals on the basis of: race; color; national origin; religion; sex; sexual orientation; disability; age; status as a veteran or special disabled veteran; **gender identity and expression**; genetic information and any other characteristic prohibited by law (i.e., creed, marital status, citizenship status)." (University, 2017) (emphasis added)

I had heard that Philadelphia also has strong protections for gender identity. Bill number 130224 section § 9-1103 for the City of Philadelphia states that "It shall be an unlawful employment practice to deny or interfere with the employment opportunities of an individual based upon his or her race, ethnicity, color, sex, sexual orientation, **gender identity**, religion, national origin, ancestry, age, disability, marital status, familial status, genetic information, or domestic or sexual violence victim status, including, but not limited to, the following: (j) For any employer to fail to permit employees to **dress consistently in accordance with their gender identity**. (k) For any employer to fail, upon the request of an individual to change that individual's name or gender on any forms or records under the control of that employer, to make such changes to the extent permitted by law." (Council, 2013) (emphasis added)

Based on these two reassurances, I hoped that coming out publicly wouldn't result in losing my job. People in many other cities are not so fortunate. A quarter of transgender people have reported losing a job as a result of coming out, and three quarters have faced harassment or discrimination on the job. (NCTE, 2009)

To pass or what?

Another key question in coming out was to address whether I was going to try to 'pass' as cisgender woman. To 'pass' means that people on the street typically won't question whether you are a woman. I realized that I have several strikes against me in trying to pass.

For one, my broad shoulders and naturally muscular build were great as a man, but certainly don't scream 'feminine.' Furthermore, other than estrogen reducing my muscle bulk, there is nothing that can be done to reduce this.

Another strike was how late I started hormone therapy, and the effect that would have on my breast development. The closer to puberty that you start hormone therapy, the more your breasts look like original equipment (Jones et al., 2018). I started hormone therapy at age 50, which even for a late bloomer was quite a while after puberty, so I knew that my breasts would not get very large. An obvious possible remedy for this strike was to get breast implants, as about half of all trans women want to do, but that is another major expense (about $5,000 to $10,000 (WebMD, 2018a)) and risks reducing the sensitivity of my breasts. From a logistical perspective, I had already started to appreciate how inconvenient large breasts are for women. Sure, they are highly valued in American culture, but women with them (technically known as having macromastia) often suffer from back pain, need expensive bras, and find that men often talk to their boobs instead of making eye contact (Snodgrass, 2018).

The third and most challenging strike was the most obvious to the public. I'm bald. Androgenetic alopecia, if you want to be fancy about it, or 'male pattern baldness.' While genes from the maternal grandfather were attributed to causing this, more recent studies have identified more significant genetic factors. (Heguy, 2016) Sorry Grandpa!

Hair is one of the most quintessential female traits in many cultures, so this strike has been the most painful to face. The most common suggestion is to 'just wear a wig' all the time. I'm naturally warm, so the thought of wearing insulation on my head all the time is at best uncomfortable. A more significant objection to this was more fundamental. I came out to be my most authentic self. How authentic is it to hide under a wig all the time?

Another possible solution would be to get surgery to rearrange my existing hair to provide better coverage of my sizeable head. Hair transplants, as they are known, cost from $4,000 to $15,000 (WebMD, 2017) and could alleviate some of the impact of this strike. I'm still seriously considering this option.

Friends

Coming out to my closest friends was mostly easy. Many of my friends had heard the readings at the Erotic Literary Salon and knew a lot of my journey already. My coming out was welcome with open arms and loving hearts. Here is the piece I read to the Erotic Literary Salon only two weeks after coming out to myself.

Letter to Jennifer

This is a love letter that was inspired after working with Monica Day and Michele Younger over the last two months. Most of the pronouns in this piece are wrong. English is quite inadequate sometimes.

Dear Jennifer,

Thank you for being patient with me. It's taken a long time to acknowledge you. Welcome. In perfect hindsight, the clues were building for a long time. Finding girls' hair accessories on the ground as a boy, and examining them like an archeologist trying to decipher a long lost civilization. Mom always hid in the bathroom to do her hair and makeup, so those female mysteries remained ... just that. The home ec class I really wanted to take in junior high as my very first elective, but couldn't because boys don't take things like that. My pickup truck had your name, and I hopped in and greeted her out loud so many times. Was that the seed of recognizing you? The curiosity to buy a pair of pantyhose by mail order shortly after leaving home, but soon gave in to the forbidden nature of such a thing and threw them away. Shopping in recent years for 'unisex' clothes from American Apparel, and yet not knowing why. These were hints that I was missing something.

I was missing you. [try not to cry here]

As someone wise said, it doesn't have to be difficult now, it doesn't have to be painful. That's over. Gone. Let those memories be a movie you can watch safely and calmly. They can't hurt you now. Now is the time for joy! Now is the time for celebration of life and your body and all dimensions of your Self. You have earned this gift, this rebirth, so take it and run.

You can't have a pussy or give birth, and I suspect a fake pussy is about as satisfying as a fake orgasm. But that won't stop us from exploring other ways to be receptive and savor all aspects of us. We can make a time and place to explore being receptive in enthusiastic and loving ways. Ok, how about many times and places?!

It's okay to be truly masculine too, as we discovered driving home last week. We can be strong and confident, assertive, and peacefully in control. Power without oppression. We claim that aspect too.

I feel like you're both very grown up and an innocent little girl. I delight in getting to know each other, and celebrate this new connection. A new awakening.

Your clothes feel so much more expressive and alive and downright SEXY! Delicate fabric fluttering against my calves is so delicious I can't imagine why anyone wouldn't enjoy it. A suit feels like a cage to me, but an Eileen Fisher skirt is simply delicious! I know we often have to conform to society's bullshit, but at least we can find more ways to let you come out and play.

For now we can be whole, and that will ease stress, produce calm, and confidence, and open doors for new friendships and new intimacies. Only when we embody our genuine authentic selves can be connect with others who appreciate and love us for exactly who we are, not who we pretend to be. Put aside the masks, lower the shields, be ready to accept more possibilities and more love than you ever imagined.

And no more 'me' and 'you' crap. We are one.

Hello! I am Glenn, and I am Jennifer.

Notice in this piece that I was making connections between my newly recognized feelings and seeing how they fit into past events. I started to recognize that I was going to be living in different ages at the same time "you're both very grown up and an innocent little girl." I didn't expect to pursue gender confirmation surgery, "I suspect a fake pussy is about as satisfying as a fake orgasm."

The reactions among my broader social circles were a little more mixed. My tennis league, though in theory LGBT, seemed very confused and distant when I came out and started wearing cute little skorts to play. The league was almost entirely made up of gay men, and my best guess is that they couldn't imagine how someone would not want to be male. As a result of their very lukewarm reception, I stopped being involved with that league except staying friends with a few people on social media (e.g. Facebook). I might return in the future.

My soccer league, the Falcons (Falcons, 2018), was very supportive when I came out. While the men and women are often self-segregating – some women didn't like to play in coed leagues, for example – I have felt nothing but love and support from them.

Family

As it became clear that I was truly transgender and I got more comfortable in that identity, I knew I'd have to face the challenge of telling my family about it. My stepmother was most understanding in liberal matters, so I consulted with her about the best approach to coming out to everyone else. She had the brilliant idea of writing a letter to my family to explain what was going on, and answer some of their questions. This seemed like a great idea, since I knew my coming out would result in a million questions. I composed a three-page letter in which I came out, then had a large Q&A section to explain what transgender was, and what the implications of my coming out would be. Specifically, I asked and answered:

- What does transgender mean?
- Have I seen a shrink about this?
- Am I crazy?
- How did this come about?
- What caused this?
- What does this mean?
- Does that mean I'm cross-dressing?
- Is my job in danger?
- Does this mean I'm gay?
- Am I going to get surgery 'down there?'
- Am I changing my name?
- What do I hope for from you?

After the Q&A I explained that I was on hormone therapy, and what that meant for my body. The full letter I sent to my family is in Appendix D.

I mailed the letter to my parents and brother, then held my breath for a couple of days. Unfortunately, my mother and brother got the letter a day before my father, so he found out via a panicked phone call before he got his letter the next day.

Responses were predictably mixed, mostly negative. My mother and stepmother have both been very supportive and positive. My father is firmly in denial. He was offended that I wanted to change my name, since he chose my name in the first place. He also said something to the effect that he thought he knew me well but now wasn't sure who I was. I don't think he has any understanding of what it means to be transgender, so he's pretending this hasn't happened. He still calls me by the name he gave me, and I seriously doubt he'll ever change. My brother has been an odd duck. He has given up calling me by any name or pronoun. He only refers to me as 'you' or other ungendered terms.

News of my coming out spread like wildfire through the family. Of my six first cousins, one was supportive, and two came out vehemently opposed to my coming out. The latter so much so, that they sent me long letters explaining in detail how wrong I was to be coming out, and what a bad misguided choice this was for me. Bear in mind, I've barely seen these cousins in the last three decades, and we've never been close either geographically or emotionally, so I was quite amused that they had suddenly become experts on my true psychological state and gender identity. My brother also chimed in with a long letter, so I decided to kill three birds with one stone (horrible cliché) and I combined all three letters into one and responded to all of them paragraph by paragraph. The result is in Appendix E. My cousins both took a very emotional track, but my brother was quite analytical and pseudo-scientific in his memo. I later challenged him on that point, and he explained that I had had enough emotional responses, and I probably didn't need to hear another one.

I doubt my responses to my family members made a difference in their views, but at least I felt better for putting myself out there. None of them formally responded, until my brother published a very public letter about me a few years later. That letter is discussed in Chapter 10.

Work

After coming out to my family, I came out on social media. I finally changed my Facebook name to Jennifer. My coming out on Facebook was quite brief; "to the surprise of some and no surprise to a few, I just came out as transgender. now that the cat's out of the bag, let the litter fall where it may. My mom took it well, my brother didn't say much, but my dad is having a rough time. I can see how it could be surprising, to say the least. But he's strong and loves me, so he'll come around before long."

Dozens of friends cheered my social media coming out. While some people manage multiple Facebook accounts to keep family and work and friends separate, I have them all in the same account, so a handful of friends from work also saw me coming out there.

After about six months, some of my work colleagues were getting confused as what to call me. I hadn't come out at work yet, but they knew I had online. I had even started coming out in other capacities on campus, such as getting a locker in the ladies' locker room at the gym. An incident where someone called the campus police after seeing me there led to a meeting with an attorney (Michele Rovinsky-Mayer) who specialized in diversity issues. I decided it was time to break the ice formally with my college, with an email sent to my Dean and the Associate Deans:

Subject: Inclusion and Diversity FYI

Hi,

Just to let you know, I met with Michele Rovinsky-Mayer today at her request to discuss my experiences and recommendations for Drexel's handling of transgender faculty, staff, and students, since I now identify as a transgender woman. Michele is using my rare situation as an opportunity to educate Drexel staff (especially from the DAC/Rec Center, public safety office, and sports coaches) about appropriate ways to ensure sensitive treatment of many special populations (such as minors, Muslims, and transgender people) in the locker room facilities without compromising safety measures. She is working on signage for the DAC/Rec Center to remind patrons to be respectful of special populations, but to contact their staff or public safety if they have questions or concerns.

As my transition progresses, I was going to formally start using my new name (Jennifer) full time in January and start the legal name change process, but it's getting awkward as more and more colleagues know me by both names and it's hard for ME to remember which name I'm using at the moment. ☺

Thank you for being so supportive during this time of rapid and novel changes in my life.

Glenn/Jennifer

I found the meeting with the attorney very satisfying, because we were developing elements which would eventually go into formal Drexel policies for transgender faculty, staff, and students. We were very deliberate in balancing the needs of transgender users of the gym, with being sensitive to populations that might be more troubled by our presence (Muslim students, minors, etc.). We didn't want accommodation of diversity to reduce the safety of the gym members, so we had to make sure that proper procedures for people who felt threatened by anyone of any gender in the locker rooms had appropriate ways to report those incidents. We also learned from my experience with the campus police and made sure to include them in the scope of people who needed to be trained in basic LGBT concepts such as distinguishing sex vs gender vs sexual preference, and how to determine the correct pronouns to use when there's any doubt.

I met with my Dean shortly after this memo, nervous how he'd respond to my coming out. To my pleasant surprise, he was quite accepting and open about the whole thing. He said that as long as I did my job well, he didn't care how I identified. Cool! When I probably looked a little confused at his open-mindedness, he explained "I used to work around a lot of musicians." I'm not quite sure what that means, but okay, as long as he's happy!

A few days later, I accidentally outed myself to the rest of the college when I was invited to participate in a transgender panel cohosted by my University and the University of Pennsylvania. I decided to invite my colleagues to attend. Only after sending the email did I realize that it only took a tiny hint of logic to deduce that, since I was going to be **on** a transgender panel, I was probably transgender! This led to my coming out email to all of the faculty and staff in my college, and the members of the University's LGBT faculty and staff organization:

Subject: Name change

Hi everyone,

Since I formally outed myself last week with the trans panel, I'm moving up the schedule for my name change to ... right now. While not legally official yet, I'm changing my name to Jennifer. (I know, not very original, and apologies to Ms. Lally and Dr. Rode.) Accordingly you should use feminine pronouns for me now, and ladies don't be shocked that I'm changing [ahem] facilities too.

And no, I won't be upset if you goof and use my former name once in a while; after all some of you have known me for upwards of 16 years.

Thank you for your kind support during this exciting and challenging time.

Sincerely,

Dr. Jennifer Booker

Notice that I included a subtle cue to the other ladies in my College that I was switching bathroom facilities. Response to my coming out at work was immediate and almost 100% positive. Literally within hours of sending my coming out email, the staff people had 1) changed the name on my mailbox, 2) changed my name on the college website, and 3) asked if I wanted new business cards and a new nameplate for my office door. A day later, the Dean sent an email to all faculty welcoming me under my new name. Dozens of supportive emails came in from colleagues. One or two colleagues seemed to have a lot of trouble changing over to my new name, but that was the most negative response. If anyone felt strongly otherwise, at least they were kind enough not to say it to my face.

With friends, family, and work all now knowing of my transgender status, it was time to complete my transition. I wanted to be legally recognized as the woman I am.

Reflection

1. Where you live, is it legal to be transgender? To be homosexual? Look up and cite relevant local regulations.
2. Are any of your local politicians LGBT or clear allies? If so, what legislation have they sponsored to improve the lives of the LGBT community?
3. How do you react on the street when you see someone who is outside the gender binary? In other words, they look gender neutral, or both masculine and feminine in different respects.
4. Find at least five sets of pronouns for non-binary people, other than he/him, she/her, and they/them. Do you know anyone who uses non-traditional pronouns? If so, how do you feel about using them?
5. How would (or did) your friends react to you coming out? Are many of your friends in the LGBT community?

6. How would (or did) your family react to you coming out? Are many of your family members in the LGBT community?
7. How would (or did) your co-workers or classmates react to you coming out? Are many of them in the LGBT community?

Chapter 7 – Gender Confirmation

After being on hormones for several months and coming out to everyone in my immediate and not-so-immediate life, I considered undergoing gender confirmation surgery (GCS), formerly known as gender reassignment surgery (GRS) or a sex change operation. This was a huge thing to even consider, since it's very expensive major elective surgery, and very permanent. The main reasons I wanted to investigate it were 1) to explore sexuality with plumbing that made more sense to me, 2) to obtain legal status as a woman[12], and 3) to have the ultimate trump card to eliminate any doubt about my sex, especially for locker rooms and other settings.

Much of this chapter is based on detailed notes I took throughout transition. I took about seven pages of single-spaced notes, starting a few days before surgery and ending about three months afterward.

Research

Being a good little academic, I knew the first step was to research what I was considering getting into. This was about seven months after starting hormone therapy. The Philadelphia Trans Health Conference (PHTC) is held every June, so this provided a great and terribly convenient resource for learning

---

12 At the time (2014), most states required genital surgery to change one's gender markers. In some states and countries this requirement has been removed since it discriminates against less wealthy trans people, those who simply don't want surgery, and some people with intersex conditions who were assigned an incorrect sex at birth. (Mottet, 2013)

about surgical options. They describe the mission of PHTC as "to educate and empower trans individuals on issues of health and well-being; educate and inform allies and health service providers; and facilitate networking, community-building, and systemic change." (M. Center, 2017c)

I went to two presentations on GCS, one from a local Dr. Kathy Rumer, and the other from a well-known doctor who recently moved from Colorado to San Francisco, Dr. Marci Bowers. Dr. Bowers gave a much more dynamic presentation, but Dr. Rumer was very nearby. Both gave the same information.

GCS for male-to-female clients is called vaginoplasty (plastic surgery of the vagina), and consists of removing the penis and testes, and inverting much of the scrotal skin tissue to form a vagina. A recent refinement to the procedure uses the inside of the unused urethra to help form a mucous membrane down the center of the vulva. The tip of the penis becomes the clitoris. Many videos on YouTube show the procedure in more detail than I care to discuss. (Morrison, 2017)

When GCS was first developed, it was a two-stage procedure – one to create the vagina, then heal from that, then a second procedure to form the vulva. This was the example in the fictitious movie *The Danish Girl* (IMDb.com, 2018a). The stages were merged into one procedure over a decade ago. Nevertheless, many trans women get a second surgery to refine the aesthetic appearance of their vulvas.

Recovery from GCS typically takes three days in the hospital, another four days of closely supported care, then long-term recovery takes about a year. I was a bit surprised by the last bit – a year to recover from surgery? Recovery from a broken bone takes two or three months, how can it take that long for this? I was afraid to ask. Literally.

In order to qualify for GCS, you need letters from two psychiatrists or therapists to verify you are a psychologically sound candidate for it. I was told that cost of surgery is about $20,000 to $25,000 and wasn't covered by most insurance plans. Minor expenses like prescriptions might be covered by health insurance, but the cost of surgery itself and associated fees was not covered because of a specific exclusion in the policy obtained by my employer. This is changing quickly, as there is more and more pressure for insurance companies to cover GCS expenses. (HRC, 2018a)

Mazzoni provided me with a list of doctors they recommended. Charles Garamone was in Florida (heck, I'd go see Marci in California first!), Christine McGinn wouldn't take patients with a BMI over 28 (that ruled me out), Beverly Fischer in Maryland was a referral, but she doesn't do MTF GCS. The last one was Dr. Kathy Rumer; whose office is in the Philadelphia suburb of Ardmore.

I met with Dr. Rumer, and after asking her a slew of questions to make sure my medical history wasn't a conflict, felt confident I could trust her with my most intimate bits. We scheduled my surgery for that winter. I planned it to be at the end of Fall term for school, so I had as much time as possible for recovery before classes started for Winter term.

Legal and Social Preparations

As I accepted that I was going to go through with this, I had a lot of legal and social issues to deal with. From the legal perspective, I knew that there was a tiny chance of something going badly wrong during surgery, and I needed to designate someone as having medical power of attorney for me.

Having a wonderful girlfriend at the time, the legal parts were relatively easy to deal with. After some awkward discussions (what should be done if I become a vegetable? Fun stuff like that), I filled out power of medical attorney forms, wrote a living will, and updated my will for the first time in ages. I even adjusted my life insurance policy to give my girlfriend some of that ... just in case. Bear in mind we had only been going out about six months at this point, so this was quite a jump in our level of relationship! I literally gave her authority to make life and death decisions about me.

I was in a quandary over how to tell my family about the upcoming surgery. I turned to my stepmom, who at twelve years my senior has been more of a big sister than a maternal figure. She wisely told me that it was a perfectly legitimate option **not to tell my family**. After all, my genitals are a very private matter (!) and to a large extent it isn't any of their business. This revelation was a huge relief! After all, most of my family freaked out when I came out, just imagine how they'd respond to this! We agreed she would be my family point of contact immediately after surgery, and the rest of the family wouldn't be told until much later (such as reading this book!).

In addition to the legal documents, I put together a list of key contact people for my girlfriend and my housemates. I broke the list into three parts. The first few people were who to notify after surgery to let them know everything was okay. The next part was people who had volunteered to help during recovery who I thought might actually do so. (You get a lot of people who say things like 'oh yes let me know if I can do anything' but would probably find a hundred excuses not to actually do anything.) The last part was the immediate family contact information only to use in dire emergency. This approach gave me piece of mind that I had covered all the major bases and contingencies.

Advice

As I prepared for surgery, I got advice from the close friends that knew it was going to happen. My stepmother offered the following bits of wisdom:

- Your new theme song is "I enjoy being a girl"
- Can't scratch (crotch) in public
- Don't wear patent leather shoes with a skirt! (Took me a while to think about this one. Patent leather is shiny enough to act like a mirror.)
- No white shoes in winter unless they're winter white and have faux fur on them
- It's a woman's prerogative to change her mind
- Keep your knees together when wearing a short skirt
- Cotton crotches in undies help with reducing feminine odor

- Never try to match your eye shadow to the color of your blouse.
- Never wear brown shoes with blue pants or skirt. Shoes should match the color of your hose or pants and the handbag too.
- It's OK for women to wear men's clothing so don't be too hasty to get rid of all of the men's clothing you have.
- Always check to make sure the toilet seat is down if you decide to visit the bathroom and don't turn on the lights first! Of course, you live in a house full of women, so it shouldn't be a problem. However, if you ever happen to find yourself in the same house as your father or brother, you'll want to make sure of that. While it's only a matter of an inch or two lower, it's the cold enamel against warm skin that can be a nasty surprise.

Cost of GCS

To pay for the surgery, I cashed out a small 401(k) retirement account and took out a signature (unsecured) loan. I knew some people had used public fundraising sites like GoFundMe (GoFundMe, 2018) to pay for GCS, but since I'm middle class I didn't feel like begging from my mostly poorer friends to pay for it. Class privilege has its price. The costs for Dr. Rumer and the rest of GCS (excluding the cost of prescriptions and therapist visits) are shown in Table 2.

Table 2. Cost of GCS

Item	Cost
Male to Female Intersex Surgery[13]	$12,980
Anesthesia Fee	$1,120
Hospital facility fee	$2,500
Three nights in hospital	$3,600
Total	$20,200

Dr. Rumer offered a place next to her office to stay after the hospital visit where I could get additional support (kind of a recovery hotel?), but since I had support from my girlfriend, I decided to save the money and just go home from the hospital. I could sleep on the living room futon for a few days without any problem.

Getting Therapist Letters

I had to get two letters from psychiatrists or therapists to prove I was crazy enough to become a woman. I still think that's the funniest part of my transition!

The first one was easy – I used a therapist from my healthcare provider (Mazzoni Center), Ms. Elaine Dutton. I met with her, discussed my situation in detail, why I wanted surgery, etc., and she wrote a letter for me promptly. She holds an LSW degree (Licensed Social Worker), which is adequate for one of the two

13 That's how Dr. Rumer described it on the invoice!

letters. The other letter has to come from someone with an MD or PsyD or PhD – some relevant terminal degree.

In this letter, Ms. Dutton cites appropriate terms for the basis for her recommendation (I like "*thorough biopsychosocial assessment*") and the standards upon which she makes that recommendation – WPATH (WPATH, 2018b).

First Therapist Letter

I am writing this letter in support of Jennifer Booker (legal name: Glenn Booker, DOB: <date1>), who has been a patient under our care since <date2>. Ms. Booker has been living full time as female for the past year and has stable and persistent female gender identity and mental health.

Since Ms. Booker became a patient at Mazzoni Center, she has consistently been engaged in our multi-disciplinary approach to care, which involves medical monitoring of hormone therapy, a thorough biopsychosocial assessment, and ongoing counseling and resource allocation as needed. Informed consent was obtained from Ms. Booker before she began receiving care.

Ms. Booker has demonstrated an understanding of the risks and benefits of surgical procedures and per the Standards of Care set forth by the World Professional Association for Transgender Health, she has met both the eligibility and readiness guidelines for further sex and gender affirming surgery. I believe that Ms. Booker is an excellent candidate for vaginoplasty and this is the appropriate next step in her transition.

The second therapist letter was more challenging to get, since I had to find an outside therapist. I was given contact information for a few possible choices, and finally met twice with Dr. Raquel Romirowsky, after which she wrote the following letter for me.

Second Therapist Letter

I am writing on behalf of Jennifer Booker (legal name, Robert Glenn Booker, D.O.B. <date1>), a queeridentified transgender female who is seeking a vaginoplasty. I am a licensed psychologist with a private psychotherapy practice and I follow the WPATH standards of care in my clinical practice. For the purposes of this letter I will be using the female pronouns to refer to Ms. Booker, as she is living full time as a female and has done so for the past year.

I evaluated Ms. Booker on <date3> and <date4> to determine her awareness of the risks and implications of getting the vaginoplasty recommended by her treatment team at the Mazzoni Center. A biopsychosocial intake was conducted with a review of her gender history and identity. Ms. Booker fully meets the criteria for Gender Dysphoria, but no other mental health issues at the time of evaluation. She is a biological male diagnosed with transsexualism for which the effective treatment is the combination of psychotherapy and medical intervention aimed at her living as a female. She reports consistent crossgender identification for the past year. She has also been taking hormones under the care of the treatment team at Mazzoni Center since <date2>.

Ms. Booker is in a supportive and loving relationship with her partner since <date5>, and her partner supports and embraces her gender identity. Her family is aware of her gender *identity since <date6>. She has a strong social network in Philadelphia, in her place of employment, and online.*

Ms. Booker presents herself as a female through dress, psychologically and in her social and professional relationships. She has discussed the impact, side effects and risks of this surgery with her doctor and informed consent has been obtained. Psychotherapy continues to be available to her with her therapist at the Mazzoni Center if she needs additional support. In my opinion, Ms. Booker is prepared for this procedure.

Notice in the second letter that the same WPATH standards are being invoked, and my new favorite word "biopsychosocial" is also used. Dr. Romirowsky diagnosed me with transsexualism after meeting the criteria for Gender Dysphoria, which is the DSM-5 version of what had been called Gender Identity Disorder (Parekh, 2016). DSM-5 is the Diagnostic and Statistical Manual of Mental Disorders, version 5, which is the standard psychologist's handbook for diagnosing mental disorders. (APA, 2013a) In order to get approved for GCS, you need to have lived for a year as your chosen sex and be on hormone therapy for a year. By the time I was going to get surgery, I qualified on both counts.

This letter also cited the fact that I was in a relationship with my girlfriend – I'm sure that added part of my support network was helpful (thanks Lucy!). I was comforted to see that I had "no other mental health issues at the time of evaluation" – yay, I'm mostly sane! *giggles, falls over*

Getting two authoritative letters to recommend GCS was a critical step before surgery.

Biopsychosocial?

Since both letters cited using a biopsychosocial approach, I was curious what this meant. It was first defined by George L. Engel in 1977 as an alternative to the existing reductionistic and dehumanizing biomedical model that was in vogue at the time (Borrell-Carrió, Suchman, & Epstein, 2004). The biopsychosocial approach attacked the dominant biomedical model in three major ways, first for believing in the separation of body and mind. While that assumption makes analyses easier, and led to the scientific study of anatomy and physiology, it has been known incorrect for centuries (Lieberman, 2012; Mehta, 2011). The second critique was the belief that "anything that could not be objectively verified...was ignored or devalued," which ignores critical concepts like human suffering. The third critique was to recognize that the observer has an effect on the observed. Trying to measure and understand a patient changes that patient. The way a scientist structures an experiment influences the outcomes of that experiment. This is consistent with the anthropology sense of reflexivity, which requires that investigators consider their own biases and their impact on the people they are studying (Nazaruk, 2011). In contrast, traditional scientific method assumes that experiments can be conducted without the scientists affecting the outcome of those experiments. (Reiss & Sprenger, 2014)

The reflexive approach has some commonality with a phenomenological approach recommended by David Fryer. (Fryer, 2011) This approach can help "uncover a radially self-reflective understanding" of how we experience gender in the world by helping us determine which experiences "need to be exposed and called into question." Even if an event is not statistically valid, it may still have been a foundation for some aspect of our identity. The scope of this book was largely selected this way, as I examined my life and chose the experiences that played a role in molding my identity.

The biopsychosocial approach recognizes that the origins of illness can occur through interaction among many levels of scale, such as molecular, organs, individual, and societal levels. Complex interactions across many levels produce health, physical illness, or mental illness. This approach is consistent with multiscale modeling attempts in biology, where ideally we'll be able to predict the effect of, say, speeding up flow through an ion channel in cardiac muscle on the resulting clinical observations of the patient. (Marsden & Esmaily-Moghadam, 2015) My dissertation used multiscale modeling to analyze healthy aging. (G. Booker, 2011)

Medical Preparation

Gender confirmation surgery is major elective surgery, so it isn't surprising that massive preparation is made to ensure that risks are minimized. Table 3 summarizes major milestones leading up to the morning of surgery.

Table 3. Surgery Preparation Timeline

Days Before Surgery	Time of day	Action
30		Stop hormone therapy
30		Get medical history done and baseline EKG
21		Payment is due to the doctor, hospital, and anesthetist
14		Stop taking medications on the list
10		No ibuprofen, aspirin, or Vitamin E
3		Start taking arnica
1	8 am	Start clear liquid diet
1	12 pm	Start bowel prep
0	12 am	Begin complete p.o. fast
0	4 am	Give self enema
0	4:30 am	Use antiseptic soap during shower
0	6 am	Arrive at hospital – no nail polish, jewelry, perfume or deodorant

*Zero Days Before Surgery means the day of surgery

A month before surgery I stopped hormone therapy. This is because estrogen affects blood clotting (Bonnar, 1987). Within a month before surgery I had to get a full medical history done and get a baseline EKG to make sure my heart is strong enough to handle the stress of surgery. For the medical professionals out there, the lab tests for the medical history included CBC, PT/PTT, complete urinalysis, CMP, MRSA screening, prolactin, and total testosterone. Three weeks before surgery I had to resolve payments to the doctor, hospital, and anesthetist. Yes, all three had to be paid up front well before surgery.

Two weeks before surgery I had to stop taking any medications or homeopathic remedies or vitamin supplements that were on huge lists provided by my doctor (Appendix F). I found it particularly interesting that such a wide range of substances were included – it wasn't just prescription and over-the-counter drugs, it includes herbal supplements, diet aids, foods, and vitamins. They gave the reasons for excluding each type of substance was given – it affects blood clotting, or heart rhythm, or how you respond to anesthesia, etc.

Disclaimer for Appendix F: Brand names are owned by their trademark holders. The list was that given to me in 2014; there may be more drugs and foods and supplements which are not included. I have included the full list I was given to show the extent of possible interactions, especially with ordinary foods or food supplements.

Ten days before surgery I was not to take ibuprofen, aspirin, or Vitamin E, all of which are blood thinners (Supplements, 2018). Not shown in Table 3, my doctors didn't run the MRSA test right, so I had to start a horrible nasal crème five days before surgery to make sure I didn't have an active MRSA virus in my sinuses.

Three days before surgery I started taking four arnica pills under my tongue four times a day. Arnica is well known in the homeopathic community for its ability to help healing. (Iannitti, Morales-Medina, Bellavite, Rottigni, & Palmieri, 2016) I first became familiar with it as statistician for the California Association of Midwives, (G. Booker, 1992) because it was the homeopathic remedy most often used by lay midwives for their clients postpartum. Apparently, the purpose here was to preload my body with it to make it readily available after surgery.

Things got messier as the day of surgery approached. About 24 hours before going to the hospital, I had to start a liquid diet. That excluded so much (Figure 22) that I basically had some fruit juice and that was about it. My "clear liquid diet" consisted of three bottles of fruit juice (apple, cranberry, and grape, for variety) plus a lot of water. Noon the day before surgery I had to start a bowel prep routine (Figure 23) to clear my colon using fun things like Dulcolax and Magnesium Citrate. I noted that bowel prep was far less intense than the one I had had years earlier for a colonoscopy, thank goodness. I lost 4.4 lbs the day before surgery.

Clear Liquid Diet Details

A clear liquid diet helps maintain adequate hydration, provides some important electrolytes, such as sodium and potassium, and gives some energy at a time when a full diet isn't possible or recommended.

The following foods are allowed in a clear liquid diet (any foods not on the following list should be avoided):

- Plain water
- Fruit juices without pulp, such as apple juice, grape juice or cranberry juice
- Strained lemonade or fruit punch
- Clear, fat-free broth (bouillon or consommé)
- Clear sodas
- Plain gelatin
- Honey
- Ice pops without bits of fruit or fruit pulp
- Tea or coffee without milk or cream

Figure 22. Clear liquid diet

On the day prior to your surgery you must follow these bowel prep instructions:

a. At 12 PM (noon):
    i. Drink one (1) bottle of **Mag Citrate** and take three (3) **Dulcolax** laxatives by mouth. Make sure you have access to a bathroom from this point on throughout the day.
b. At 1 PM:
    i. Take two (2) 500 mg tablets of Neomycin
    ii. Take one (1) 500 mg tablet of Flagyl
c. At 2 PM:
    i. Take two (2) 500 mg tablets of Neomycin
    ii. Take one (1) 500 mg tablet of Flagyl
d. At 10PM:
    i. Drink ½ bottle of Mag Citrate by mouth
    ii. Take two (2) 500 mg tablets of Neomycin
    iii. Take one (1) 500 mg tablet of Flagyl
e. At 4:00AM the day of your surgery give yourself one (1) Fleets Enema rectally for a final bowel evacuation.

Figure 23. Bowel preparation routine

A summary of the supplies needed before and after surgery, including prescription and over-the-counter (OTC) supplies, is shown in Table 4. Many of the OTC supplies I ordered online before surgery, so I had them on hand. Yes, it was embarrassing to buy adult diapers in the drug store. But I'll give them credit, it's clever to use them as a huge bandage after leaving the hospital. After all, they're designed to soak up liquids and hold your hips snugly!

At some point the day before surgery I removed my nail polish, since that was forbidden. It used to be that pulse ox meters (which measure how well oxygenated your blood is) couldn't read through nail polish, but now I think it's just to eliminate another foreign substance from the operating room.

Midnight before surgery I started a complete fast – no food or liquid by mouth (p.o. or *per os* in medical lingo). This is routine for any surgery to help keep you from choking on your puke, a decidedly unglamorous way to die. At 4 am I gave myself an enema to finish clearing anything from my colon. I took a shower and used special antiseptic soap all over, to help avoid any possible sources of infection.

Hungry, odorless, and lacking sleep, my girlfriend drove me to the hospital. I was ready.

Table 4. Supplies before and after surgery

Item	Purpose	When used
Prescription Supplies		
Neomycin	Antibiotic cream	Post-surgery
Percocet	Pain relief	Post-surgery
Flagyl	Prevent vaginal infections	Post-surgery
EKG	Assess heart	Part of pre-surgery medical history
Bactrim	Antibiotic	Post-surgery
MRSA nasal swab	Prevent MRSA infection	Pre-surgery five days
OTC Supplies*		
Arnica Montana 30x	Promote healing	Pre- and Post-surgery
Depends (~20) adult diapers	Giant bandage	Post-surgery
Mag Citrate (2 bottles)	Laxative	Part of bowel prep
Dulcolax (tablets not suppository)	Laxative	Part of bowel prep

Item	Purpose	When used
Fleet enema (1)	Clean colon	Last step in bowel prep
Underpads for bed	Prevent staining bed mattress	Post-surgery
Unscented feminine wipes	General feminine hygiene	Post-surgery
Unscented sterile greaseless lube	Lube for dilation therapy	Post-surgery and forever
Medicated (iodine) douche	Clean vagina	Post-surgery

*OTC = Over The Counter (i.e. non-prescription)

Surgery and Immediate Aftermath

My girlfriend and I showed up at the hospital at 6 am and found a nurse to start my intake process. She pulled my file and started going through the checklist of all the tests and preparations I was supposed to have done. I didn't use the MRSA crème enough days (four instead of five), so they had to make up for that. They ran down the list of blood tests done for my medical history, and the nurse paused.

"Did you pee in a cup?" she asked me.

"No, what's that for" I replied.

"Pregnancy test" was the surprising response. I tried very hard to suppress outright laughter, and my girlfriend and I exchanged terribly amused looks as the nurse studied my chart very intently.

She asked me how long I had been on hormone therapy, and I replied 13 months. She seemed surprised by this and kept pushing for me to pee in a cup. I reassured her that I had NEVER been pregnant and could not be. She finally gave up, shortly before I was going to lift my gown and flash my junk at her. Really honey, I have never been pregnant. I'm sure!

Other than not fully reading my chart, the source of her confusion could have been the name of the procedure. GCS is 'vaginoplasty' or plastic surgery of the vagina, so maybe she assumed I already had one. From her odd reactions, and how surprised she was how little time I had been on hormones, my best guess is she thought that I was FTM and not MTF.

We got a nurse to witness our signing the legal papers, so I knew I was in good hands in case something went terribly wrong. Bear in mind that this was a huge step for our relationship. It's not typical at 6 months into a relationship to ask your girlfriend to have legal power over your emergency medical decisions!

A nurse came in and put two large cuffs on my lower legs, kind of like blood pressure cuffs. Once installed, they inflated themselves and deflated about 15 times a minute (that's a guess). Their purpose was to provide support for blood pressure to my extremities and help avoid blood clots. Those ^&%$^ cuffs were on my legs from that point until I left the hospital 3-1/2 days later. The cuffs made sleeping a challenge, and I grew to hate them completely by the time I was released.

The anesthetist came and started an IV in my right hand (I'm left-handed, so I wanted that one free). Dr. Rumer appeared briefly to say Hi. I had wracked my brain to think of something to say to the doctor who is about to fix your most intimate plumbing. The best I came up with was "I hope this morning you do your best work ever." She looked mildly insulted by this and said "I do my best work every day." Ok, fair enough. I was sleepy and hungry and scared and excited.

Between visits from various nurses and doctors, I had a little time to myself. I was sitting up on a gurney, separated from other surgical patients by white curtains. I paused to ponder the enormity of what I was about to do and realized this was the last possible moment to change my mind. I was about the give up the cock and balls that had been part of my body and identity for 51 years. I was paying someone a small fortune to give me a vulva and vagina.

I wrote in my notes "During a brief undisturbed moment, I cradled the family jewels in my left hand and thought about what I was about to do. I tried to make peace with them, and let them know I didn't hate them. We just could never communicate well or even seem to speak the same language. I stroked my scrotum a little, paused to savor it, and looked forward to that becoming part of my new vagina." I have shared that with live audiences a few times, and invariably a few people laugh uncomfortably because I just shared what was possible the most intimate moment of my life.

The anesthetist came back and told me he was going to start three drugs in my IV. One was a muscle relaxant, one was to make me happy and a little loopy, and the third was the start of actual anesthetic.

Shortly after the drugs started flowing into me, they wheeled me toward the operating room. My girlfriend met me in the hallway. I reached for her with my left hand and held her as long as I could. I've never known anyone who produced such strong feelings in me from simple touch. A thousand butterflies danced in my stomach and I was on the verge of tears. I told her I loved her and felt her squeeze my hand gently. To this point she had never used the L word[14] yet, but she moved mountains to be there for me in every way possible. I reluctantly let go of her as I was wheeled toward the operating room.

The happy drug must have been very generously given, because a massive wave of euphoria swept over me. As we passed strangers in the nurse's station near the operating room, I started waving to them, saying hello, good morning, and anything else that came into my mind. I was briefly higher and giddier than I've ever been in my life.

I passed out before getting to the operating room, so I never saw the operating room.

---

[14] The L word here is Love, not Lesbian.

Recovery – the First Week

I woke up about five hours later in the recovery room. My first thoughts were 1) hmm, guess I survived surgery, and 2) why am I not in any pain? I soon deduced I was probably on really good pain medication. I was told that Dr. Rumer got done about 11:10 am, after starting about 7:30 am.

As I examined my surroundings, I realized I was hooked up to a ton of monitoring equipment, flat on my back, and with those infernal cuffs still hugging my calves. Yay 21st century technology! I had a urinary catheter (which I expected), two drains flanking each side of my vulva, the two leg cuffs, an ECG, and an IV all hanging off of me, so changing position at all was a logistical nightmare anyway. My IV included a box with a magic button I could press to get morphine on demand. I had never seen such a thing before and thought this must be a perk of elective surgery!

When I first tried to move, such as for the nurses to change the pads under me, I was told to roll like a log. Any attempt to use core muscles was massively painful immediately. When the nurses came in to change my gauze panties and bedding, I quipped "I've only had a vagina for less than 12 hours and already I have bloody panties."

First full day after surgery I was uncomfortable, especially since I couldn't roll to one side yet. I was still amazed how little I needed the morphine. Got my first glimpse of my girl bits as the doctor changed the dressings for the first time. Massive amounts of bruising all across the front of my hips was a surprise. I knew my vulva would be a mess, and it was. My mons was huge, I couldn't see anything below that. **It finally really sank in that girls can't see their own vaginas without a mirror.**

This later led to lots of interesting discussions with my girlfriend around "When did you discover your vagina?" and "When did you discover your clit?" and what happened afterward. I never occurred to me that self-discovery would even be an issue for girls, since boy plumbing is so obvious. A well-educated 25-year-old friend admitted that she didn't know exactly where her urethra was, it was just down there somewhere. Clearly, she had not watched as much porn as I had.

Lucy and my dear friend Jennifer came to visit but left by the end of visiting hours at 8:30. I was asleep shortly after 9 pm anyway. The major events after surgery are summarized in Table 5.

Table 5. Recovery timeline

Days after surgery	Event
3	Release from hospital
3	Resume arnica, 4 pills sublingual 4x/day
3	Start taking Bactrim, 1 pill 2x/day with breakfast and dinner
6	Doc removes packing and catheter (nominally day 7)
6	First shower allowed
6	Start dilation therapy, 4x/day for first month (3 meals plus before bed)

Days after surgery	Event
6	Start doing arnica massage 2-3x/day
6	Start doing medicated (iodine) douche & rinse once per week for 2 months
10	End taking arnica
10	End taking Bactrim
14	Resume estrogen therapy. Spironolactone is no longer needed.
34	Reduce dilation therapy to 3x/day (4 wks after start of dilation therapy)
36	Change frequency of douche to 1-2x/month
94	Reduce dilation therapy to 2x/day (2 months after start of 3x)
184	Reduce dilation therapy to 1x/day (3 months after start of 2x)

The night after the first full day, I initially had three blankets to keep warm, and the nurses got concerned I was running a fever from "not breathing fully enough." They brought me this weird plastic inhale meter (an inspirometer) and told me to use it once an hour. While asleep. Instead, I took off two of the blankets and my temp returned to normal. *duh* (This was another example of a medical professional just reading the measurements and responding with a treatment, without consulting the patient.) It was rare to get more than two hours of sleep at a time, since I kept getting interrupted for taking vital signs, changing the IV bags, or an alarm going off from the leg pressure cuffs, IV system, or morphine pump.

On the second full day after surgery I was allowed to turn sideways and was getting bored from being in the hospital. I had to keep a pillow between my knees (for 2+ weeks) when sideways to keep pressure off my vulva, which added to the awkwardness. And the back of my bed isn't supposed to tilt up more than 30 degrees, which keeps my weight off of tender new parts. Vitals were all doing fine, and the catheter wasn't as annoying as I feared it might be. Got flowers from Jennifer and some mystery person/people who sent yellow flowers. Thank you whoever that was! Next time attach a card!

On the third day after surgery I was released from the hospital about noon. Jennifer picked me up and took me home. Walking up even a couple of stairs is a little painful for my adductors (inner thighs), but otherwise I could walk slowly and stand up just fine.

Shortly after getting home Lucy arrived, and stayed until my doctor's appointment that Monday morning. She bought a ton of food, cooked everything in sight and filled the freezer with most of it, and stayed with me basically 24x7. Weirdest. Date. Ever. Seriously, I'm crying right now just thinking of how wonderful she's been about being there for me and providing amazing support, just because "she'd be a lousy girlfriend otherwise" as she put it. And Jen did great filling in when Lucy couldn't. Great support team, even if they barely met each other beforehand.

The fourth day after surgery went mostly well – I didn't move much except to turn from side to side. Started seeing a hint of blood in my urine toward the end of that day. Lucy and I spent a lot of the day watching sports or silly movies. Fortunately, my living room has a futon, which we used for my bed for the first few days home until I could walk up stairs again. Lucy slept on the couch, so she'd be nearby if I needed anything in the night.

Day five after surgery became a nightmare for a while. A blood clot got stuck in my catheter, causing my bladder to spasm. That meant for a while I'd go to the bathroom, and by the time I finished getting cleaned up, I'd need to pee again before I got back to the living room. Peed myself a little bit one time because I didn't make it back to the bathroom in time. Very frustrating to lose control over something as basic as peeing. As I sat on the toilet baffled why I couldn't stop peeing (I didn't know about the spasms yet), I realized this was the kind of complication I most feared from GCS.

That few minutes was the only time I questioned whether I should have done GCS.

Later that day the spasms stopped, urine flowed into the collection bag just fine, and no longer had a trace of blood. I had changed my doctor's appointment from the afternoon on day seven to first thing in the morning of day six. I didn't change the appointment again because I was terrified of going through the bladder spasms again. I was so afraid I barely slept. Lucy slept on the sofa minus its cushions.

The morning of day six after surgery Lucy drove me to the doctor's office, and the doctor removed the tubes (two drains and catheter) and vaginal packing. I was shown how to do dilations. For 20 minutes each time??? Way longer than I was expecting. I had expected the dilations to be maybe five minutes each, so 20 minutes each time was a bit of a shock. Oh well. Was told to douche once a week with an iodine solution and use some arnica cream on my mons 2-3 times per day. Good, I get to massage myself!

I got a tour of my girl parts courtesy of my surgeon. My clit was hiding behind a big blood clot and won't appear for a couple weeks. Don't rush it. The sutures are all going to dissolve eventually, and for the moment look predictably nasty. My inner labia were very thin, and my outer labia were swollen and seemed huge.

For the record, I took many pictures of my girlbits before and many times after surgery. I have deliberately not included them in this book because, well, that would be over-sharing, even by my standards.

Later that day I tried to do dilations for the first time. Why can't I find my vagina??? And why am I bleeding like a stuck pig??? I was bent over, using a mirror behind my legs to help see what I was doing, trying to insert the dilator, and every time it touched my skin, I started dripping blood everywhere. After a very panicked phone call to my doctor's answering service, I finally got answers why I was bleeding like I had never seen any girl bleed.

The answer to the first question was mostly due to having the wrong angle; I thought the vagina was more in line with the body, and it's about 30 degrees anterior from that. The second question was due to my urethra being very annoyed by the catheter, and so ANY contact nearby would make it start spewing blood. The cure was to look for the vagina from back to front, and don't let the dilator touch the urethra EVER. I hired a housemate to clean the bathroom – it looked like an episode of Dexter[15] in there.

As I soon discovered doing the douches and mons massage, my new parts had a very weird attribute at first. I couldn't feel them! I had normal feeling in my legs and hips and up to my outer labia, but my inner labia and vagina had no sensation! I realized that the surgery had probably cut major nerves in that area, so while blood flow was fine and the tissues were healthy, it would take many months before the new nerve connections would form. In fact, much of the second six months of recovery was all related to the reestablishment of sensation in that area.

The night after day six, Lucy and I could finally sleep together again. I had to get up a lot in the night, but the company was wonderful. She left the next afternoon to visit her family; she had stayed with me for three solid days after getting out of the hospital.

Peeing

When I was preparing for surgery, I asked my girlfriend what the biggest change from transition would be. To my surprise, in response to this somewhat tongue in cheek question, she paused thoughtfully and said 'peeing.' She was right. Girls need a staggering amount of toilet paper compared to boys.

---

[15] Dexter is the title character of a TV series on the Showtime network. He's a serial killer, who often ritually stabs his victims to death. (IMDb.com, 2018b)

My first time peeing with girl plumbing was six days after surgery, after we went to the doctor and she removed the catheter and drainage tubes. After we got to my home, it wasn't long before nature called and I dutifully toddled to the bathroom. I sat on the toilet, released the grip on my urethra, and started peeing. Quickly one important question came to mind.

What the $&%^&$%#%@ do I do with my hands??

After all, with boy plumbing, one hand is dedicated to aiming into the toilet, or you'll pee all over your leg and other awkward places. With girl plumbing, your hands are not needed. Nevertheless, I immediately realized that girl plumbing is much MUCH messier than boy plumbing, because pee was wandering all over my butt cheeks and mons, in a decidedly non-ladylike fashion.

Therefore, I soon concluded that the main job of your hands while peeing is to start collecting toilet paper. Now from my observation of various female significant others over the years, I knew that most girls grab a handful of toilet paper and pat their vulvas and they're done.

My plumbing was not nearly so tidy. I had to collect toilet paper at least three times to dry off my mons and butt cheeks. I hoped that this was a temporary condition given the fact that my mons was in the early stages of healing, but unfortunately some four years later, this doesn't seem to be the case.

Peeing with boy plumbing takes no toilet paper. With girl plumbing, at least six squares of high-quality toilet paper seemed to be the minimum for me, and with cheap public bathroom single ply toilet paper, 4-6 feet can be needed.

Ten days after surgery, I went to the toilet and stood in front of it. I reached in my sweatpants, and only then realized I couldn't pee effectively that way any longer. *duh* Mistakes like this kept occurring for months afterward. Old habits die hard!

Another issue that emerged over the next few months was that it was far easier to leak pee with girl plumbing. The reason seems clear from an anatomy perspective; the urethra for girls is much shorter than for boys (1-2" versus 7-8") (Martini, Nath, & Bartholomew, 2017), so there is less room for muscles to clamp down on it. I've discovered that sitting on very hard surfaces, like wooden or metal benches, can especially encourage a little leakage unless I consciously clamp down to prevent it. Leaks while running during soccer can also occur.

I remembered in my church youth group when I was in high school, the pastor's daughter was legendary for peeing involuntarily whenever she laughed hard. She was quite open about it, and often shared with us when it occurred. I found this odd and amusing at the time, but now I have a lot more sympathy for her!

A logistical issue emerged in connection with clothing. Sometimes, particularly in the winter, it's possible to put on layers of clothing that mean you have to essentially strip before you can go to the bathroom. I accidentally did this to myself at work a couple months after surgery, when I wore tights that had clear suspenders over your shoulders, plus a skirt and top and cardigan. In order to go to the bathroom, you had to remove all of the other layers to pull down the tights! Now I plan outfits with an eye toward how complex peeing will be.

In public places, lines for ladies' restrooms are common, so that is also a factor in planning bathroom breaks. As a result of all this, I have to pay closer attention when nature calls. If I think I might need to pee, don't EVER ignore it!

I've also been amused by the importance of toilet paper in ladies' public bathrooms. Everyone completely understands how critical it is to have a proper supply, so if someone gets in a stall with no paper, a daisy chain will form instantly to pass a roll to them.

Good hygiene isn't optional

I've learned the hard way that being a girl is fundamentally messier than being a boy; mostly because of peeing. A little while after transition, I decided I might be getting overzealous about washing my hands after peeing and stopped doing it all the time. Combine this with regular cuticle care that can result in small breaks in the skin, and I managed a very weird infection. I got an infection under a fingernail! It started swelling up and became throbbing and a little painful that I finally couldn't sleep one night and took myself to the hospital emergency department down the street. They diagnosed it, gave me antibiotics, and told me to keep it warm. The pus from the infection eventually drained (ick), and the fingernail fell off! The nail grew back over the next several months and is fine now.

The lesson from this, boys and girls, is that once you become a girl you have to take better care of yourself than boys do! When the US military was debating allowing women on ships and in combat, they had to consider that the health care costs for women soldiers and sailors was higher per person than for men (Farrell, 2013). Maybe soap and toilet paper costs are part of that!

Healing timeline after surgery

I made detailed records of my progress in recovering from GCS, so I've broken the information into categories to give an idea what it was like in many aspects. Naturally everyone recovers differently, so anyone else's recovery might be different. Overall, I'd say that short term recovery took about two weeks, more functionality by two months, but full recovery took a year.

Dilation therapy

A week after surgery, my doctor removed the gauze packing material from my vagina, and I started doing dilation therapy. I was given a set of dilation tools (plastic dildos) to use with odorless lubricant cream. Dilation therapy just means you lube up a dildo and stick it in your vagina and leave it there for 20 minutes. The frequency of doing this tapers off very slowly – four times per day for a month, then three times a day for two months, then twice a day for three months, then once a day forever thereafter. Yes, forever.

The crazy part is that initially you have to bend over and use a mirror to see where to insert the dildo. You're standing bare assed, legs apart, bending over to look between your legs. One hand holds the dildo, and the other holds a hand mirror behind your butt to help see your vulva. Once the dildo is in place, keeping your legs together holds the dildo in place, and I could sit down near the edge of a chair to wait out the twenty minutes. The whole business with the mirror took me a while to understand...why not just feel for your vagina? The answer came after I had had some minor surgery on my labia during recovery. My doctor used no anesthesia yet trimmed my inner labia without causing pain. How? My nerves around my vagina weren't working yet. I had no touch or pain sensation for many months after surgery, so I had to use a mirror to see where my vagina was! How bizarre.

I finished doing dilation four times a day 34 days post-surgery. Before day 44, I had a little sharp pain when inserting a dildo, but now that's gone. Just feel pressure and a little stretching.

Once I got sensation in my pussy, dilation therapy became much easier. I could leave panties loosely on, lube and insert the dildo while in bed, pull up the panties or use my thighs to help hold it in place, and relax in bed for the twenty minutes. I check my email, or social media, or play games on my phone. It's not a sexual act, it just makes sure that my vagina doesn't seal up. If I have sex that counts the same as doing dilation therapy. And is a lot more fun. Over a year after surgery, I've discovered that if I miss a day's dilation once in a while, nothing bad happens. I don't push it beyond that.

Body position

Immediately after surgery I was flat on my back and had to stay that way for the first day. Then I could log roll to either side, with a pillow between my legs. After leaving the hospital, I was taken home by my girlfriend. I had set up a futon in the living room, so for the rest of the first week post-surgery I could stay entirely on the first floor with a living room/bedroom, bathroom, and kitchen all there. Only after getting out the catheter and drainage tubes, would I brave going upstairs. Stairs were difficult because pushing down with my legs apparently activated some core abdominal muscles, and those were all **very** tender.

Day 13 I was given the ok to sleep on my stomach again, but it wasn't at all comfortable. At most I can sleep mostly on one side, with the upper leg extended to tilt me a little face down. Day 21 Got okay to end the pillow between my knees if it's not helping (it isn't). Day 27 Can sleep on tummy, but too much pressure on mons is uncomfy. Day 34 - Still uncomfortable to sit on hard chairs, I tend to slouch to one side or back to sit more on my sacrum. Day 42 Mons is still a bit tender to sleep on my tummy, and there's a hint more swelling on the right side.

Energy level and general activity

Day seven after surgery, I was home alone for the first time. Getting up and down from a chair or sofa is a little uncomfortable, but otherwise I'm doing amazingly well. I did two loads of laundry and got most of the living room back in order. That was a bit overdoing it, so afterward I collapsed into a deep happy sleep for an extended nap. Have to remember to take care of myself! I'm recovering so fast I forget my body needs time to fix itself, and that takes a lot of energy too.

Ten days after surgery I went to see the movie Into The Woods (IMDb.com, 2018e) with a friend. Two flights of stairs and driving on Philly streets were a bit much for my weak constitution, but it was nice to get out of the house and spend some time with her.

Day 12 – I was tempted to try to go to the burlesque brunch at Tabu (a local gay bar), but then realized that 1) the loud music might be painful, and 2) sitting on the hard, wooden chairs would certainly be painful. Reluctantly skipped that, instead went shopping in a mall with a friend and then drove to visit Lucy as she got back from traveling. During shopping, I noticed some light vaginal bleeding and realized I had walked too far. My friend got her car to pick me up. This was a wakeup call that I had to pay close attention to my body and not expect healing to occur quickly.

Day 13 got the letter from my doctor saying I'm medically recognized as a girl. *blush* This letter became the basis for my legally recognized status as a woman.

Day 21 – Starting work yesterday was completely exhausting. (I had planned the surgery date to give me the most possible time between surgery and the start of classes. It wasn't financially feasible to take a term off work!) I keep forgetting my mind and body aren't even close to being on the same page. Laurie (my doctor's assistant) said it takes six weeks to feel yourself again, and I'm only halfway there. Patience.

Day 32 - went to Ikea. Managed to walk the whole store but was exhausted afterward.

Day 38 - saw Michele Younger for the first time since Jennifer came out. Main discovery was relationship versus relating (static baggage versus open and curious) and realizing that I needed to vent the pain of my body being violated during surgery, even if it was consensual. She was extremely positive toward Lucy (called her a 'very healing force' in my life). Michele cried with joy when she saw my vulva. Told her I realized recently that I was not expecting the possibility of doing well at sports; a leftover from the 'pathetic' self-image pattern.

Day 42 It's getting easier to sit through classes & meetings but standing for 2 hours of lecture was exhausting.

Day 49 – wore tights comfortably for the first time. Starting to sit up straight without annoying pressure on my vulva. Ran a little to catch the bus, and it felt fine.

Day 51 - pants are ok to wear now, still a little mons swelling. Got pants back from a friend who hemmed several pairs of them, just in time. Up to this point, I was only wearing skirts or dresses to work, even though it was in the middle of winter!

Day 44 In a week it's okay to start being sexually active again!!! Doctor said it's okay to start using the (larger) blue dildo after warming up with the (smaller) orange one for ten minutes first, if I want to try it. (I later gave up on the larger dildo.)

Day 46 – A month and a half after surgery, light contact on my mons and outer labia is nice, but harder (deeper) pressure is uncomfortable. Really starting to feel one with my new parts. Sitting a long time is getting much more comfortable.

Day 56 - Really feeling like myself. Sitting through class is no problem now. Signed up to rejoin the Sunday night soccer league! Will probably try to swim in a couple days. Only a trace of leakage at this point. I walk confidently now, and I'm restoring good posture.

Day 61 I played soccer for the first time. Really felt good to get my pulse racing again, but also realized that I am badly out of shape! Running at this point is mostly a suggestion.

Day 64 – my girlfriend played with my clit some – it feels like getting an erection! Still no sensation on my inner labia.

Doctor visits

My doctor saw me daily in the hospital for three days following surgery, then at one week and two weeks, and six weeks and twelve weeks post-surgery. The final visits were at six and twelve months after surgery.

Driving

Nine days after surgery I drove a few miles without any problem. A long trip would be hard on my girlbits, but a short trip was no problem. Sitting upright is painful, but a reclining sitting position is fine for hours or even sleeping on the sofa. I went to the grocery store and got comfort food – cinnamon rolls, mac and cheese, Pepsi.

Wound care

Day 12 - After today's shower I noticed my labia are getting closer together, and my mons is getting softer and smaller. Yay!

Day 34 - Getting more comfy for my knees to come together. Girl bits are feeling more like me and less foreign. Mons swelling and tenderness are almost gone. Transverse scars are still nasty, but the labia are coming closer together.

Day 42 – my vulva is still leaking, but very little at this point. Can't wait to swim and sleep naked again. Knees even more comfy coming together; can sit somewhat like a lady now. Day 42 Vulva is really feeling like part of me now.

DIAPERS/PADS After leaving the hospital, I was wearing a diaper to help absorb blood and other stray liquids from my girl bits. In addition, pads were put on my bed to help catch any leaks during the night. I didn't find them effective, since they tended to get scrunched up in the night anyway. Day 13 after surgery – I used the last of the diapers, and switch to (feminine hygiene maxi) pads and feel slightly less silly. It's never dignified to wear a diaper, even if it isn't for incontinence!

Day 31 - Amount of light brown gunk oozing from the scars is getting less. I'm using overnight pads with wings, about four per day, to catch it. Also go through 2-3 pair of panties per day. Laundry nightmare?

Day 44 – Everything healing very well, too fast in fact. My doctor trimmed some tissue from my inner labia and around the os of my vagina. Some bleeding but not painful. No nerves there yet apparently. She also touched my clit, which was a strong ZING

– not sexual but intense. It was awkward to be touched that intimately, by a doctor, with my girlfriend in the room. It was very clinical – she pushed my clit like you'd push a doorbell, noted that I jumped out of my skin, and continued with the examination. My mons still has some swelling, a little more on the right side.

Day 52 - I switched from pads to pantiliners.

Day 70 – I gave up on panties at night. Now back to sleeping nude. Not enough leakage to be an issue, just change the sheets every week or so.

ARNICA CREAM After leaving the hospital, I started using an arnica cream on my mons daily to help healing. I was familiar with arnica from my midwifery days, since many lay midwives use it for their clients postpartum to help healing. I used the arnica cream until 22 days after surgery.

DOUCHE Ten days after surgery I did the medicated (iodine) douche for the first time. I kind of like the cool swirly feeling before it comes out, but I can't figure out how to stop the dripping forever afterward! The next day I had to do laundry since the douche leaked a little on the sheets and mattress pad. Got no great advice for the douche drip problem, just use some extra padding to soak up the leaks afterward. Day 27 Now just dilation, weekly douches, and Tylenol. The medicated douches continued weekly for two months, followed by plain water douches.

Unlike original equipment vaginas, mine isn't self-cleaning, so even long after surgery I'm expected to douche every 2-4 weeks to help keep mine happy. About six months after surgery I switched to regular over the counter douches – rain scented, floral, whatever.

When I do dilation therapy, I monitor my vaginal odor to keep alert for anything abnormal or signs I need to clean her up.

DEBRIDEMENT CREAM Day 13 Some necrosis of the tissue flaps near the opening of my vagina was found by my doctor during my two-week checkup. The necrotic tissue will die off and be replaced. Only issue is that will slow getting to the final finished appearance of my labia. Doc prescribed some debridement cream to help speed the healing process there, to be used daily for two weeks.

Day 18 a thin strip of left labial tissue came off as a result of that cream. Day 27 – end of debridement cream treatment.

ANTIBIOTIC OINTMENT Day 44 Use antibiotic ointment to clean up my vulva for a week. This was in response to the trimming of labial tissue, to prevent infection.

Pain management

For the first three days after surgery, I was in the hospital and had morphine on demand through my IV. After going home, I was taking Percocet regularly to keep comfortable.

Day 11, I stopped taking Percocet, and substituted Tylenol. Day 27 Now just dilation, weekly douches, and Tylenol.

Day 34 Tried stopping Tylenol for a day or so; not bad but it still helps. Main signs I still need it are a slight fever and increased discomfort when standing or sitting.

Medication

Ran out of the arnica pills and antibiotics on Day 10, and don't need more of either.

Day 13 Given the okay to restart hormones (estrogen therapy). As a result of going through surgery, I went six weeks before surgery with no estrogen or spironolactone, so effectively I was back on male hormones for that time. The reason for this is that estrogen affects blood clotting, so they didn't want it to interfere with the early healing post-surgery. Then the next two weeks after surgery I had no girl or boy hormones, since I was still not back on estrogen yet and had no testes to produce testosterone. I was hormonally neutral!

Recovery beyond two months

Day 66 spoke to Laurie (RN) and confirmed that vaginal leakage could occur for months or stop soon. Still haven't tried swimming, partly due to school duties (grading).

Day 70 days since surgery. Court hearing for name change is set for Day 92.

Day 72 I finally feel really comfortable sleeping on my stomach. Still some mons swelling. Dilation is getting to be a little fun, feeling the return of my sex drive. Getting the urge to play with my clit. Still haven't been to the gym or paddle pool. (I was trying to be in a competitive dragon boat racing team, and some winter practice sessions were in a paddle pool, i.e. an indoor pool where you can simulate paddling.)

By the six-month checkup, I was fully active in every respect, and was given the ok to resume sexual activity.

Vaginal leakage continued slightly for well over a year after surgery. I kept wearing pantiliners for about a year and a half, then eventually decided it had stopped enough to be not worth the hassle of using the pads. I still keep one or two in my purse in case a sister needs one for a period emergency.

It wasn't until about month 9 or 10 after surgery before I regained sensation in all of my girl bits. Healing of nerves takes that long. Having sex was permitted six months after surgery, and most girls have their first orgasm between 6 and 12 months.

As I was doing dilation therapy, I was concerned that I couldn't use larger diameter dilators. I asked about this at my last doctor visit at 12 months. She said I had healed perfectly, and the only way to change the vaginal diameter would be to do another surgery for that purpose. It was clear she strongly recommended against doing so, so I dropped it. It would be a bigger issue if I expected to have sex with men.

Reflection

1. If you had unlimited resources for it, would you get plastic surgery? If so, which one(s)? If not, why?
2. If you had time to prepare for major surgery, who would you designate to make medical decisions for you if you couldn't make them?
3. Do you have a will? If not, write one. There are lots of free or cheap legal resources.

4. If gender confirmation surgery covered by insurance where you live? It might also be specific to your employer, if it's not covered by socialized medicine.
5. Look up the criteria for Gender Dysphoria in DSM-5. What are the diagnostic criteria? Do you exhibit any of them?
6. Have you or close friends or family had any surgeries or major injuries? How long did it take to recover?
7. I got narcotic pain killers after surgery. How severe is the opioid epidemic in your area? More generally, how are people with drug addiction treated? Are they treated with prison time, or counseling, or is it treated as a medical problem? Some combination of those?

Chapter 8 – Name Change

Before surgery I asked Dr. Rumer if I should do my legal name change before or after the surgery. Since I met with her only a few months before the date for surgery, she recommended waiting until afterward, otherwise insurance forms would get confused. Even though the surgery itself wasn't covered by insurance, incidentals like prescriptions were covered, so I needed a consistent name through the process to avoid confusion and rejected claims. Besides, this way I could do name and sex change at the same time.

The name change process along with recognizing my sex change involved getting a letter from my doctor to prove I'm a girl, then a court order for the name change, then social security card and driver's license updates, then passport and all other ID could change. The major documents took about six months to get correct, but the miscellaneous other documents can easily take another year.

Doctor's Letter

As I was recovering from GCS, about two weeks afterward, I got a very important piece of paper in the mail from my doctor. This was the magic piece of paper that meant I could be legally recognized as a woman[16]. It read in part:

---

16 Recent changes have made it possible to be legally recognized as a different sex than assigned at birth, even without undergoing GCS, but at the time this was required in most states.

To Whom It May Concern:

The above captioned patient underwent gender reassignment surgery on <date> at <hospital name and address>. She is presenting full-time as a female, is on a regimen of hormone therapy and fulfills all requirements set forth by the World Professional Association for Transgender Health (WPATH). She now requests to have her records changed to reflect her gender.

I, Dr. Rumer, have treated and reviewed the medical history of this patient. I have also personally performed her surgery, examined this patient and can attest that an irreversible surgical change of gender has been completed.

I declare under penalty of perjury under the laws of the United States that the forgoing is true and correct.

The magic letter was on her practice's letterhead, was notarized, and also contained the license and contact information for Dr. Rumer. Now the name change process could begin, and I could be legally recognized as a woman at the same time.

From coming out to myself to completing medical transition, only 620 days (1.7 years) had elapsed. Getting to legal recognition took a total of 719 days, just under two years.

During a routine checkup with my primary care doctor many months later, I commented on how fast my transition had been, and asked if many others had done so. He responded that many wanted to, but few could. It was a tactful reminder of my class privilege to be able to make my transition occur so quickly.

Choosing My Name

How did I choose my name? What a monumental choice!

When I was working with Michele Younger, Jennifer was the name that came to mind for myself. As I tried this new moniker on for size, it felt like the right choice, but I decided before making it legal I'd make sure I really wanted it. I turned to the Internet. I looked up Jennifer on babynames.com, where I was told it is from old English for "Fair Phantom or White Wave." (Babynames.com, 2018a) They also pointed out that it was the most common girl's name through the 1970's and half of the 80's, which could explain why I liked it so much – it was very familiar! This is a classic example of the Familiarity Effect from sociology. "When we are familiar with someone or something, we start liking him/her because the person or thing does not appear to be strange or remote or threatening." (Chabra, Rai, Hegde, V, & Devan, 2015)

I also have always liked the name Sarah, but that's from Hebrew for Princess, and I'm neither Hebrew nor a princess. The names of my grandmothers (Adeline and Esther) were too antiquated to be of interest. I also wanted a common name that's easy to spell, having spent too many years correcting people how to spell my name and always wanting a silly license plate or mug from tourist shops with my name on it. As a result, I decided to stick with Jennifer for my first name.

I chose my middle name of Margaret in honor of Margaret Hansen, a great aunt on my father's side. She was a strong, independent woman, and I admired her for that. By the way,

Margaret is from English for Pearl (Babynames.com, 2018b). Given that my ethnic heritage is at least 50% German, it was a little odd to choose two English names, but I have a lot of English ancestry too. I somehow never considered taking my mom's middle name, Marie. This was pointed out to me by my girlfriend, who shared that middle name.

Changing my name has been a sore point with my father, since he picked my original name, and named me after two World War II veterans from his side of the family. I suspect he's more struggling with the whole 'my son is now my daughter' part than the name change itself, though he still calls me by the name he gave me. He's not likely to change any time soon, so it's not worth arguing it.

Court Ordered Name Change

Now that I had the magic letter from my doctor and chose my name, I could get my formal name change done. I applied for Mazzoni Legal Services (M. Center, 2017a) to help with my name change, but I was too old and/or wealthy for them to help me.

A little asking around revealed that Ben Jerner, of Jerner & Palmer, P.C. (Palmer, 2015), had experience working with the LGBT community and had specifically helped transgender people with name changes. I met with Ben, thought he was an awesome person, and hired him on the spot. Here is another example of where my class privilege allowed me to do things that many transgender people can't. It cost $2000 to have my name change done.

To prepare for the name change, Ben needed my social security card and birth certificate. The latter proved more difficult than I expected. All my life, my birth certificate had been a document called a Form 240, "Report of Birth Abroad of a Citizen of the United States of America." Come to find out from Ben that that document isn't really my birth certificate. The real one is a Form 360, "Report of Child Born of American Parent(s)." Imagine my surprise! I had to ask my mom to dig through her files and find the Form 360 and send it to me. Good thing she had it!

Then Ben did his thing behind the scenes to prepare an affidavit which would be presented to the court. A newspaper announcement of my name change was published in the Philadelphia Daily News and in the Legal Intelligencer. A credit check was run to make sure I wasn't changing my name to avoid debt. The courts had to verify that I had no outstanding judgments or warrants out against me – so I wasn't changing my name to avoid prosecution. A background check complete with fingerprints was done to ensure I had no felony convictions.

The legal basis of a name change in Pennsylvania is apparently "54 Pa. Cons. Stat. §701." The name change itself is routine, since you can change your name to almost anything that isn't obscene or a trademark. (LegalZoom, 2018) The interesting part is that there is no law explicitly allowing a court to correct a person's sex, so it was justified because "Article V, Section 5B of the Pennsylvania Constitution and 42 Pa.C.S. § 931 confer upon this Court unlimited original jurisdiction in all cases except as may otherwise be provided by law." The court can change one's sex legally based on "the Court's equity jurisdiction in the furtherance of justice." (Jerner, 2015) For that matter, as I read that passage, a court can do *anything* outside the scope of the law, as long as it's in the interests of justice. This is why we hire lawyers to do stuff like this!

On this basis the Court of Common Pleas of Philadelphia County– Civil issued my legal name change:

DECREE

AND NOW, to wit this <date>, upon hearing of the within Petition and upon motion of Benjamin L. Jerner, Esquire, attorney for the petitioner, and upon presentation of proof of publication of notice as required by law together with proof that there are no judgments or decrees of record or any other matter of like effects against the petitioner, and it appearing that there is no legal objection to the granting of the prayer of the petition.

IT IS ORDERED AND DECREED that the name of petitioner Robert Glenn Booker is changed to Jennifer Margaret Booker.

IT IS FURTHER ORDERED AND DECREED that the sex of Petitioner is changed to female.

BY THE COURT

Yay! Now I have a less medical (no creepy "*irreversible surgical change of gender*" business) but very official piece of paper that says I have a new name and I'm now legally recognized as female.

Once this was done, my initial contract with Ben Jerner was finished. I got three official notarized copies of the court order (at $42 each!) in case some places kept their copy. The first page of the decree is what I generally sent out to places needing proof of name change; no one cares about the supporting documents after that.

Birth Certificate

For another $750 I hired Ben to get my birth certificate reissued. Part of the reason I hired Ben instead of trying to do it myself was that I was born on a US Army base overseas. Ben knew how to work with the State Department to find the right documents needed.

This is one of the weirdest parts of transition for me. It's one thing to say I'm going to change my name and recognize I'm female, but it's quite different to effectively go back in time and issue a different birth certificate. I chose to do it, so all of my identifying documents are consistent with each other. (That's part of my German heritage, wanting all my papers to be in order. That was a joke.)

Surprisingly, there were no problems with getting this done, and it only took a month or two to get my new birth certificate in the mail. Only then did I realize that my original birth certificate had a typo in my mother's maiden name ("Clanmeier" wasn't correct), but it wasn't worth starting the process all over again to correct it.

Social Security Card

With court order in hand, I went to the local Social Security office to get my SS card reissued. They insisted on seeing an original and notarized letter from my doctor before they would comply, even though that was exactly what the courts had needed. I quickly learned that every organization might have different requirements to meet before they'd update my records. Other than that, they didn't give me any grief.

Driver's License

Pennsylvania (PA) is notorious for weird requirements at the DMV (Pennsylvania, 2018) (Department of Motor Vehicles). When I got my first PA driver's license, they wouldn't accept the social security card that I had used my entire life in at least three other states' DMVs and for numerous federal agencies. They said it was just a receipt for the real card and made me get it reissued at the local Social Security office before they'd accept it.

Not surprisingly, they couldn't just process a name change, they had to add a special form for the change of gender marker (the M or F to indicate your sex) which doesn't appear on their website. Once I jumped through an extra hoop or two, I got a new license without any problem. Fortunately, I needed to renew my license anyway, so the name change was a nice bonus on top of that.

Passport

Once you have a current social security card and driver's license, most other forms of ID are easy to get. My passport had expired within a year of transition, so I waited to renew it after the name change was completed. A local post office also processes passport applications, so I just needed new passport photos and took my pile of identification forms to that office. A little over a month later my passport arrived in the mail.

A month after my passport was reissued, I went on a business trip to Japan. When flying I tend to wear dresses because they are easier to manage in airplane bathrooms, and because the extra femininity helps avoid people questioning me. The only issue I had with airport security was them wanting to check my back; I think the camisole under my dress confused them since it wasn't a bra but produced a line across my back. None of the ladies in Japan questioned me being in the ladies' restroom. I'm not sure if that was simply out of courtesy, or because I was obviously a foreigner, or maybe a combination of the two.

All the other stuff

With all of my major forms of ID updated, I started doing change of name for various organizations. This was an epic task, and it still isn't over three years later. Some places are fussier about what documentation they want, such as banks, whereas others will update their records just based on you asking them to do so. Table 6 summarizes the myriad places where name changes have been needed, plus I added a few categories that don't apply to me just to make the list more inclusive for others.

I'm one of those people who join *every* organization, so updating those is still under way for me years later. I also support a wide range of charities to varying degrees, so getting them all up to speed with my new information has been no trivial effort. I updated my driver's license right away, but later realized that I hadn't updated the *title* for my car yet, which requires another trip to the DMV. Oh joy.

My mortgage company wouldn't change my name because my previous name is still on the deed to my home. In order to change the latter, it's apparently a $400 process to get the deed reissued. I haven't tried to do that yet. With the help of experienced legal counsel (a big qualifier!), my name change process went very smoothly, with few exceptions.

Table 6. Name Change Needs

The core documents:	Doctor's Letter Court order (decree) Birth certificate Social Security card Driver's license Passport
Work	Employer Professional organizations and memberships
Education	Current schools, student ID cards Alumni associations
Family	All of them!
Banking	Bank accounts Credit cards Retirement accounts (401(k), 403(b), Swiss bank accounts, etc.) PayPal (online payment service) Patreon (support for artist friends) Any loans other than car or mortgage (student loans)

(continued)	
Home	Mortgage company or landlord Deed (if you're a homeowner) Utility companies (gas, electricity, water, sewer, garbage collection) City (property tax collector)
Communication	Phone bill (land line) Phone bill (cell phone) TV and Internet services (such as Cable TV, FiOS, Satellite, etc.)
Transportation	Car title/registration (is separate from driver's license) EZ-Pass (toll payment system) Parking permit (I have to pay to park in front of my own home) Car loan(s) Travel services (Expedia, Travelocity, etc.)
Entertainment	Magazines (a huge category for me) Non-professional memberships and subscriptions (also huge) Does shopping count as entertainment? eBay, Amazon, Groupon Ticketing services (Ticketmaster, Ticketleap, Eventbrite, Live Nation, Fandango, Ticketfly, Vivid Seats, Yelp, etc.) Social media and online services (Facebook, Twitter, Google, etc.)

(continued)	
Insurance	Health insurance (often notified by employer)
	Dental and vision insurance (often notified by employer)
	Life insurance (often notified by employer)
	Car insurance
	Renter's or homeowner's insurance
Charity	Automatic deductions for charities

Reflection

1. Were you named after a relative or someone famous? How do you feel about the names you were given? If you changed your name, what would it be?
2. What are the most common names when you were born?
3. How do you feel about novel spellings of common names, or very unusual names? Weigh the need for individuality versus how easy it is for people to spell it or other considerations.
4. Where were you born? How has that influenced your life in terms of language and culture?
5. Socioeconomic class has been a recurring issue. What class were you born into? How has that affected your social life growing up? How has it affected your career choices?
6. In the 'All the other stuff' section, there are tons of possible categories of name change areas that might be needed (Table

6). Which of these would be the most challenging or tedious for you to update? Can you think of other areas I omitted?

Chapter 9 – Social and Sexual Transition

Beyond the medical and legal aspects of coming out and transition, I was in for a shock when I realized how complex the social and sexual aspects of transition would be. After all, I was raised and socialized to be a man, not a woman, and I was about to learn just how different those worlds are.

Clothing – after coming out

After coming out to myself, suddenly my sudden skirt spree made sense! As I was deciding whether to go public with my identity, I tried to get feminine clothes that would still be safe for staying in the closet.

I bought panties. Dozens of panties! Ruffled panties, lace panties, panties in every color. Panties were an easy starting point, since I could wear those regardless of the rest of my wardrobe, and they are very blatantly feminine. Slowly I started to sneak more obviously feminine clothes into my work wardrobe. Less than two months after coming out to myself, I wrote:

I'm doing a lot of covert cross-dressing at work, since they either won't notice or won't care if I'm wearing a girl's sweater or blouse or jeans, as long as it isn't obnoxiously feminine. Six inch stilettos and a miniskirt would probably be a little over the line.

After months of more subtle wardrobe changes at work, I saw knowing looks from staff women in my college. My office was on the same floor with the main office of my college, so I saw many of them often. As I started to introduce blouses or jeggings into my wardrobe, as I passed ladies in the hall, I saw them glancing down at my outfit and give the slightest smile.

In contrast, my friend was talking to a male manager in my college, and she mentioned my change in wardrobe for the last several months. I had spoken with him several times and been in meetings with him, but he literally had no idea my wardrobe had changed.

Once I decided to go public with my newly-realized identity, I faced a massive problem. Women's clothing is incredibly complex! I started looking at women's clothing from the point of view of a consumer, not just someone who enjoyed beautiful women in them. How do I decide what looks good on me? What do I like? Are those the same styles? I was consoled to realize that most women I had known had settled on a handful of looks that work well for them, and that way they can safely ignore most of the rest of women's fashion. "Fashion is very complex. I may never really understand it. But I've been noticing my classmates, and they tend to stick to fairly simple combinations, so maybe I can find a few patterns I like (and vice versa) and keep my head from exploding." (Glenn Booker, 2013b)

I barreled ahead without answers to those questions or knowing what 'my style' was. I wasn't even brave enough to measure myself to help judge sizes, I just guessed my dimensions and bought stuff that struck my whimsy. I had to figure out what size I was for skirts and dresses. It took me ages to figure out that even sizes (18-20) were women's sizes (also called misses or plus sizes), but odd sizes were Junior sizes. As a kind sales lady explained, Junior sizes were for younger women who hadn't filled out all their curves yet, e.g. their butts. I later found out that a male friend who cross-dresses wears Junior sizes, just because they fit him better!

I found sales on American Apparel and got some things from them. I bought dozens of pieces on eBay, without any idea if they'd go together or not. I started rearranging my closet to make room for my new clothes; the first time of seven or eight times I rearranged my closet for that reason.

I needed some reliable feedback on fashion, so I went to visit two friends from the Salon and Mark Groups to help. After all, they both cross-dressed, so they could provide insights on my new wardrobe. I gathered some of my new clothes and drove to their home. We spent the day playing dress-up! They looked at the clothes I had bought, and 'frumpy' and 'Mrs. Doubtfire' got a lot of mention. I had developed body hair in my 30's and so I was very self-conscious about that. I hadn't started hormone therapy yet and hadn't shaved anything but my face, so I picked high-necked tops and long ("maxi") skirts and dresses. I was afraid to get anything too feminine or sexy, so I had bought clothes better suited for grandmas than me. The odd part was that I was afraid of getting anything too flashy. I hadn't realized that me wearing **anything** feminine was going to attract attention!

One outfit I soon wore to a Mark Group was particularly memorable in a tragic way. One of the worst pairings of styles in recorded history, it was nonetheless a sensual win. The top was a heavy red cashmere sweater with big gold buttons on the shoulders, kind of like epaulets. The skirt was white silk. In February. Ok, I didn't know that rule about not wearing white in winter. But sensually, the outfit was great! The cashmere was soft as can be, and I loved how the silk skirt brushed against my legs. I learned from this fashion *faux pas*, but also noticed that I'm heavily drawn to clothing that makes my skin happy.

I tried on a bra, and got advice where to find good 'falsies' – fake boobs (GlamourBoutique.com, 2018). After pondering the cup size I wanted (there's a choice you don't get to make every day!), I settled on a C cup. I decided that a C cup was big enough to be clearly feminine, without the logistical challenges of having really large breasts. I learned that dresses were easier to pick out than skirts, because you have to pair a good top with skirts, and that can be tricky sometimes.

Gisela

After getting some advice from friends, I decided to get help from a friend I met through Monica, a charming lady named Gisela Vera (Viera, 2018). Gisela is from New York City, and is an insanely well-trained fashion guru. She went to fashion school in Italy for three years and is good enough to help do final preparation of models for New York's Fashion Week runway shows. Again, taking advantage of my class privilege, I hired her to help me determine my clothing style.

After some discussion and emails, she came down from NYC and we played dress up in my home. She brought a few pieces she got to try on me and went through my chaotic wardrobe to see what might work well for me. She paired tops and skirts in ways I hadn't thought of and helped me figure out what clothes worked well for me and which didn't, and most importantly for my education, WHY they worked or didn't. She confirmed that square necklines are terrible for me, because they accentuate how broad my shoulders are. Instead, V necks and cowl necks are much more flattering. She showed me that the peplum tops I had gotten were horrible on me, since they exaggerated my already large tummy. Likewise, anything with belts was generally not a good idea, since I don't have a well-defined waist.

I was getting ready for my first black tie event as Jennifer and Gisela helped me pick out an evening gown and earrings (Figure 24). She also set an example for modifying clothes, like cutting off those plastic hanging straps inside many dresses. I had found a lovely tiered skirt that was too long for me, so she just cut off an entire tier from the bottom of it – perfect solution!

Figure 24. My first black tie event as Jennifer (R)

I don't recall who the lady is on the left, sorry.

About a year later, she came down again and helped me refine my looks again and filter out stuff that simply didn't work. As a result, I'm getting a lot more confident in my clothing choices and can trust whether something feels good on my body or not. I have since gone through my wardrobe several times, and systematically eliminated (i.e. given to charity) anything that doesn't make me happy to wear.

Shoes are a nightmare

As my wardrobe started filling out, I started braving the world of shoes. Shoes are challenging for most women. For me they are truly a nightmare. Thanks to my leg issues, I need to build up shoes in order to wear them for any significant length of time. At first, I'd buy shoes online, find ones that fit, then take them to the shoe store I had been using for over 15 years. Then they'd tell me that they couldn't build up that pair of shoes. I repeated this process many many times. I had had a lift put on dress shoes and sneakers, so I was shocked how many limitations there were on building up women's shoes.

- The toe can't be pointed, or the lift tapers too much.
- There must be a strap to keep the shoe on, or the left one will fall off all the time. This eliminates flats and pumps.
- The heel can't be a stiletto, it has to be chunky. Apparently, it's impossible to replace a stiletto with one that's 1.5" taller.
- Oh, and my feet are terribly wide (thanks Dad) so I typically need at least an EE width. Sometimes a D width will work if I'm lucky. This eliminates entire brands of shoes that don't come in wide widths.

As a result of these limits, there are stunningly few kinds of women's shoes that I can wear, such as Mary Janes, boots, sneakers, a few shoes with low heels, and sandals.

Swimsuits are a nightmare too

As I filled out my wardrobe with more and more feminine elements, I realized I'd have to face the challenge that makes the strongest women shudder in fear. I'd have to buy a swimsuit.

For comparison, consider what men must do to buy a swimsuit. Go to the store. Find a suit that you like. Pick out your size (small, medium, large, etc.). Buy it. This process could take as much as five minutes if you're a bit indecisive.

Now consider the challenge of getting a swimsuit for women. Are you getting a one-piece or two-piece suit? A one-piece is easier, but you still have to make sure it fits your hips and chest and torso length. Since I'm in the 'plus size' category, most suits in that range assume you have at least C cup breasts or up, which I don't have. Sometimes the top will fit well, but not the bottoms.

A two-piece swimsuit is a supreme challenge. The top needs to fit your band size (the circumference below your breasts), and the cups have to be the right distance apart to fit your breasts, as well as be the right cup size (depth). The bikini bottom has to fit your hips and waist and go with the top in terms of colors and pattern(s). Coverage of the suit is also an issue – how much skin to you want to expose? Are you showing off a lot, or do you want to cover up more? Most of the tops I've purchased have extra material to cover your tummy, since in my case that's not something I want to show off. A friend referred to my tummy as a 'problem area.'

Often tops and bottoms are purchased separately, since it's rare a given combination of top and bottom will fit you unless you happen to have a typical body shape imagined by the swimsuit maker. I'd bet that 99% of transgender women do not have that typical body shape, especially if they transition well after puberty. As a result, it's quite possible to spend an hour or more looking for a swimsuit, and then simply give up without success.

Makeup Basics

Since my mom did her makeup in the bathroom behind closed doors, and I had no close female friends while growing up, the world of makeup was a huge mystery. I knew this was a complex world and I knew NOTHING about it. I barely knew what lipstick and mascara were, and those were from ads on TV.

For my class on fashion and feminism, I contrasted the difference in what might be expected for a man and a woman to wear on their faces (Table 7). (Glenn Booker, 2013a) After all, most men rarely touch their faces except to shave in the morning, whereas women might be expected to use a dozen or more products to achieve a 'natural' look.

Table 7. Face makeup for men versus women

Men		Women
Face Sunblock		**Face** Sunblock Foundation Powder Tinted moisturizer BB or CC creams Primer Concealer Blush Bronzer Luminizer Toner

Men		Women
Eyes Nothing		**Eyes** Mascara Eye liner Eye shadow (maybe many colors) Eyebrow pencil False eyelashes Concealer Corrective
Lips Lip balm		**Lips** Lip balm Tinted lip balm Lip gloss Lipstick Lip liner Lip plumper Lip stain

I finally braved learning more about makeup about six months after coming out to myself. I spoke with friends and got to choose between going to MAC (Cosmetics, 2018) or Sephora (USA, 2018) to start my journey into the world of face painting. Both seemed to be transgender-friendly, so that was a plus. I picked Sephora and made sure to ask for a consultant who was happy to with a transgender client who knew *nothing* about makeup.

I scheduled a "Personal One on One" makeover. It was supposed to be about 1-1/2 hours but in my case took three hours. I was told to ask the nice lady for help with a "neutral palette" for work. I had little idea what that meant, other than it sounded like nothing too weird or flashy.

When my makeover started, my Personal Beauty Advisor, one Sue Bostani, asked me what my face care regimen was. I told her I didn't have one. She smiled. She complimented my skin for being in good shape, and then launched into a million steps to apply a full-face neutral palette. When she was done, I bought ALL of the products she recommended, which ran over $600. I had little idea how much makeup cost, though I guess that was a lot. When I got home, I cleared space on my dresser and laid out the products in the order they were applied and wrote down everything in painful detail (Tables 8 to 11). I haven't been very good about using the face mask; in the four years since I got it, I haven't tried it yet.

Table 8. Skin care (both AM and PM, except skip UVB at night duh)

Type	Apply where	Apply with	Product
Cleaner	Whole face	Fingers	Dior Gentle Cleaning Milk
Eye moisturizer	Near eyes	Fingers	Dior Hydralife eye cream
Face moisturizer	Face except near eyes	Fingers	Dior Hydralife silk cream
Sunblock	Nose and forehead & up	Fingers	Diorsnow UVB Protection
and 2x/week:			
Mask	Whole face	Fingers?	Manuka Doctor Rejuvenating Face Mask

Table 9. Foundation Makeup

Type	Apply where	Apply with	Product	Color
Primer	Whole face	Fingers	Hourglass Veil	None
Foundation	Whole face	Big brush & foundation brush	Cover | FX Total Cover Cream Foundation	N25
Corrective	Purple spots	Concealer brush	Bobbi Brown Corrector	Lt. peach
Concealer	Arch below eye	Concealer brush	Hourglass Hidden	Sand
Setting powder	Whole face	Big brush	Nars Translucent Crystal	None

Table 10. Eye Makeup

Type	Apply where	Apply with	Product	Color
Eye shadow primer	Above eyes	Fingers	Urban Decay Eyeshadow Primer Potion	Original
Eyebrows	Eyebrows	Brow brush	Anastasia Brow Powder Duo	Blonde

(continued)				
Eye shadow	Above eyes	Shadow brush	Smashbox Master Class Palette 2	Sable/ taupe, champagne, etc.
Eye liner	Barely above & below eyes	Liner brush	Nars Larger Than Life	Brown
Mascara	Mid & outer eyelashes	Its applicator	Various; see big box (Smashbox Pak)	Black

Table 11. Other face makeup

Type	Apply where	Apply with	Product	Color
Blush	Cheeks	Big brush	Marc Jacobs Shameless	Rebellious (night) Reckless (day)
Bronzer	Above cheekbones & toward temples; upper forehead into hairline	Big brush	Guerlain Terracotta Light	03 Brunette

(continued)				
Lipstick	Lips!	Lip brush or its stick	Urban decay Super-saturated high gloss lip color	Big bang
Lip liner	Outer lips	Lip brush or its stick	Urban decay 24/7 glide-on lip pencil	Anarchy

I've asked several makeup professionals about the different between corrective and concealer, and I have yet to get a coherent answer whether to use one, the other, or both. Corrective is supposed to correct discoloration of the skin near the eyes, whereas concealer just covers over it. In my notes after getting the makeover, I was careful to note that "corrective ... is applied under the concealer around the eye area" so I apply them in that order, but I'm still not sure if both are really needed.

Sue emailed me after my visit with some additional tips. "Yes... lips and eyes will tend to be the primary focus of the face and the complexion: concealer, foundation, primer and bronzer all balance and perfect for a more harmonious face. REMEMBER THINK SYMMETRY."

So how do we get this stuff off? My early exploration with my cross-dressing friends introduced me to the concept that there is a separate kind of makeup remover for near your eyes, then a more general-purpose remover for the rest of your face. Apparently, I had bought a fancy cleaner, but I don't recall ever using it. I wrote "Remove makeup with the Dior cleaning milk (light circular motion), then wipe off with cleaning wipe or a white washcloth." I've just been using Neutrogena eye makeup remover on cotton balls to clean around my eyes, and that brand's makeup remover towelettes for the rest of the face.

This whole makeup introduction didn't even address nail polish, which I got later. I picked up a big box of polishes to get started, called "Formula X The Twenty-Two." I added some very soft pastel polishes a few months later, but then realized that pretending to have subtle nail polish on a 50-something-year-old trans woman was quite silly. I usually wear some shade of pink nail polish now.

On the rare occasions when I do my nails myself, I do the whole five-step process. First use acetone to remove dead polish, cleanse the surface of the nails, then apply a primer polish, two coats of colored polish, and finally a top coat of clear polish. I prefer to have someone else do it at a salon, because my cuticles get really unhappy (split, painful), and a manicure keeps them in good shape.

By the time I got nail polish and other makeup accessories, I had spent over $1000 in the first year. Since I rarely wear makeup, my costs have been far less in later years, probably well under $100. Yes, this is another aspect of my class privilege, being able to get a makeover done and buy everything they recommended.

Most of my friends get makeup from drug stores, at a fraction of the cost I paid.

I've asked a lot of cisgender women what they do for makeup every day, and I get a wide range of responses. Very few do full face makeup, and most just do two or three things. Lipstick is common, many do mascara, some add blush or a little eye shadow, maybe some eye liner. Some of my pale redhead friends wear sunblock every day, even in winter. Everyone seems to find what accents the parts of their face they like the most. This is a really practical approach, since most don't want to spend the time needed to do full face, or the expense of going through makeup that quickly. I think my ex-wife spent about $600/year on MAC makeup, which she wore every work day.

As for me, I rarely wear makeup. For one, the time is an issue, and for another, in order to put on makeup, I have to wear contact lenses to see what I'm doing. I first got contacts about ten years ago and initially wore them all the time, but then my eye doctor said that was hurting my eyes. The lack of oxygen to my corneas was making them create new blood vessels to feed themselves, and that's not a good thing. As a result, I cut back to wearing contacts only for active sports (soccer, etc.) and for special evening occasions.

Advanced makeup

Beyond the sheer equipment for doing makeup, there is a whole world of learning how to apply makeup for various kinds of looks, from subtle to dramatic to silly. There are hundreds (probably thousands?) of YouTube videos on makeup techniques. Some of the artists recommended to me include:

- Sam and Nic from pixiwoo
- Tanya Burr for makeup application
- Lisaeldridge
- Gossmakeupartist
- Jaclyn Hill

I'm sure their videos are great. I haven't watched a single one of them. It takes a huge investment of time to learn to do makeup well, and I haven't done more than scratch the surface of it yet. Doing full face makeup takes me at least 45 minutes, and my friends say that applying makeup for burlesque shows can run 1.5 to two hours. And then at the end of the day you wipe it all off!

I attended a drag makeup workshop by Farrah Thorne (Thorne, 2018), a local hyper queen. A hyper queen is a female-identified performer who dresses in exaggerated hyperfeminine makeup and costumes. Over the course of two hours, she transformed the face of Tiel, an amazing local burlesque performer, into half hyper queen and half drag king (Figure 25). A drag king, the opposite of the more familiar drag queen, is a female performer who dresses as an exaggerated male. This showed off stage techniques like hiding your eyebrows with a glue stick and foundation, using multiple sets of false eye lashes, creating false facial hair, and incredible levels of blending for eye shadow and highlighting.

Figure 25. Hyper queen (L) and drag king (R) makeup on Tiel by Farrah Thorne

I think part of my learning process for makeup is learning that it's okay to break the rules. I don't care if the pencil says it's "eye liner," you can use it to draw on a moustache. Eye shadow doesn't only go near your eyes if you want it to. Just because you have thin lips doesn't mean you can't overdraw them with lipstick to make them bigger. A lot of learning to do makeup seems to be just playing with it and seeing what it looks like. A look that would be disastrous for the office might be fabulous for the stage! This will be a major part of my next explorations, I'm predicting, mostly for stage use. A challenge I face is the fact that I'm noticeably red-green color blind, so I can't tell what others see.

Time Management

A huge amount of time goes into being a woman than most men never have to expend. I first came to appreciate this when I found out that a conventionally attractive classmate got up at 6 am every day to work out in the gym for an hour, then shower do her hair and get made up for the day, which took another hour. Two hours of every day were spent maintaining her appearance for the world, two hours where she wasn't sleeping, or studying, or having fun. In contrast, at the time I might have spent 20 minutes to shower, and that was about it.

When I was in California, I was getting ready to go to the ballet for the first time with two friends. I watched in amazement as my female friend spent over an hour in her underwear getting made up, then half an hour doing her hair, then carefully slipped her dress over her head. My preparation for this formal night out (dressed as a cisgender man) consisted of putting on a suit and tie and brushing my hair. Done in five minutes.

The wage gap between men and women has barely budged in decades, in part because gains in women's education and income are being offset by more men working over 50 hours per week. (Cha & Weeden, 2014)

And yet if women choose to ignore social conventions for looking 'good,' we pay a price for it. Attractive women make 5-10% more, on average, than those who are average, and plain looking people earn 5-10% less than average. Women in low-paying jobs get a higher premium for being attractive. (Doorley & Sierminska, 2012)

In hiring decisions, attractive men can be viewed as being more competent, but the opposite is true for attractive women. (Lee, Pitesa, Pillutla, & Thaud, 2015) Men are more likely to get called back for an interview than women, a larger effect than racial discrimination. (Busetta, Fiorillo, & Visalli, 2013) Politicians are 20% more likely to get elected if they are one standard deviation above average in attractiveness. (Berggren, Jordahl, & Poutvaara, 2010) The 1960 election of President Kennedy may have been swayed by his polished appearance in a televised debate. (Staff, 2017)

There are so many other forms of discrimination (race, religion, size, sexual preference, ethnicity, etc.) that it's a challenge to keep track of all the ways of analyzing them from various perspectives, such as legal, sociological, economic and computer science. (Romei & Ruggieri, 2013)

As a woman I have learned how profoundly we are judged based on our clothing choices. Having dozens more choices more than men opens the door for criticism by ourselves and others whether we have chosen the right outfit for a given situation. A huge component of this is assessing how sexual an outfit is. (Montemurro & Gillen, 2013) How low is the neckline? How high is the hem? How high are the heels? How sparkly is the fabric? Am I exposing too much skin? Is the fabric too sensual? Is this outfit appropriate for my age, parental status, and marital status?

Consider other issues like childbirth. If women choose to have children, they lose months or possibly years of time to develop their careers. At a minimum, they might take a few months of maternity leave ("family leave" or "parental leave") and must face the impact of that on their careers. Women can face an income penalty of 5-10% per child early in their careers, with more penalty for both low income women and highly skilled workers. That penalty diminishes later in life unless they have three or more children. (Kahn, García-Manglano, & Bianchi, 2014) In contrast, men get a bonus for being fathers, with white men getting more than black men, and labor non-intensive jobs get a larger bonus for men. (Hodges & Budi, 2010)

Women have to decide on priorities. How much time and expense are we willing to put into makeup, hair, clothing, and family? What price will our careers pay for those decisions?

In my case, I benefitted from white male middle class privilege for a huge part of my career. My wife and I looked like a straight couple, so my income might have benefitted from the men's bonus for having children, even though they were step kids to me. I'm too old for having children even if I was fertile. The main challenge I face is managing the enormity of fashion choices and navigating the waters of criticism. Oddly enough, almost all of the criticism is from other women, not from men. Most men are oblivious to fashion, but women need more practice at supporting and praising each other. This has been a great benefit of Mama Gena's School of Womanly Arts (Regena Thomashauer, 2018), which gives tools and practice for encouraging self-praise (bragging, but not in the egotistical sense often associated with that word), identifying our desires, and helping each other achieve them.

Street Harassment

Of course, any discussion of transition to female would be incomplete without mention of harassment. As soon as I started changing my wardrobe to more obviously feminine clothes, I started getting street harassment.

Most of the harassment was verbal, and from the people near my home in West Philadelphia. Most of it came from men or boys, though to my surprise some was from young adult women.

Typical verbal harassment was loud comments to themselves or to a friend with them, such as "What the fuck?!" or "That man's wearing a dress!" or the occasional wolf whistle or just laughing really loudly after looking me up and down. Sometimes pairs of people will be chatting as they walk toward me, then go silent when they're about ten feet away, and shortly after passing me they burst into loud and obvious laughter. If laughter really is the best medicine, then I'm an asset for the public health of Philadelphia!

A dear friend produced a video and we acted out some of the forms of harassment I have faced. (Orenstein, 2017) Once as I passed a construction site, one worker gestured toward me and said to his friend "That's you, next year." Somehow, I doubt that was a compliment.

More threatening harassment was when I'm followed by people. Some men have rambled ongoing narratives to their male or female friends as they follow me, speculating whether I'm a man or woman, plenty loudly for me to hear. Some have changed direction to start following me even though they were headed the opposite direction.

The challenge from the very first incident of harassment was deciding what to do about it. My initial instincts were correct. Do nothing. Don't react. Ignore them. In the more extreme cases of harassment, I have given serious thought to responding verbally to them. I haven't. I'm terrified what would happen if I do respond.

Sometimes I fantasize about how I'd respond. My favorite fantasy was when I was harassed by a boy maybe 10 years old with his friends. He was making fun of my clothes, and I wanted to say to him "Wow, that's really brave of you! I'm impressed, because most boys your age wouldn't admit to caring so much about fashion. When you get older, maybe you should consider a career in fashion design. There are some great programs here in Philly you should look into." In my fantasy, this is enough to make the boy slink away with his proverbial tail between his legs.

I was shocked when my fashion choices were criticized by a college-aged, conventionally attractive woman who was apparently walking toward the Penn campus with some of her friends. I was shocked because she's the sort of person most likely to get street harassment on a daily basis. What the holy fuck are you doing harassing someone else? Aren't you tired of being on the receiving end of this?

As my first burlesque performance approached (discussed in the Sexuality section), I created a Facebook page for my alias, Apple Teeny. Many of my existing friends soon friended me, plus a few people I didn't know. About a week after my performance, a man I didn't know started chatting with me. I got a funny feeling about the conversation, and after a few generic pleasantries, he finally got to the point and asked for a picture of my pussy. I blocked him.

A couple of days later, another unknown man started chatting with me, and before long I was gifted with my first Unsolicited Dick Pic. I blocked him. Seriously, does any man actually think that sending someone a picture of their penis is an acceptable or effective way to seduce them? Soon the Name Police for Facebook challenged my account name, and Apple Teeny has been locked out ever since.

Ages 5 and 15 and adult

As I got more accustomed to my new life as a transgender woman (this is the new normal for me), I started to notice that I'm effectively several ages at once, depending on the occasion.

At first, I referred to transition as Second Puberty. After all, I was experiencing an influx of hormones for the first time and watching how my body responded in terms of emotional changes and physical changes (not just growing boobs!). But then I realized that I was also undergoing more fundamental changes as I observed women around me for cues as to accepted behavior in our society.

I'm part five-year-old, because I'm looking around at the women around me and learning basic social skills. How do they move? How do they talk? How do they respond in different situations? What are the rules for being a woman in our society? What is normal behavior?

For example, I have known forever that women are expected to keep their legs together when they sit down while wearing a skirt or dress. Teaching myself to do this has been a whole other challenge! In some of my first times wearing a skirt to a Mark Group, I was gently told that I was sitting like a soccer player. I wanted to reject this as an insult, since after all I WAS a soccer player! Nevertheless, it took me months to finally grasp the secret of keeping your legs crossed. Ready? In order to keep your legs together when you sit down, YOU HAVE TO PUT YOUR LEGS TOGETHER BEFORE SITTING DOWN. I kept trying to fix my leg position *after* sitting down, and this was the fundamental problem that made it so hard for me.

And other times, I'm age 15 because I'm learning about my body and how she responds. How big will my boobs get? Do I want to risk enhancing them? What is my new sexuality? What parts are more sensitive now? What arouses me? How do I reach orgasm? How do I date as a transgender lesbian?

At the same time, I question those rules and behaviors as a hypereducated adult trained in feminist theory. Do I *want* to follow the rules I observe? Are they good rules to follow? If not, what rules should replace them? Are there role models for the world I want to create, or do I have to forge new territory? After all, I'm already violating some basic precepts of Western European culture (e.g. the gender binary), so that gives me license to cause trouble in other areas. If I do create new rules, am I willing to pay the price for doing so?

While processing all these physical and emotional changes and learning what it's like to be a woman in our society, I'm holding down a full-time professional job, paying a mortgage, taking care of my home, and lots of other typical adult responsibilities.

These three ages take place all the time for me now, often in rapid succession. This is part of my new normal.

Dating

The world of dating has taken on new dimensions since my transition. Since I identify as a transgender lesbian, I have made a completely non-shocking revelation.

THERE ARE A LOT FEWER LESBIANS THAN STRAIGHT WOMEN!

As I look around at my friends and acquaintances, I keep an eye out for possible dating candidates, and I'm saddened each time I find someone of interest is ... straight. Dammit! Something like 5-10% of the population are homosexual, so that means 90-95% of the women I'll meet are likely not interested in my fabulous pussy, never mind what percent of lesbians would consider dating a tranny. Damn. Never mind the number of women who are already in monogamous relationships with someone. The bottom line of this bitchfest is that my dating pool has gotten a lot smaller since coming out!!

To be fair, I haven't been actively looking for dates a lot recently, so I need to get over my fear of rejection and start pretending to be more confident than I really am. There is no shortage of lesbian dating sites but finding someone who is interested in me is a challenge.

Family Relations

As I write this, four years after coming out to my family, the long-term implications are becoming clear. Only three family members are openly supportive of me; my mother, stepmother, and a cousin's daughter. My father still addresses me by the name he gave me. I don't fight it because he's old and stubborn, so it's not a battle worth fighting.

My brother has been an interesting tale. For years on the rare occasions we would speak, he bent over backwards to avoid calling me by either my original name or Jennifer. He also refused to use a gendered pronoun for me, doing mental gymnastics to contrive how to only address me as 'you.' I interpreted this oddity as him fervently not wanting to take sides on my coming out and name change.

That changed in late 2017 when he called me early one Monday morning. He quickly assured me that no one had died; it was that rare for him to call me outside of a birthday or Christmas call. He told me I might get some weird Facebook friend requests, because he had just gotten a letter published online. After repeating that a few times with slight rephrasing and commenting that he had often written letters which weren't published, he said he'd send me a link to where it was published. (M. Booker, 2017)

The letter is in its entirety in Appendix G. Its opening paragraph reads "The demand that I refer to my sibling using a female pronoun is nothing less than thought policing. It is a demand that I assert what I do not believe." He launched into a linguistic discussion of pronouns, then proceeded to cite me as an example of "where preferred pronouns become critically intrusive." He admits to the sins of transphobia and deadnaming me but justifies them because "To call my sibling *she* is to concede a reality that I do not believe to be the case." He claims that humans only have two sexes (!) and equates having hobbies which are traditionally associated with the other sex (e.g. cooking for a man) is the same thing as having a different gender identity than that assigned at birth.

The article produced over 1500 comments, with some siding with my brother and some not, and others digressing to unrelated subjects.

I was aghast by my brother's article. In addition to the sins he acknowledged, he didn't realize that by publishing this article in a right-wing publication, he was producing a very real threat on my life. I turned to social media, shared the article, and well over 100 friends came to my support.

At the time of the article's publication, I was teaching a class on Gender and Technology for Rutgers University in New Jersey. (Information, 2018) I was teaching information technology and informatics students about gender theory, transgender issues, intersex conditions, feminist theory, and how these subjects relate to the design of products. A week after the article was published, I had recovered enough to share it with my students as the basis for class discussion. One student said my brother's understanding of biology appeared to have stopped at fifth grade level. Another noted that it seems my brother was protesting too much. Are you hiding a secret, "Michael?" A third student went to the article online and started reading the comments. One caught his attention, where the author said he was going to address my brother as Mr. Booker, because he didn't believe he had completed a doctorate, and would refuse to believe any evidence he might present to the contrary. It was perfect satire and made my day.

From an analytical perspective, my brother ignores basic understanding of the cultural influence on the definition of one's 'sex,' which Anne Fausto-Sterling has studied extensively (Fausto-Sterling, 2018). To say there are only two sexes also ignores the existence of intersex conditions (APA, 2006), which are typically based on hormonal and/or chromosomal differences from typical male or female. He ignores the fact that publicly deadnaming me could threaten my job prospects and could be life-threatening as well. Most importantly to me, his primitive understanding of transgender issues means that he is showing the supreme arrogance to assume that his unsupported opinion of how to address my gender dysphoria is somehow superior to that of the APA (APA, 2017) and WPATH (WPATH, 2018b), whose expert members have spent their lives learning the best ways to do so. In short, my brother's article ignores not only my own declaration of my gender identity, but also:

- The professional opinion of two mental health professionals and one medical doctor

- The acknowledgement by the City and County of Philadelphia (court order recognizing me as female)
- The acknowledgement by the Commonwealth of Pennsylvania (driver's license)
- Acknowledgement by three branches of the United States government (social security card, birth certificate, and passport)

His limited concept of gender identity flies in the face of decades of research, summarized nicely by Hyde *et al* (2018). After discussing five specific dimensions of how the gender binary is incorrect, they conclude that "Gender and sex are closely intertwined such that sex cannot be studied without consideration of gender, and studies of gender can often benefit from considering sex as well. Use of the term gender/sex will be helpful in expressing this close interconnection and overcoming a tendency to use gender and sex as binary categories." As a result, "the multidimensional, complex, interactive, and dynamic nature of gender/sex cannot be captured by a categorical variable, much less by a categorical variable with only two categories." (Hyde, Bigler, Joel, Tate, & van Anders, 2018)

My brother also put his own career in jeopardy, since his employer has a very clear policy on non-discrimination (College, 2018). His article shows blatant disregard for such principles.

I don't expect to contact my brother for the foreseeable future.

Sexuality

My transition gave me a whole new world sexually. It took until about six months after surgery before I was healed well enough to try out my new plumbing. Even then, it wasn't very satisfying for a while because of a factor I hadn't thought of in previous surgeries. I couldn't feel anything. My outer labia and clit were fine, but my inner labia and vagina literally had no sensation for nearly a year after surgery, because nerves had to be cut during the procedure, and took that long to reconnect. This was more than a little awkward, since the tissues were alive and pink and happy, they just couldn't feel anything!

The following piece was read at the Erotic Literary Salon, and graphically describes the pure joy of reinventing my sexuality.

The Awakening

Prologue: Being a scientific sort like some people (look at Susana), I've noticed that readings here tend to fall into three categories. Some pieces are wishful thinking; I don't tend to do those. Some are introspective, I do a lot of those. But this piece is the third category: just bragging!

*Backstory: Hi, I'm Jennifer, and I'm a transsexual lesbian. *wave* Two and a half years ago I came out to myself as transgender. Since then I've come out to my friends, family and work; and am now legally recognized as Jennifer by a host of state and federal agencies. Ten months ago I underwent gender confirmation surgery, so in addition to going through second puberty from hormone therapy (lift boob), I've been exploring* *my new body (spelled p-u-s-s-y) sexually and sensually. These are my stories.*

A very fine lady was my girlfriend through transition and recovery, but she finally had to admit she wasn't 100% comfortable with my being trans, so we parted ways romantically in the last couple of months. This left me with the problem and opportunity of being a free agent. In the past I became reclusive after a breakup, and I was determined not to do that again. Loneliness sucks.

A good friend was going to a play party last weekend, so with their implied endorsement I braved coming too. It was held in a big apartment in the gayborhood that doubled as a yoga studio. Well worn carpeting, tons of cushions and pillows everywhere, meditation sayings on the walls, you get the idea. I expected Ringo Starr to be just around the corner.

The party was led by two people from the Deep South who led the fifteen of us through games for the first couple of hours. Learning to explore someone using all five senses one at a time. I had never consciously just smelled someone's body before. We fed each other fruit and chocolate and pretzels with the receiver's eyes closed. We practiced enthusiastic consent. Asking to touch someone and asking to be touched, without always getting a 'yes' response. Asking for the absurd with guaranteed acceptance. (Ask a man in the audience if he's fuck me in the ass with a pink sparkly dildo while singing an aria from Carmen. Answer for him "Yes, I'd love to do that!") Telling a stranger our sexual identity and preferences, STD testing status, and how often we use protection for sex.

All this was preparation for Open Play Time. Now I had been to play parties for the mostly BDSM scene, but they had clear limits on nudity and sexual activity, so those were a lot of whipping and bondage scenes. Here everyone was sober but there were no limits beyond getting consent, so I raised an eyebrow the first time I walked past a couple happily lost in a blowjob, or someone eagerly spanking a very exposed and wet pussy. The moans filling the air made my clit tingle with anticipation.

I knew a couple at the party, and so we soon fell onto an air bed on the floor and started petting each other. Trixie was in the middle between Janet and I, and we lavished attention on her very full breasts and stroked up and down her legs, teasing her pantied pussy along the way. Meanwhile soft flogging and deep cries filled the air from the St. Andrew's Cross17 around the corner. I remembered how much I love the sound of ecstasy. My clothes found a pile in the corner as I got comfortable.

Then it was my turn to be the center of attention. I laid on the air bed, naked as a jaybird, as Trixie and Janet admired my new body for the first time. Janet was a little shy, and contented herself with sucking my breasts and flicking my nipples now and then. Trixie kept stroking me closer and closer to my pussy, and finally mustered the courage to ask if she could play with my pussy. I eagerly agreed. Copious lube helped slide my pussy to a very warm state, as Trixie cautiously explored inside me for the first time. I noticed occasional people passing by our little party, and thought what a brazen hussy I must look like. I quickly went back to the moment. Valerie came along, and seemed very interested, so we invited her to join the party. She took over fucking my pussy, getting more

[17] A St. Andrew's Cross is a large heavy wooden X, used for restraining people for assorted adult activities. Use your imagination or ask your friendly neighborhood dominatrix.

aggressive than Trixie had been and started slapping my clit. I jumped the first few times at the intense sensation, but then started enjoying it more and more. Janet got braver and started stroking my clit while Valerie focused on finger-fucking my pussy. I heard myself added to the chorus of moans, drawing more and more attention from others. I savored their happy and approving gazes. There I was with three people licking and fucking my body as I moaned like a whore in heat and writhed on the bed, and I came to accept and fully own the most obvious realization for anyone who knows me:

I am completely and utterly a slut!

As I observed the huge shift in my sexuality and how it could be expressed, I compared it to the masculine perspective I had tried to follow for so many years. The masculine model of sexuality was all about conquest and release; release in the orgasm sense. Consider how many 'coming of age' teen movies show the boys or young men focusing on 'getting laid' and how much men are praised for being very promiscuous. That means you're a player or a stud! I was trying to be a good lover by being responsive to the needs of my partners, but often went overboard and lost touch with (or was never in touch with) what my body wanted. My focus was almost entirely outside of my own body. As a result, I was often impotent because my mind was completely into the idea of having sex or making love, but my body was disconnected. This led to far too many deeply embarrassing episodes of "it's not your fault, it's me" said by both parties, and a lot of fear around partnered sexuality because it was so difficult to maintain an erection. In order to be successful sexually,

I had to have confidence that I was going to be successful, but that confidence could only come from being successful in the past. This was a very hard pattern to get started!

After recovering from gender confirmation surgery, all the performance anxiety went away. Now I just had to ask for lots of lube and could be completely receptive to the sensations that my partner(s) gave me, or I gave them. Having sex wasn't five minutes of fear and awkwardness, it could be two hours of trading off giving and receiving.

Around this time period, I had become quite a fan of the burlesque community in Philadelphia and had even taken a few classes on how to do it. My motive was really simple, but kind of embarrassing. I wanted to feel sexy. Sexy had been the last adjective anyone would use to describe me. "Sweet" was usually the kiss of death adjective. Puppies are sweet. Kittens are sweet. Sweet is devoid of sexual power, devoid of sex appeal, devoid of connection. I crave connection to others. I crave to feel my sexual energy.

I picked my stage name. Apple Teeny. A double play on words, it's based on a favorite cocktail (the apple martini) and poked fun of my large size with 'Teeny.' There are many variations on the apple martini, but mine tend to have equal parts plain or green apple vodka and sour apple pucker (Distillers, 2018), plus a splash of sour mix and a maraschino cherry or two. I use Teeny ironically, like how the biggest guy in prison has a nickname of Tiny.

I finally braved my first burlesque performance at an event called SEXx 3.0. Based on the TEDx (Conferences, Unknown) talks but allowing much racier content, I took my familiar spoken word pieces and recombined some of them and stripped while reading them.

SEXx 3.0

Described as "a series of live performances about sexuality."

Costume: Full makeup, brown wig, little black dress?, lace cardigan, pasties, no cami, thong and granny panties. Need mic, mic stand, chair, bottle of body lotion.

INTRO: Hi I'm Apple Teeny, I'm a transsexual lesbian. I love to tell people that because 1) it's true, and 2) it makes a lot of them go HUH? I came out as trans to myself only three years ago, and have undergone a lightning fast transition. This piece is about the joys and challenges of tranny sexuality. (take off cardigan) Let's go back to a more innocent time in our lives, because I'm going through a second puberty. It's ok, this one is fun.

LEGS: Legs get a lot of attention for women, but as a good feminist I realized that I DON'T HAVE TO SHAVE MY LEGS. That idea lasted about a month. Shortly after coming out, I wanted to go to a slumber party themed event, so I got a cute pink nightgown. I realized my calves were showing, so I decided to shave them for the first time. When I was done, I was putting lotion on my somewhat confused legs (do it), and realized how wonderfully sensual it felt, even over the unhappy scars from my childhood. As a man it was expected to mostly ignore your body, but now I seemed to have permission or even obligation to pay attention to my body.

TITS: A few months later, I was convinced that I really was trans, so I started hormone therapy. Goodbye testosterone, hello estrogen! I heard the effects took a while, so I was shocked after only a month when something brushed against my chest and inside I went ZING! Sensitivity of my chest had gone through the roof! (take off dress) I asked some lady friends who were raised female, and many of them had similar experiences when going through puberty. As a male I was never told this! I obviously knew that girl boobs grow, but no one ever mentioned the sensual aspect. Wouldn't it be nice if boys knew that's WHY you warm up a girlfriend before going near second base? Hello?

BUTT GRAB: Of course I've gotten introduced to the more challenging aspects of being female in our lovely society. A month ago I was leaving very early in the morning to go to a soccer tournament, and stopped at a 24-hour convenience store near my home. A homeless man followed me into the store, and begged for money. As he got closer he realized I was female, and apologized for misgendering me. After I politely declined his request for money, he turned to leave the building, but not before brushing his hand across my ass like this (take off granny panties and show them). I was shocked by the initial physical reaction, because on that level it felt really good for my ass to be petted, but it was followed a millisecond later by the horror of realizing that it wasn't consensual.

SEX: I'll end on a positive story. During my recent transition, I had a girlfriend who generously introduced me to lesbian sex. Now as a mostly straight man, I had seen many videos of such things, but I knew reality has little to do with porn. Straight sex seemed heavily focused on 'getting him off' because that was the main measure of 1) how manly you are, and 2) how desirable she is. I didn't care so much about proving either of those, I just wanted to eat her. When there's no penis involved, that pressure goes away, and it becomes a matter of taking turns. Maybe she'll take the lead, straddle my hips and grind her clit against mine. Finger fuck me and nibble on my boobs. Lick my pussy until I can't breathe. After a pause to catch my breath, it's my turn to lead. Eventually we realize we need to stop for a break to recover and cuddle. Two hours passed, and the room smells like a French brothel.

Real lesbian sex is FAR better than porn can ever capture. Second puberty rocks!

Reflection

1. What role does fashion play in your life? How important is it? Do you have a style?
2. What drives your fashion choices when you're shopping? Price? Texture? Trendiness? Modesty? How appealing a possible date might find it?
3. How important are different activities in your time budget? Sleep, work, school, exercise, eating, etc. How much of your time on a typical day are spent on each type of activity?
4. Have you been harassed on the street? How did you respond? How did you WANT to respond?
5. Have you harassed others? How did it make you feel? How did they respond?
6. How have your relationships with your family evolved over time? Is it substantially different from when you were a child? Do your parents treat you as an adult or child or somewhere in between?
7. Are there aspects of sexuality that you want to explore but haven't yet? Are some of them considered edgy or forbidden?

Chapter 10 – The Future

This chapter focuses on the future and long-term views of both my own situation and more generally the prospects for transgender people.

More transition?

By 2016, I had completed enough transition to be legally recognized as a woman, and that was a huge accomplishment. Thanks to my baldness, the main other procedure I'd consider is some form of hair transplant. I've heard estimates from $10,000 to $20,000 for that, depending on the procedure and provider. (M. W. Smith, 2017)

Much lower priority might be more body hair removal. Hormone therapy has done a good job of minimizing the hair I didn't get rid of before surgery, but it might be nice to nuke some more of it. A problem with the laser removal approach is that it doesn't work on lightly colored hair, so blonde or grey hair isn't affected by it. To get rid of those would take another method, such as electrolysis. (Jaliman, 2017)

Many trans women seem to get a second vaginoplasty to improve the appearance of their vulvas. I've considered such a procedure, but I'm not sure if I'm vain enough to spend however much it costs for such a thing. After all, aren't all vulvas supposed to be beautiful?

Dozens of other surgical procedures have been developed. For example, trans women with a prominent Adam's apple can get a shaving procedure done to reduce that, called chondrolargynoplasty. Liposuction, raising cheekbones, butt implants, enhancing eyelids (blepharoplasty), and many other possibilities exist, none of which are personally appealing. (Trimarchi & Edmonds, 2011) Some of these procedures are discussed in more detail in *Trans Bodies, Trans Selves*. (Erickson-Schroth, 2014)

Challenging physical limits

The added physical risk of coming out as trans has had an odd side effect. Since I have already done something very risky by daring to be myself, it has loosened up the restraints on activities I've been doing. In the past, even as a child, I have expected to live a long time, and between that and the problems with my legs, I've been very cautious about what I've done to challenge myself physically. Coming out has made me braver about trying new things!

I've been playing soccer for several years, and a major frustration for me was getting tired too easily running up and down the field. I decided to start running to improve my cardiovascular endurance. Bear in mind, the longest I had ever run in my life was about 3.5 miles with my father when I was maybe in second grade, and a nearly one-mile run in high school gym class. Running was the least likely sport for me to take up, given my history of orthopedic surgeries. I started off really gently, running a lap of the track at the Drexel gym, then walk a half lap to catch my breath, and repeat. I built up the distance I could walk/run this way, until I made the mistake of mentioning it to a friend at a burlesque show. Come to find out, she's a very active runner, and she challenged me to do the Broad Street Run that spring. That Run is ten miles down the middle of Philadelphia!

I ran a little more until I found out that I got in the Run through its lottery system, about 10 weeks before the event. Then I had to get serious and started running more and more to build up the distance I could cover and improve my speed. The Broad Street Run is time limited; they open up the streets after 2.5 hours, so you have to average under 15 minutes per mile to finish before traffic returns. I kept practicing and building up until I did a couple of practice runs of around seven or eight miles – pretty amazing given my history!

The big day for the Run came, and the weather was awful. The temperature was barely above freezing and was raining steadily all day. I seriously questioned my sanity for doing this but did it. My first three miles were a healthy 12 minutes per mile, and I slowed later but managed to finish the Run in 2 hours and 15 minutes – 15 minutes to spare!

In addition to the pride of completing such a long run for the first time in my life, the added endurance certainly helped my soccer game. Thanks to indoor facilities and artificial turf, soccer season runs all year around. The Falcons league (Falcons, 2018) in Philadelphia has been wonderfully supportive, and I've traveled with them to compete in soccer tournaments on the East Coast.

I've also taken up figure skating again. I had done so for a couple years before coming out but stopped to focus on finishing my dissertation. When I got back on the ice after an eight- or nine-year hiatus, I quickly learned that my body had forgotten everything I once knew! The challenge of balancing on not only one foot, but on a narrow steel blade on one foot is doing wonders for restoring bilateral strength. The joy of gliding across the ice, and inherent grace of the sport speak to my soul.

I have dabbled briefly in a variety of dance forms. Tap dancing was fun, but my body doesn't move that fast readily. Salsa dancing is also fun but too fast for me to keep up. Tango was more my speed, but not knowing Spanish made it difficult to become part of that community. Contact improvisation is thoroughly enjoyable. I love the intimacy of it, the sensuality of so much immediate contact and weight sharing with your partner. I think I stopped that only because I was doing so many other things! I tried hula hooping too, which is a great way to connect to your hips.

Rocky Horror Picture Show

My brother introduced me to the Rocky Horror Picture Show (RHPS) when we were in High School through a comic book (graphic novel) about it. I went to see the movie and was quite amused by its absurdity. (IMDb.com, 2018j) I saw it a few times while attending the University of Minnesota, and even took a girl to see it on our first date. Okay, maybe that wasn't the best idea, it was a bit much for her. I enjoyed the soundtrack when not seeing the movie and went to see it a couple times in Los Angeles when I was working nearby. A few people tried to act out the movie, but they had few props, no makeup, no costumes, and it was kind of sad. While at Drexel, they put on the theatrical version, the first time I saw that form of it.

After getting on my own in Philadelphia, I stumbled upon Transylvania Nipple Productions (TNP). (TNP, 2018) Founded some 15 years earlier by Nick and Erica, TNP was a mature shadowcast with over 20 members, and well-crafted costumes and props. A shadowcast dresses up and acts out the movie while it plays behind them on the screen. They performed monthly at a theater in Philadelphia, plus occasional other shows. I came across TNP right as I was starting to transition, so I was a little extra nervous. They welcomed me with open arms, literally and figuratively. RHPS is a fun movie, I especially love the lyric "Don't dream it, be it!" but on its own I could take it or leave it. I'm approaching my fifth anniversary with TNP because the people in it are incredible. Diverse, silly, bright, pleasantly warped (not just Time Warp-ed), and dedicated to putting on a professional quality show, they have become my closest friends. Figure 26 shows me as Dr. Scott, a role I love to play.

Figure 26. Me as Dr. Scott in 2015

Skydiving

A friend was posting frequent Facebook check-ins at a skydiving center (drop zone) in New Jersey, close to Philadelphia. (Keys, 2016) I had been interested in skydiving many years ago, even looked into it when I was first in college. One abnormally warm December day, I finally went to the Cross Keys drop zone and met up with my friend Emmy. People were packing parachutes on the floor of a big carpeted airplane hangar and going up in a Cessna Caravan airplane and falling to earth. I summoned my bravery and signed up for my first tandem jump. I watched a video (yes, you can die from this. All good?), went through a brief lesson, and did my first jump from 13,500 feet altitude. I was amazed by the sensation of having the sky coming at you in a 120mph freefall, then a huge tug as the parachute deployed, and the instructor flying the canopy like a little airplane to land on a huge grassy area next to the airport.

As I walked back to the hangar after my first jump, I realized that I had more adrenaline flowing in my veins than I had ever experienced! This was completely incredible!!! I spoke with Emmy about starting lessons, and she pointed out that winter was a terrible time to do that, and I should wait until spring. The next April, I started lessons. I got through most of the student curriculum, started doing solo jumps, and was very close to getting my skydiving license, when I made a big mistake. I didn't plan a solo jump well and after five or six mistakes which could have saved me, couldn't get back to the landing area. Not quite, I missed by 40 or 50 feet, and landed in trees. I would have been fine, except for one pesky branch that broke my left tibia and fibula (lower leg) about ten feet before I reached the ground. I landed safely using only my right leg, and quickly realized that my left leg was broken. I was easily in sight of the drop zone, so people arrived promptly and called 911.

Recovering from that put a crimp in my skydiving and soccer activities but taught me important lessons. One lesson – I can still heal a broken leg. It's slow and tedious, but I can do it. Two – skydiving, like many sports, is very unforgiving of mistakes. Three – I have amazing friends. I got massive levels of support from friends in many different parts of my life – soccer friends, burlesque friends, Rocky Horror friends, and friends from work – all eager to help me out and support me during recovery. I can't think of any time in my life when I've had such a strong and diverse support network. Okay it was a terrible price to pay to learn that, but reassuring nonetheless.

I went on to complete my A level skydiving license the next Spring. (USPA, 2018) The next step is to get good at diving with others, making formations during freefall, interacting with others while under canopy, and many other possible directions. The skydiving community is a wonderful bunch of lunatics, very accepting of fellow adrenaline junkies. They're meticulous about safety and getting lots of 'sky therapy' during the day, and party vigorously at night.

Performing

In addition to challenging my physical limits through soccer and skydiving, I have continued to explore performing to express my new sexuality and body in a way to challenge my creativity and artistry. After all, nudity has always been my friend, so performing partially nude isn't shocking, just beautiful. I've taken beginner burlesque classes from three different performers and started to learn about stage makeup techniques, how to create costumes, and how to compose a burlesque number. (J. Booker, 2017a) Since I've already studied sewing, music and dance composition, this adds a new sexy element to the foundation I've developed over the last decade.

The next major challenge for me in this arena is to go from the safe world of telling people about myself (like the readings for the Erotic Literary Salon) to doing storytelling about characters who aren't me. Can I pick a song and make up a routine to go with it? Can I take a theme someone gave me and create an act related to that theme? These are fun directions I'd like to explore. I even joined the Burlesque Hall of Fame, (BHoF, 2018) and hope to attend their annual four-day Weekend convention.

A major mental block for me is developing a concept of myself as a sexy, sensual woman. My self-image for decades was focused only on being a brain (smart) or a cripple. Can I be desirable? Can I connect fully with my sexuality? If so, what would that look like? What would that feel like? These are the questions I want to be able to answer in the next couple of years. When someone tells me I'm beautiful or sexy, I assume they're just being polite, since I've never been conventionally attractive.

I expanded my training to include pole dancing as another way to explore my body and play with kinds of movement that were taboo before coming out. (Fitness, 2018) This has become a source of massive enjoyment and has helped me re-develop upper body strength that hormone therapy took away from me. I have done a few performances of pole dancing and polesque, which is a combination of pole dancing and burlesque. I advanced to the second level of techniques, so I'm challenging myself to do things like inversions and one-handed spins. It was really discouraging at first to advance to level two, but then I remembered that pretty much all pole techniques start out nearly impossible, and only get easy after a lot of practice.

Another exploration has been the world of 'acro,' which is short for acrobatics. This involves doing handstands, lifts and counterbalances with a partner – or more than one partner! It's a lot of fun, since it means getting very close to your partner, and requires trust, excellent communication, and body awareness. For me it's making up for never having gotten to be a cheerleader!

A confusing aspect of both pole dancing and acro is that they lack a consistent set of terms to name techniques. Every studio seems to make up their own terms, so describing moves often involves demonstration or a lot of searching for videos on YouTube. My pole studio has four levels of pole techniques from beginner to advanced, but what techniques are in their levels is unique to them. The engineer in me wonders why there hasn't been more standardization.

Sex work

Some burlesque performers also do exotic dancing, are 'web cam girls,' strippers, go-go dancers, lap dancers, pole dancers, or professional dominatrices. Is burlesque sex work? Where is the line between erotic expression and sex work? Opinions vary. Some insist burlesque isn't sex work because most burlesque performers don't do it as their primary or sole source of income. (Magazine, 2016) Does that imply that professional burlesque performers are sex workers? Some claim burlesque is worse than sex work, because it pretends to empower women while objectifying them.

(Mullone, 2013) Burlesque clearly isn't sex work in the same way that turning tricks on the street is, but we're getting paid to do sexy things and generally remove most of our clothes. Isn't that sex work? Or is sex work only when you're having physical intimate contact with a client?

Some say that burlesque is given more political respect than sex work, because "stripping is about economics and labor, while burlesque is about art and feminist eroticism." (Tarrant & Jolles, 2012) Mullone quoted a friend who said that "Women control burlesque. Men control lapdancing." Does the gender identity of the person running the establishment or producing the show determine whether the activity is oppressive or empowering? A global study of the economics and sociology of sex work appears in *Sex Work Matters*. (Ditmore, Levy, & Alys, 2010) For example, they examine the role of the Hijra in Indian culture. The Hijra are a people outside of the caste system, who are identified as neither male nor female. (Dictionary, 2019a) This includes eunuchs, transgender people, and those with intersex conditions. I had a sociology instructor from India who had to pay off a group of Hijra to bless her son after his birth, or they wouldn't leave her doorstep.

Decades ago, my parents went to the Lido show in Paris. (Paris, 2018) Like classical burlesque, that show was mostly tease, and therefore was acceptable for proper mainstream people to attend. Some of my academic colleagues won't even attend a burlesque show, because they don't feel it would be professionally respectable to be seen there. Clearly, I don't embrace this view.

The arguments seem to revolve around several dimensions. One is the part time versus full time aspect. That claims if you're doing burlesque for a hobby, it doesn't count as sex work. A second dimension is titillation versus arousal. If you're teasing someone, that doesn't mean sex work, but if you arouse them, it does. This dimension is impractical to define objectively, I would say. A third dimension could be the extent of nudity. In Philadelphia, burlesque performers must cover their genitals, anuses, nipples and areolas in any establishment that serves liquor. More nudity than that requires a strip club license. (FindLaw, 2019) Some strip clubs get around this by allowing patrons to bring their own liquor (BYOB). Nude events without liquor are therefore allowed, such as the annual Naked Bike Ride, which I've enjoyed several times. (PNBR, 2018)

The World Health Organization defines sex workers very broadly, as "people who receive money or goods in exchange for sexual services, either regularly or occasionally, and who may or may not consciously define those activities as income-generating." (WHO, 2002) The key then becomes what they define as 'sexual services.' They don't. Some define sexual services as being synonymous with prostitution. (Collins, 2019; Dictionary, 2019b) Canadian law defines a sexual service as "a service that is sexual in nature and whose purpose is to sexually gratify the person who receives it." (Justice, 2014) Since gratification is a source of satisfaction or pleasure (Merriam-Webster, 2019), anything that is sexually pleasurable could support the WHO definition. In the WHO's view, whether the work is full time or part time doesn't matter, and whether you get paid for it or receive other compensation still counts as sex work. If I do a lap dance for an audience challenge during a show and win a free drink, WHO might count that as sex work.

For me the legal issue is important because my employment is based on very traditional professions and doing illegal things on the side could jeopardize my continued employment. In that sense, I'm safe because what I've done is clearly legal, but prudish employers could still try to use it against me.

On a broader scale, legalization of sex work has been an area I've supported for several years. Nationally, groups such as COYOTE have been around since the early 1970's, calling for the legalization of sex work. (Almodovar, 2004) COYOTE stands for Call Off Your Old Tired Ethics, pointing to the morality play that often accompanies judgment of sex work. More general work has been done in recent years by the Woodhull Freedom Foundation, who is "the only national human rights organization that works full-time to affirm and protect sexual freedom as a fundamental human right." (W. F. Foundation, 2019) Woodhull's scope is vast, covering first amendment rights related to sexuality, HIV/AIDS, LGBTQAI, racial justice, reproductive health, and more. Attendees of their annual Sexual Freedom Summit include sex educators, legal and medical professionals, and human rights activists.

The history of sex workers "fighting for their right to work, for respect and justice" from the late 1960's to the Slutwalk era is well documented in Sex Workers Unite. (Melinda, 2015) I participated in several Slutwalks in Philadelphia, more so before they changed their name to the more accurate but far less concise March to End Rape Culture. (Philadelphia, 2019) The original title came from 2011 when a Toronto police officer stated that "women should avoid dressing like sluts to in order not to be victimized." (Mendes, 2015) This statement epitomized blaming women for violence committed against them, instead of blaming the actual perpetrator. That's rape culture. Slutwalks originated to emphasize that, regardless of what we're wearing, our clothing or lack thereof does not constitute consent to be sexually assaulted.

Many attempts to legislate sex work often conflate voluntary sex work with sex trafficking. Some simply can't believe that people would voluntarily choose to do sex work. They assume that anyone doing sex work must be under the control of a pimp or otherwise coerced into doing it. That assumption simply isn't true. Some women are empowered by the ability to get men to give them money for minimal effort; and in our culture, money is power. My ex-wife was a sex worker in the early 1970's and made as much as $1000/week doing so. That was when $10,000 a year was a good salary.

Nightmares such as the deceptively named "Fight Online Sex Trafficking Act" and "Stop Enabling Sex Traffickers Act" (FOSTA-SESTA) legislation of 2018 have pretended to fight sex trafficking, while in reality being enormously harmful to sex workers and forcing many of them into more dangerous work environments. (R. H. A. JUSTICE, 2018) The threat of liability from closing the 'safe harbor' rule of the internet has led to major networking and social media sites closing personals ads (e.g. Tumblr, Facebook, Reddit, Craigslist, and Google), which were used by sex workers to screen potential clients. (Romano, 2018) As a result, more sex workers will be forced to working on the streets where client screening isn't possible, and people being trafficked will be more isolated and less able to reach help. Yes, legislation to help fight sex trafficking is hurting victims of trafficking. Thanks to the reach of the Internet, FOSTA-SESTA has had global negative impact.

FOSTA-SESTA has also squashed harm reduction efforts for sex workers. Organizations like the Red Umbrella Alliance, Project SAFE, and the Sex Workers Outreach Project (SWOP) are run by or in close collaboration with sex workers to help warn them of unsafe clients ('bad date sheets') and provide safer sex supplies and clean injection supplies to improve public health in street economies. (PhillyRUA, 2019; safephila, 2019; SWOP-USA, 2019) FOSTA-SESTA makes these activities subject to civil liability lawsuits, further reducing the safety of consensual sex work.

That's not to say that sex trafficking isn't a real problem. Organizations such as the Girls Education and Mentoring Service (GEMS) in New York City have made huge strides in helping girls and women escape from coerced sex work. (GEMS, 2018) GEMS was founded by Rachel Lloyd, who was trafficked herself and has since devoted her life to fighting Commercial Sexual Exploitation of Children (CSEC). (Lloyd, 2012) Before my coming out as transgender, I attended a 3-day GEMS workshop on how to train people about CSEC. Nationally, GEMS publications and training, as well as increased awareness of trafficking by flight attendants, law enforcement personnel, long distance bus drivers, and others has led to rescuing many girls and women.

As a cripple I was treated by many as less than human. Sex workers are often treated the same way. Serial killers often target sex workers because they know most people won't miss a missing sex worker. (Quinet, 2011) To honor and remember sex workers lost to violent crime, December 17th is the International Day to End Violence Against Sex Workers. In 2018, events to mark this day occurred on four continents. It started in "2003 as a memorial and vigil for the victims of the Green River Killer in Seattle Washington." (Unknown, 2019)

This section turned out to be much longer than I expected. Dozens of my friends are involved in sex work; when their safety and fundamental human rights are threatened, I can't keep quiet. My political bent is heavily toward personal freedom. If you can get naked and eat pizza in front of a web cam and get paid for it, hey, more power to you! If you want to relieve men of their semen and money, go for it. People are allowed to get paid for destroying their bodies in a boxing ring or coal mine. People can sell their minds for performing in front of a classroom to help educate students. Whether your job involves your body or mind or both, as long as you consent to the work, I'm okay with it. Sex work is no exception.

Long term self-care

Nominally, recovery from gender confirmation surgery takes a year. Beyond that, there is ongoing self-care needed to take keep everything happy. Every day, dilation therapy is needed unless I had some form of penetrative sex. I generally do dilation every morning right after waking up and facing the day. It gives me time to check email, Facebook status, and ponder what I'm going to do that day.

In theory I should be doing douches about once a month. Unlike original equipment (cisgender) vaginas, which are self-cleaning, there is nothing to replace that function in my case. I say 'in theory' because I don't do that very often, but I make sure my pussy smells about the same, which I assume would be a good indicator of something unusual.

About a year and a half after surgery, I decided it was time for my first annual well-woman appointment. I scheduled an appointment with my local Planned Parenthood (America, 2018), since I figured they are experts in such things. Even though the office I went to was in the middle of the Gayborhood[18] in Philadelphia, they seemed really confused by having a trans woman show up. Of course, my visit omitted many steps from a typical OB/GYN visit, since I have no cervix to check for cervical cancer, and I don't need birth control.

The clearly confused doctor took a vaginal swab and disappeared to run tests on it and run the STD tests. She returned

18 The Gayborhood refers to an area in Philadelphia where there are many LGBT-friendly bars. It's so well known as such that the city put up little rainbows below the street signs.

a while later and had me explain GCS. She was confused, because apparently the swab showed skin cells, which normally wouldn't be the case. An original equipment cisgender vagina is lined with mucous membranes (specifically "basal, intermediate and superficial squamous epithelium"). (Pernick, 2017) After GCS the vagina is lined with skin tissue from what used to be the scrotum ("keratinized squamous epithelium" tissue). (Cubilla & Chaux, 2018) I got the distinct impression that I was the first trans woman to appear at that Planned Parenthood. When I told this story to my regular doctor at Mazzoni, he said they can handle such visits in the future.

While I have a vulva and vagina, they aren't exactly the same as original equipment ones, and I don't have the deeper internal organs (cervix, uterus, uterine tubes, ovaries) more like a cisgender woman who had a hysterectomy and bilateral salpingectomy-oophorectomy (WebMD.com, 2018). Since I have no menstrual cycle and no cervix (and hence don't need a Pap smear), my needs for Well Woman care are minimal.

Another oddity of my long-term health is that I still have a prostate gland, like cisgender men typically do. As noted earlier, my doctor indicated that removal of the prostate during gender confirmation surgery is very bloody, so it's left in place to avoid the danger of that blood loss. This produces the seeming contradiction of a medically recognized woman who has a prostate.

Thanks to hormone therapy, I have wonderful sensitive breasts, but no one knows what risk I have for breast cancer. I got baseline breast X-rays (mammogram), but neither my doctor nor the

American Cancer Society knows what risk trans women have for breast cancer. There are too few trans women to establish a meaningful statistical assessment of our risk yet. I do self-exam occasionally and will get X-rays done every few years just to be cautious. UCSF recommends screening every two years, based on the limited research available to date. (M. B. Deutsch, 2018)

I'm concerned that I have gained a lot of weight lately, starting with the recovery from the sky-diving accident. I was ravenously hungry during recovery, and couldn't exercise, so I gained 20+ pounds. The current administration and the stress associated with that has invited more overeating (I stress eat, not the opposite), so I'm 30-35 pounds above where I'd like to be. Instead of panicking, I'm focusing on a good amount of exercise to help balance my health picture, and I'll focus on weight loss when I feel safer.

Clothing evolution

As I get more and more comfortable with my gender presentation, my wardrobe is continuing to evolve accordingly. I'm wearing mostly knits instead of woven clothes, because they move with me more easily and are often softer. I wore mostly skirts and dresses for a while right after transition, but now I listen more to what mood I'm in, and wear jeans or sweatpants or whatever I feel like. I'm getting better at listening to my own sense of what feels good on me. Lucy proved a good role model in this regard. She would take six or more items into a dressing room, try them all on, and maybe only buy one at most. If you close your eyes and it doesn't feel good on you, don't buy it! I used to talk myself into buying clothes that felt questionable and realized that I never wore them.

I'm slowly getting more adventurous with clothing choices, especially for going to clubs or parties. Even though I'm not conventionally attractive, I still have fun buying wilder outfits, whether it's something gothic in black and red, or a racy leather bikini, or having too many corsets to choose from. My first venture along these lines was getting an authentic German dirndl (traditional dress) in the Bavarian colors of blue and white for a Halloween costume. When visiting Germany with my father and brother's family, some three years before coming out, I found myself taking pictures of racks of dirndls. I had no excuse to go look at them in detail, but I was inexplicably drawn to them. Now I have one!

As a result of one polesque class I learned the basics of applying rhinestones (E6000 glue is my friend!), and have plans to use them liberally on several pieces, including a hot pink felt hat from Lady Gaga's Joanne song. (24/7, 2017) The glitter bug has bitten! I keep realizing that I'm really obvious as a trans woman, so a little glitter or some rhinestones aren't that much flashier. For the same reason, I don't bother with subtle nail polish. Hot pink is a favorite, with glitter overlay for special occasions.

Mama Gena

An innocent sponsored ad on Facebook led me to a new world through a speaker and author called Mama Gena (a.k.a. Regena Thomashauer). As she opens her web page, "I am here to reclaim the eternal, grief-soaked majesty of the Feminine." (Regena Thomashauer, 2018) The ad said there was a free two-day seminar in New York City called The Experience to introduce her approach. I decided to take a gamble on it, rented a hotel room for one night, and took an early train to NYC one Saturday morning.

I was suspicious of the happy bouncing women who greeted us, wearing T-shirts that said '8,000 nerve endings at your service,' a reference to the clitoris I got right away from the Vagina Monologues. They waved huge pink feathers and danced, welcoming thousands of women into a large conference facility. Mama Gena is a consummate speaker and took a lot of time explaining about the patriarchy, male privilege, and showing statistics about women's income disadvantage, the extent of being threatened by intimate partner violence, and other depressing topics that I already knew from my study of feminism.

I found it beautiful how everyone was referred to as Sister Goddess (SG), reflecting both our sisterhood (which would become deeper than I ever imagined!) and the divinity within each woman. The latter fit in perfectly with the idea from the Church of All Worlds to greet one another with Thou Art Goddess, also recognizing the divine within all of us and we don't need a third party to access Her.

What impressed me was the tools she showed us for releasing the pain of oppression and celebrating ourselves and each other. There was a huge emphasis on sisterhood, supporting each other, and learning how to feel ALL of our emotions safely. She recognized and praised the power of pussy, the center of our power, and the importance of listening to our pussy and not just our brains.

The purpose of The Experience was to give some 2,000 women a taste of Mama Gena's approach to empowering women, and offer signing up for Mastery, an expensive three-month intensive with three weekends in NYC and lots of support and activities online between them. Bear in mind that while attending this I was quite depressed after being let go by my employer and spent most of my time frantically looking for a new job.

Many women heard of Mama Gena through her four books, the most recent of which is *Pussy: A Reclamation*. (Regena Thomashauer, 2018) Accordingly I wasn't shocked by the frequent use of 'pussy,' though some women clearly were. As she says in that book, "Reclaiming pussy is about reclaiming the erotic power that is your Source as a woman." Frequent references to the divine feminine appealed to me, and I'd guess there are more than a few pagans among her fans.

I set aside my logical engineer brain (no small feat!), listened to my pussy, and signed up for Mastery. I wondered how 500 women could connect and establish intimate bonds in a three-weekend program, but pussy screamed that this was something I needed, and I listened to her.

Mama Gena spent decades developing the contents of Mastery, so I can't reveal details here, but it was life changing, as cliched as that sounds. After the first weekend I realized that I needed a major career change and was led by a sister of choice to nursing, specifically SANE nursing. (Nurses, 2017) That specialization beyond a Registered Nurse (RN) supports women who are being examined after rape or other sexual assault. As I write this in late 2018, I'm actively making this career change happen.

Mastery became far more than a set of interesting workshops. By the end of it, we realized that the bonds we had established were more like an adult sorority, forged by powerful shared experiences and deep connections with women around the world. It's an emotional support network for cheering each other on, helping each other through challenges, and networking for shared interests and career changes or advancement.

Many Mastery graduates are life coaches, bodyworkers, or other kinds of counselors or therapists. I connected with SG Jennifer Peterson, who is a Certified Equus & Life Coach in upstate New York. (Peterson, 2018) I hadn't been near horses in 25 years, but I was drawn to working with her and her horses. In doing so I've learned that I have a huge connection to horses, and they are very sensitive mirrors of what you are projecting. When you speak your truth near a horse, they are drawn to you. If you are telling lies or speaking solely from your intellect, they walk away. It's kind of like having a 1200-pound lie detector who can tell when you're lying to yourself. I look forward to continuing to learn from SG Jennifer and her babies.

Another delightful connection via Mama Gena was with Sheila Kamara Hay (Hay, 2018), a previous Mastery graduate and guest speaker during my Mastery. Her corporate baby is Ecstatic Birth, which focuses on teaching a pleasure-centered approach to not only physical birth of babies (for which she is a doula and has done four times personally), but also for birth of new careers, projects, and other symbolic births. She emphasizes that ecstatic birth doesn't mean it is easy (it might be!), but it can be deeply ecstatic physically, mentally, spiritually, and/or emotionally. In an initial session, she taught me how to check in with my body systematically to see how each part feels, then ask my body what she wants today. The magic for me was to take that technique and apply it to my life **every day**, to make checking in and searching for more pleasure an everyday activity. She also reminded me to take care of the financial aspects of my career change, so that I create a safe space for my new life. Giving birth needs safe space, so I need to make sure I'm creating a safe environment physically and financially so I can birth my new career with pleasure. I've spent so much time focusing on the medical side of recovering from surgeries and accidents, I really needed a reminder it was okay to make physical pleasure a regular practice, not just a special treat.

Completion and publication of this book is also a result of Mastery. I met SG Nicola Humber and got her first two books, (Humber, 2016, 2018a) then was thrilled to see her start of The Unbound Press. (Humber, 2018b) Her mission of providing support and a forum for helping "more women live a fully expressed life" was a perfect fit for my story.

Legal and career impact

When I came out, I was working for an employer that had nominally been very supportive and was living in a city that explicitly bans discrimination based on gender identity and gender presentation. As I change careers, I face a whole new and very scary world, consisting of possible employer and residential discrimination.

Employers vary wildly in their level of support for gender non-conforming employees. (NCTE, 2009) As a result, I have to face the fact that there may be employers who are appealing and for which I'm well qualified, but they wouldn't hire me.

Similarly, I now have to consider where I'm going to live if I leave Philadelphia. State and city laws may or may not provide protection for transgender people like myself. For example, as a straight white man I would have faced no problems living in any part of Texas. But as a transgender lesbian, the only major city in Texas that I'm aware of being relatively safe is Austin, which seems to be the "progressive" capital of that state.

Some states have been actively hostile to transgender people, such as North Carolina. Their legislature passed a bill in early 2016 called HB2 (CAROLINA, 2016), which requires people to use bathroom and changing facilities which match their 'biological sex,' which they define as "The physical condition of being male or female, which is stated on a person's birth certificate." This openly discriminates against transgender people who don't have the resources or desire to change their birth certificate (class discrimination) and/or identify as any non-binary gender or have an intersex condition. These "bathroom bills" also place the onus on organizations to hire someone to monitor bathrooms, and whose job would be to guess what a person's gender identity is, based on their gender presentation. Gender identity and gender presentation are not necessarily the same. I know many cisgender female soccer players who have been questioned in locker rooms because their appearance is seen as masculine, so the targets of such bills goes well beyond the transgender community. The bills also presume that people always carry their original birth certificate with them, which is absurd on every level. The massive public backlash against this bill resulted in concerts and sporting events changing from North Carolina locations, and by one estimate cost them at least $395 million (E. G. Ellis, 2016).

Some states don't allow gender markers to be changed at all (Tennessee, Ohio, and Idaho), while others allow options other than M or F (Oregon). Cities like San Francisco and New York City allow people to self-identify their gender, the most liberal option. (HANSSEN, 2017)

Increased awareness of and recognition of transgender and gender non-conforming people has led to proposals at the scale of legal and policy issue to evolve past the need for binary gender markers. Heath Davis notes that many laws use 'sex' and 'gender' interchangeably, adding to the confusion. The 'M' or 'F' is often called a gender marker, even though it denotes one's sex. People use gender-neutral bathrooms in almost all private homes, yet we seem to need segregated facilities in public spaces. Why? Most forms of identification (schools, healthcare, driving, passports) include gender markers, yet they rarely affect the services or rights accorded. (H. F. Davis, 2018) Even in cases like healthcare where services might differ by sex, transgender people can defy norms, such as trans men who can get pregnant, or trans women who have a prostate gland. Once we get clear on the pointlessness of the gender binary, trying to stuff people into labeled categories is a waste of time.

The picture is far bleaker in many other countries than monitored bathroom facilities. "Several countries, including Malaysia, Kuwait, and Nigeria, enforce laws that prohibit 'posing' as the opposite sex—outlawing transgender people's very existence." Some countries are much more understanding, including Argentina, Colombia, Denmark, Ireland, and Malta, all of which have eliminated barriers to gender recognition (Watch, 2017).

Many transgender people also run afoul of the laws regarding same-sex relations. As a lesbian, I am among them. There are at least 77 countries, mostly in Africa and the Middle East, where same sex relations are illegal (Figure 27). At least ten of these countries have laws on the books providing for the death penalty for same-sex relations.

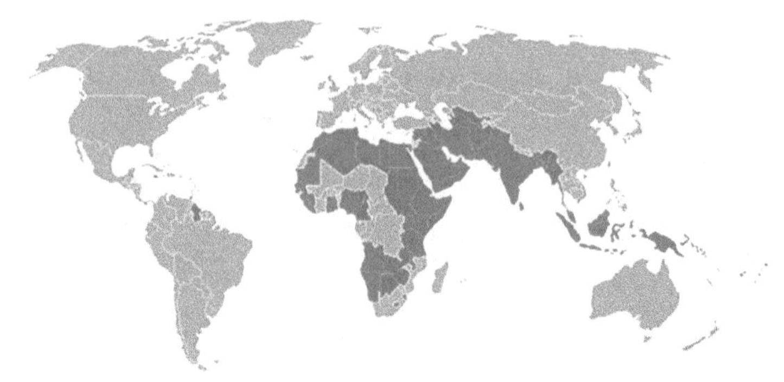

Figure 27. Countries (in red) where same sex relations are illegal (76Crimes, 2017)

The danger of these laws lies not only in employment and long-term residence but could also be a problem if even visiting any of those countries on vacation. Perhaps I'd be safe in a tour group or some other structured visit, but I doubt I'd risk it. In many literal ways, my world has gotten smaller as a result of coming out as transgender.

Recent political events in the United States have been a reminder that my legal status could change rapidly and with little notice. Under the Obama administration, there was open support for the LGBT community from the highest levels of government.

The election cycle of 2016 in the United States has produced a whole new level of fear. What happens when bigotry against the LGBT community is endorsed at the highest levels of government? (GLAAD, 2018a) As of this writing in late 2018, the current administration has launched 84 attacks against LGBT people in less than 700 days in office. What kind of message does that send to people who are already confused and/or uneducated about us? I'm in such a state of perpetual fear at this point that I'm not sure how to process this threat. Many of my friends are looking up the laws in Philadelphia regarding the carriage of concealed weapons.

My ERA

In the 1970's and 1980's, the Equal Rights Amendment (ERA) was a push to get a constitutional amendment to protect rights based on one's sex. It read in its entirety: (Institute, Unknown)

- Section 1. Equality of rights under the law shall not be denied or abridged by the United States or by any state on account of sex.
- Section 2. The Congress shall have the power to enforce, by appropriate legislation, the provisions of this article.
- Section 3. This amendment shall take effect two years after the date of ratification.

The ERA was passed by Congress in 1972 but failed to get ratified by enough states by 1982. I propose a far more inclusive version of Section 1:

- "Section 1. Equality of rights under the law shall not be denied or abridged by the United States or by any state or local government on account of sex, gender identity, gender expression, sexual orientation, or marital status." (Glenn Booker, 2013)

The retaining of 'sex' as protected and adding 'gender identity' would protect cisgender people, transgender people and people with intersex conditions. The addition of 'gender expression' would eliminate all laws which restrict clothing choices, protecting cross-dressers. Traditional clothing laws focused on outlawing cross-dressing, and many school dress codes focus almost exclusively on policing girls and blatantly violate equality principles. (Harbach, 2016; Kosciw, Greytak, Giga, Villenas, & Danischewski, 2016) The addition of 'sexual orientation' would eliminate discrimination based on being homosexual or asexual or pansexual or any other consensual form of intimacy. Enthusiastic consent isn't a good idea, it's mandatory. (Coy, Kelly, Vera-Gray, Garner, & Kanyeredzi, 2016)

The addition of "marital status" was included to protect those who want no relationship (and don't want to be penalized for being single) or want committed relationships with multiple people (polyamorous). After all, marriage is largely a special type of corporation, for which the Government Accountability Office identified "a total of 1,138 federal statutory provisions classified to the United States Code in which marital status is a factor in determining or receiving benefits, rights, and privileges." (GAO, 2004) Same sex marriage was legalized by the Supreme Court in 2015 (STATES, 2015), however other types of relationships are still not recognized or are explicitly illegal.

Just imagine how many thousands of laws could be simplified or eliminated by adopting this version of the ERA!

More acceptance?

In the first few years after coming out, I haven't seen much sign of increasing acceptance from my biological family. My brother stabbed me in the internet back, and the only hint of increased acceptance has been an occasional message from a distant relative or two. The liberal side of the family turns out to be more conservative than I thought, and no one is jumping up and down to have me visit or come to my home. I had kept a room as a guest room, complete with a fine bed and dressers, but after a few years of no one coming, I rented it out to housemates instead. It feels like a lot of my family is afraid to see me, afraid to confront the reality that I'm now recognized as a woman.

My dad's brother abandoned his three children after remarrying many years ago. My father said he could never understand how my uncle could abandon his children. And while I speak to my father every week, it feels like abandonment when he refuses to recognize my name or use correct pronouns. Research has shown how family acceptance of chosen names affects depressive symptoms and even suicide ideation. (Russell, Pollitt, Li, & Grossman, 2018) While I'm not suicidal, the lack of support is still painful.

I know this has got to be shocking and weird for him, since there was no such thing as 'transgender' when he was growing up. Transgender people existed, but the words we use to describe us now only came about in the last few decades. Before that we only had whispers about 'transvestites' and 'transsexuals.' That's why most of my coming out letter was defining what is going on and who I am. I'm trying to be understanding, but it's been several years since I came out, and there's no sign of changes, and that's frustrating for me.

The presence of more transgender people in the media has been helpful for greater public awareness, but also leads to more open discrimination by those who want to pretend we don't exist, such as by the bathroom laws. There is a lot of research ongoing about how best to serve transgender youth, (Turban & Ehrensaft, 2018) and now there are camps for gender non-conforming children such as Camp Aranu'tiq. (Aranu'tiq, 2018)

Mention of race has been conspicuously absent in the book, largely because I have benefitted from white privilege. As a trans woman, I am reminded of that privilege on November 20 every year during the Transgender Day of Remembrance (TDOR). (GLAAD, 2018b; Project, 2018) Each TDOR is a memorial service to honor the transgender people around the world who were murdered or committed suicide. The names of the transgender siblings lost that year are read. In an act of selfishness, I'm grateful each year my name isn't being read. I'm consistently shocked at how many of the victims are trans women of color, and most of the trans men are also of color. One source reported that "87% of trans people murdered from 2013 to 2015 were people of color." (Holter, 2017)

The effect of multiple forms of oppression interacting with each other in a negative sense of synergy is the basis of what Kimberle Crenshaw coined intersectionality. (Crenshaw, 1989; McCall, 2005) So while I have benefited enormously from race and class privilege (white, middle class), I have had the challenges of disability and abuse history flavoring my path.

My journey has paralleled the four phases of the Inner Roadmap of Gender Transformation described by Lee Ann Etscovitz. (Etscovitz, 2014) My physical challenges as a child and abuse history added to my confusion over gender roles, corresponding to her Suffering the Truth phase. My inner work opened up by the Sacred Whore and subsequent workshops and life coaching led to my coming out to myself and decision to be public, which were my expression of Owning the Truth. My physical transition, both hormonal and surgical, and legal transformation were Presenting the Truth. Now that my transition is complete and I'm living as fully female, empowered even more through Mama Gena, I'm Living the Truth.

My friends and family have stepped up in ways I never imagined possible. My soccer league, the Falcons, have been supportive without exception. The burlesque and pole dancing communities have been wonderful. There are burlesque shows that are produced and feature only transgender performers. Pole dancing welcomes everyone, not just the slim and young and limber. Even Mama Gena, who clearly targeted middle to upper class cisgender straight women at first, has made huge strides in welcoming transgender and bisexual or lesbian women.

The ultimate level of support has come from, oddly enough, my Rocky Horror cast. Two of the cast members, after hearing about my challenges from my biological family, stepped up to become my sisters, what I called 'sisters of choice' earlier. April-

Lynn was the first, who said things like "I can't promise to fix all your problems, but I can promise you won't face them all alone" and this applies "until you either tell me to go to hell and stay away or I die." Getting this deep committed level of love and support has meant the world to me.

Closing

This book was dedicated to describing my journey as a transgender woman, from the coming out so profoundly shocking that I literally couldn't have imagined it happening, to the joy of second puberty under hormone therapy, to the exploration of clothing and social aspects of publicly outing myself, to the physical and emotional challenge of undergoing gender confirmation surgery, to getting medical and legal recognition as a woman.

Before my coming out could occur, I had to be in a safe place emotionally, financially, and professionally. I suspect that my physically challenging childhood and emotionally devastating marriage delayed my coming out by decades. I was starting to open up when I studied massage therapy but coming to the East coast to chase my now ex-wife shut me back down.

As I approach six years since coming out, with my transition completed, my new world is a mixture of pleasures and challenges. I feel more content in my body than I've ever been. I keep learning what it means to be a woman in 21st century America and deciding which rules I want to follow and which I don't want to obey. I play with my wardrobe and enjoy seeing what makes me happy and what feels good to my body.

When I presented as male, women passing on the street would often look away, after I saw the flash of fear in their eyes. Anyone male was seen as a threat, first and foremost. Now women tend to remain neutral when they see me, and some flash a Mona Lisa smile of amusement at my wardrobe. They no longer see me as a threat. I am a gentle soul, so this makes me happy.

Being obviously transgender has an ongoing price. When I go to a public bathroom, I still have a trace of fear that someone will challenge whether I belong in the ladies' room. Even with all my identification papers in order and years of using female-defined facilities exclusively, the fear of judgment remains. The same fear emerges when shopping for clothes and looking for a changing room to try something on. I know who I am, but others will continue to try to decide for me otherwise.

Interaction with my biological family is still a challenge. Most of my family doesn't want to recognize my name or sex; only a handful of exceptions are supportive. My friends are mostly in the LGBT community (sometimes called the 'queer ghetto' for our need to self-isolate for protection) and other friends tend to be liberal or they wouldn't be my friends.

My career has been limited by coming out, since my status as a transgender woman means that there are dozens of countries and states where it would be nearly or literally suicide to live and work there. In my previous life as a straight middle-class white man, I wouldn't have had any such issues.

My religious life hasn't been affected, since as a pagan there are no issues with any consensual form of sexual preference, gender expression or gender identity.

As noted in the previous section, my legal status is highly in flux, depending on where I live and who is currently the political leader. Having the class privilege of getting all my legal forms of identification updated (birth certificate, social security card, driver's license, and passport), I am in a much stronger position than my transgender siblings who don't have that or are non-binary and can't be recognized as such by most government entities. Recent reports of transgender women having their passports revoked by the State Department mean that I could become trapped in the United States. (O'Hara, 2018)

This is the price paid for authenticity. As soon as I realized that I was transgender, I knew that I couldn't just hide away and only be myself at home or at fetish events. I have to be myself 24x7. This has exposed me to street harassment, non-consensual sexual contact from strangers, nearly constant misgendering in public, and drastically increased risk of physical assault or murder. Like I said in my coming out rebuttal letter (Appendix E):

I knew the risks of what I'm doing before I started. I knew it's at least theoretically possible lose my family, my friends, my job, and maybe even my life. Since I'm not exactly the village idiot, doesn't that tell you something about how incredibly important this has to be to me?

Coming out and transition aren't for everyone. The latter is expensive, painful, and requires lifelong dedication. It was the right choice for me. For those readers who are considering them, I hope this book gives insight as to what they might be like. For healthcare professionals and friends and family of transgender people, I hope this gives you some empathy as to the physical, emotional, and social challenges of people in a similar position.

I'm going to close with part of the poem Beloved by Sister Goddess Amy Jindra. (Jindra, 2018)

Blessed be.

You are allowed to be who you really are,
not a reaction to your past.
Yes, you've been raped.
Yes, you've been abandoned.
Yes, you've been sabotaged, beaten, isolated and left disparaged.
You are meant to be successful.
Surrounded by people you love and trust.
You can have an exciting and fulfilling life.
Being a martyr doesn't make you a good woman.
Live your life.
Do what excites you.
You are not your past.
You have permission to be
who you are supposed to be.

Reflection

1. How do you feel about *attending* racier events, like the Rocky Horror Picture Show, or a burlesque show? Is that interesting? Not appropriate? Why?
2. How do you feel about *performing in* things like Rocky Horror or burlesque? Is getting partially nude while performing appealing to you? Or revolting? Why?
3. What do you think of extreme sports like skydiving or base jumping? Is the adrenaline worth the risk? Would you try something like that? How risky are such sports?
4. Does your gender identity and/or sexual preference restrict where you can live and work? How does or would that make you feel? Are there legal efforts to reduce or increase restrictions?
5. Evaluate my proposed changes to the ERA. With which of them do you agree? Why? Would you propose other changes?

Appendix A: Terminology

Term	Definition and Source
AIS	Androgen Insensitivity Syndrome, an intersex condition that means a person's body generates testosterone but either partially (Partial AIS) or completely (Complete AIS) doesn't respond to its typical effects. (MedlinePlus, 2017a)
APA	American Psychological Association (APA, 2017)
Bottom surgery	In the context of transgender people, refers to Gender Confirmation Surgery.
BPD	Borderline Personality Disorder (NIMH, Unknown)
BYOB	Bring Your Own Bottle, a common policy for restaurants and clubs. Patrons bring their own alcoholic beverages.
CAH	Congenital Adrenal Hyperplasia, an intersex condition. "People with congenital adrenal hyperplasia lack an enzyme the adrenal gland needs to make the hormones" (MedlinePlus, 2017b) such as cortisol and aldosterone, which are both critical for survival.
COYOTE	Call Off Your Old Tired Ethics
Cross-dresser	"People who cross-dress wear clothing that is traditionally or stereotypically worn by another gender in their culture." (APA, 2014) Formerly known as a transvestite.

Term	Definition and Source
CSEC	Commercial Sexual Exploitation of Children
Deadnaming	Disrespectfully calling someone by their old name after they have changed their name. (Dictionary, 2018a)
Demisexual	"Demisexuality is a sexual orientation in which someone feels sexual attraction only to people with whom they have an emotional bond." (D. R. Center, 2015)
faux pas	A social blunder or embarrassment.
FOSTA-SESTA	"Fight Online Sex Trafficking Act" (Committee, 2018) and "Stop Enabling Sex Traffickers Act" (Senate - Commerce, 2018)
FTM	A transgender person who transitions identity from female to male. A transgender man.
Gender	"Gender refers to the socially constructed roles, behaviors, activities, and attributes that a given society considers appropriate for boys and men or girls and women." (APA, 2014)
Gender Binary	The belief that there are only two sexes, male and female.
Gender Confirmation Surgery (GCS)	GCS is plastic surgery for someone to "have their existing genitalia altered to match their identified gender." (Perry, 2017) Previously known as a sex change operation, sexual or gender reassignment surgery, and other terms.

Term	Definition and Source
Gender Essentialism	Assumes that group differences reflect inherently different natures, such as there are biological differences between men and women that makes them differently suited to certain jobs, activities, and/or emotions. (Heyman & Giles, 2006)
Gender Expression	"Gender expression refers to the way a person communicates gender identity to others through behavior, clothing, hairstyles, voice, or body characteristics." (APA, 2014)
Gender Identity	"The internal perception of one's gender, and how they label themselves." (Killermann, 2013)
Gender Marker	The M or F to indicate your sex on identifying documents (driver's license, passport, etc.). Some states and nations have started allowing other options such as an X.
Gender Presentation	"Means how a person dresses, looks, and acts, in ways that might affect how other people view their gender." (W. Foundation, 2017d) The outside world sees your gender presentation, which may be different from your gender identity.
Genderfluid	"Gender fluid is a gender identity which refers to a gender which varies over time. A gender fluid person may at any time identify as male, female, neutrois, or any other non-binary identity, or some combination of identities." (G. Wiki, Unknown)

Term	Definition and Source
Gynephilic	"Gynephilia describes the sexual attraction to women or femininity." (W. Foundation, 2017a) Gynephilic is the adjective form of gynephilia.
Handfasting	"The pre-Christian, Roman wedding ceremony also practiced in Celtic lands. As the name implies, it included tying the hands together and is the source of the expression "tying the knot" as a description of a wedding." (Franklin, 2018)
Hedonist	"A person whose life is devoted to the pursuit of pleasure and self-gratification." (Dictionary.com, 2018)
Hypogonadism	"Hypogonadism occurs when the body's sex glands produce little or no hormones." (MedlinePlus, 2017c) This results in unusually low levels of estrogen or testosterone.
Intersectionality	"The complex, cumulative manner in which the effects of different forms of discrimination combine, overlap, or intersect" (Merriam-Webster, 2018c)
Intersex conditions	"Various conditions that lead to atypical development of physical sex characteristics are collectively referred to as intersex conditions." (APA, 2014)
LGBT	Lesbian, Gay, Bisexual, Transgender. Notice that the first three terms are sexual preferences, but the last one is a gender identity.

Term	Definition and Source
LGBTQIA	There are many definitions, here's one. "Lesbian, Gay, Bisexual, Transsexual, Queer, Intersex, Asexual. LGBTQIA is a more inclusive term than LGBT for people with non-mainstream sexual orientation or gender identity.." (Dictionary, 2011) Kate Bornstein mocked the addition of many letters by giving a list of dozens of possible additions to LGBT to include every gender identity and sexual orientation she and her friends could imagine. (Bornstein, 2013)
Life coach	"Life coaches work with their clients to help them achieve goals, overcome obstacles and make changes or shifts in their lives." (Jill, N.D.)
Mani/pedi	A manicure and pedicure.
MD	Medical Doctor, a terminal degree held by many physicians and psychiatrists.
Misgendering	Addressing someone by the wrong pronoun, e.g. referring to a woman as 'he'.
Mooning	"The recreational act of baring one's ass in public with the intention of it being seen by people who don't want, or expect, to see it." (Dictiionary, 2019)
MTF	A transgender person who transitions identity from male to female. A transgender woman.

Term	Definition and Source
Passing	"Passing is the ability of a person to be regarded as a member of an identity group or category different from their own." (W. Foundation, 2018d) In the transgender context, passing would refer to, for example, a trans woman being identified by strangers as a cis-gender woman.
PhD	Doctor of Philosophy, a terminal degree held by many psychologists and lots of other professions.
Phenomenology	"Phenomenology is the study of structures of consciousness as experienced from the first-person point of view." (D. W. Smith, 2013)
Polyamory	The state or practice of having more than one open romantic relationship at a time. (Merriam-Webster, 2017)
PsyD	Doctor of Psychology, a terminal degree held by many psychologists.
PTSD	"Posttraumatic stress disorder (PTSD) is a psychiatric disorder that can occur in people who have experienced or witnessed a traumatic event such as a natural disaster, a serious accident, a terrorist act, war/combat, rape or other violent personal assault." (Parekh, 2017)
Pulse ox meter	A device to measure the percent oxygenation of blood. A normal reading is 100%, it gets a concern below 95%.

Term	Definition and Source
SAD	Seasonal Affective Disorder. "Seasonal affective disorder (SAD) is a type of depression that's related to changes in seasons — SAD begins and ends at about the same times every year." (Research, 2018b) Most people experience it during the winter.
Sex	Sex refs to male, female, or intersex labels for a person. "Sex is assigned at birth, refers to one's biological status as either male or female, and is associated primarily with physical attributes such as chromosomes, hormone prevalence, and external and internal anatomy." (APA, 2014)
Sex Change Operation	Gender Confirmation Surgery.
Sex workers	"Female, male and transgender adults and young people who receive money or goods in exchange for sexual services, either regularly or occasionally, and who may or may not consciously define those activities as income-generating." (WHO, 2002)
Sexual Preference	"The preference one shows by having a sexual interest in members of the same, opposite, or either sex." (Dictionary.com, 2002)
Sexual Reassignment Surgery	Gender Confirmation Surgery.

Term	Definition and Source
SG	Sister Goddess, a title used for all women in the School of Womanly Arts
Social construct	"An idea that has been created and accepted by the people in a society" (Merriam-Webster, 2018a)
STD	Sexually Transmitted Disease
surgery	In general, this describes any medical procedure, often involving some form of anesthetic. In this book, 'surgery' by itself refers to Gender Confirmation Surgery.
Top surgery	Refers to plastic surgery to enhance breast size (for trans women) or remove them (for trans men)
Tranny	A transmission. Formerly a derogatory term for a transgender person.
Trans	Short for Transgender.
Trans*	An umbrella term to include folks who identify as transgender, transsexual, and other identities where a person does not identify with the gender they were assigned at birth. (Dictionary, 2018b)
Transgender	A person who has thoughts and/or actions which are inconsistent with their assigned sex at birth. "Transgender is a term used to describe people whose gender identity differs from the sex the doctor marked on their birth certificate." (GLAAD, 2018c)

Term	Definition and Source
Transgendered	Sometimes regard this as the adjective form of transgender, but many maintain this is a word that shouldn't be used. (Steinmetz, 2014)
Transphobia	Irrational fear of, aversion to, or discrimination against transgender or transsexual people. (Merriam-Webster, 2018b)
Transsexual	"The term transsexual refers to people whose gender identity is different from their assigned sex. Often, transsexual people alter or wish to alter their bodies through hormones, surgery, and other means to make their bodies as congruent as possible with their gender identities." (APA, 2014)
Transvestite	Formerly a term for a person who dresses in clothing appropriate for the opposite sex. Now cross-dresser is used.
WPATH	World Professional Association for Transgender Health (WPATH, 2018b)

This book was prepared using Microsoft Word 365, with EndNote X7 for citation management in APA version 6 format. (APA, 2011) I started writing it in the summer of 2016, and completed in January 2019.

Appendix B: References

There are 342 references.

5Rhythms. (2018). 5Rhythms. Retrieved from https://www.5rhythms.com/

24/7, B. N. (2017). Breaking News | You can finally buy lady gaga's pink joanne hat. Retrieved from https://www.youtube.com/watch?v=dHo5cPV-mR0

76Crimes. (2017). 76 countries where homosexuality is illegal. Retrieved from https://76crimes.com/76-countries-where-homosexuality-is-illegal/

ajaymkalia. (2015). "Music was better back then": When do we stop keeping up with popular music? Retrieved from https://skynetandebert.com/2015/04/22/music-was-better-back-then-when-do-we-stop-keeping-up-with-popular-music/

Almodovar, N. J. (2004). What is COYOTE? Retrieved from http://www.coyotela.org/what_is.html

America, P. P. F. o. (2018). Planned Parenthood Retrieved from https://www.plannedparenthood.org/

AngelFlight.com. (2018). Angel Flight. Retrieved from http://www.angelflight.com/

APA. (2006). Answers to Your Questions About Individuals With Intersex Conditions. Retrieved from https://www.apa.org/topics/lgbt/intersex.pdf

APA. (2011). *Publication Manual of the American Psychological Association* (6 ed.): American Psychological Association.

APA. (2013a). *Diagnostic and Statistical Manual of Mental Disorders* (5 ed.): American Psychiatric Publishing.

APA. (2013b). Feeding and Eating Disorders. Retrieved from https://www.google.com/url?sa=t&rct=j&q=&esrc=s&source=web&cd=2&cad=rja&uact=8&ved=2ahUKEwjqu9vZmeHfAhXlTN8KHZd7ADkQFjABegQICBAC&url=https%3A%2F%2Fwww.psychiatry.org%2FFile%2520Library%2FPsychiatrists%2FPractice%2FDSM%2FAPA_DSM-5-Eating-Disorders.pdf&usg=AOvVaw0lvAKzc5KNcWO5UxE-grpL

APA. (2014). Answers to Your Questions ABOUT TRANSGENDER PEOPLE, GENDER IDENTITY, AND GENDER EXPRESSION. Retrieved from http://www.apa.org/topics/lgbt/transgender.pdf

APA. (2017). American Psychological Association. Retrieved from http://www.apa.org/

Aranu'tiq, C. (2018). Camp Aranu'tiq of Harbor Camps. Retrieved from http://www.camparanutiq.org/

Army, U. (2016a). Medal of Honor Recipients World War II (Recipients A-F). Retrieved from https://history.army.mil/moh/wwII-a-f.html#BOOKER

Army, U. (2016b). U.S. Army Logistics Modernization Program. Retrieved from https://www.army.mil/lmp

Arts, F. (Unknown). Fringe Arts. Retrieved from http://fringearts.com/

Azul, D. (2015). Transmasculine people's vocal situations: a critical review of gender-related discourses and empirical data. *INT J LANG COMMUN DISORD, 50*(1), 31–47. doi:10.1111/1460-6984.12121

Babynames.com. (2018a). All about Jennifer. Retrieved from http://www.babynames.com/name/Jennifer

Babynames.com. (2018b). All about Margaret. Retrieved from http://www.babynames.com/name/Margaret

Baedeker, R. (2007). Sex: Fact and Fiction. Retrieved from https://www.webmd.com/men/features/sex-fact-fiction#1

Bank, T. L. (2018). The Left Bank. Retrieved from https://www.leftbankapts.com/

Barnes, R. M., Church, R. A., & Draznin-Nagy, S. (2017). The Nature of the Arguments for Creationism, Intelligent Design, and Evolution. *Sci & Educ, 26*, 27–47. doi:10.1007/s11191-017-9875-5

Berggren, N., Jordahl, H., & Poutvaara, P. (2010). The looks of a winner: Beauty and electoral success. *Journal of Public Economics, 94*(1-2), 8-15. doi:https://doi.org/10.1016/j.jpubeco.2009.11.002

BHIG. (Unknown). Body Harmony International Guild. Retrieved from http://www.bodyharmonyinternationalguild.com/

BHoF. (2018). Burlesque Hall of Fame. Retrieved from https://www.burlesquehall.com/

Bird, A. L. (2008). PA Resource List. Retrieved from https://socialsciencepapers.wordpress.com/2017/10/18/eating-disorder-insights/

BitLove. (2018). FetLife is the Social Network for the BDSM, Fetish & Kinky Community. Retrieved from https://fetlife.com/

Bonnar, J. (1987). Coagulation effects of oral contraception. *Am J Obstet Gynecol, 157*(4), 1042-1048.

Booker, G. (1989). 12 Minutes. *Rainbow City Express 2.*

Booker, G. (1992). *A Study of 775 Midwife-Managed Births in California*. Retrieved from

Booker, G. (2002). Intersex Conditions. Retrieved from http://www.ischool.drexel.edu/faculty/gbooker/is.zip

Booker, G. (2011). *Modeling of Human Aging using a Systems Approach.* (Ph.D.), Drexel University, Philadelphia, PA. Available from ProQuest Dissertations & Theses Global (3496887)

Booker, G. (2013). A brief review of Gaga Feminism by J Jack Halberstam. Retrieved from https://socialsciencepapers.wordpress.com/2013/12/18/a-brief-review-of-gaga-feminism-by-j-jack-halberstam/

Booker, G. (2013a). Cross-dressing: Movies versus reality. Retrieved from https://wordpress.com/post/socialsciencepapers.wordpress.com/120

Booker, G. (2013b). *Deep Thoughts v9.* Notes during life coaching.

Booker, G. (2013c). *WMST 101-001*
Term Project. Retrieved from https://socialsciencepapers.wordpress.com/2013/06/07/sex-and-gender-exploration-past-and-present/

Booker, J. (2007). Analysis of Surveys. Retrieved from https://socialsciencepapers.wordpress.com/2017/10/28/eating-disorder-demographics/

Booker, J. (2017a). Burlesque act composition thoughts. Retrieved from https://socialsciencepapers.wordpress.com/2017/08/20/burlesque-act-composition-thoughts/

Booker, J. (2017b). Dedication. Retrieved from http://cci.drexel.edu/faculty/gbooker/dedication.htm

Booker, J. (2017c). Position paper on various political topics. Retrieved from https://socialsciencepapers.wordpress.com/2013/08/07/position-paper-on-various-political-topics/

Booker, J. (2018). Gun Control. Retrieved from https://socialsciencepapers.wordpress.com/2013/01/01/gun-control/

Booker, M. (2017). Why I Don't Use Female Pronouns For My Transgender Brother. Retrieved from http://thefederalist.com/2017/09/11/dont-use-female-pronouns-transgender-brother/

Bornstein, K. (2013). *My New Gender Workbook: A Step-by-Step Guide to Achieving World Peace Through Gender Anarchy and Sex Positivity* (2 ed.): Routledge.

Borrell-Carrió, F., Suchman, A. L., & Epstein, R. M. (2004). The Biopsychosocial Model 25 Years Later: Principles, Practice, and Scientific Inquiry. *Ann Fam Med*, 576-582.

Bruce, E. J. (2000). Grief, trauma and parenting children with disability. *Grief Matters: The Australian Journal of Grief and Bereavement, 3*(2), 27-31.

busaste. (2009). Viscount bicycles!! Retrieved from https://forum.cyclinguk.org/viewtopic.php?t=21010

Busetta, G., Fiorillo, F., & Visalli, E. (2013). *Searching for a Job is a Beauty Contest* (Paper No. 49825). Retrieved from

Caplan-Bricker, N. (2017). Their Time. Retrieved from http://www.washingtonpost.com/sf/style/2017/10/05/the-intersex-rights-movement-is-ready-for-its-moment/?utm_term=.bd169ab2fc71

CardGameHeaven. (2017). Tripoley. Retrieved from http://cardgameheaven.com/tripoley/

Care, U. T. (2015). Information on Estrogen Hormone Therapy. Retrieved from https://transcare.ucsf.edu/article/information-estrogen-hormone-therapy

CAROLINA, G. A. O. N. (2016). SESSION LAW 2016-3 HOUSE BILL 2. Retrieved from http://www.ncleg.net/sessions/2015e2/bills/house/pdf/h2v4.pdf

CAW. (Unknown-a). CAW Rings. Retrieved from http://caw.org/content/?q=cawrings

CAW. (Unknown-b). CAW.ORG - Official Website of The Church of All Worlds Retrieved from http://caw.org/content/

cbuethics. (2014). The Man Box. Retrieved from http://cbuethics.blogspot.com/2014/11/the-man-box.html

CDC. (2017). About Adult BMI. Retrieved from https://www.cdc.gov/healthyweight/assessing/bmi/adult_bmi/index.html

Center, D. R. (2015). What is Demisexuality? Retrieved from http://demisexuality.org/articles/what-is-demisexuality/

Center, M. (2017a). Legal Services.

Center, M. (2017b). Mazzoni Center. Retrieved from https://www.mazzonicenter.org/

Center, M. (2017c). Philadelphia Trans Wellness Conference. Retrieved from https://www.mazzonicenter.org/trans-health/about-the-conference

Center, W. a. G. A. (2018). Men and Masculinities. Retrieved from http://www.wgac.colostate.edu/men-and-masculinities

Cha, Y., & Weeden, K. A. (2014). Overwork and the Slow Convergence in the Gender Gap in Wages. *American Sociological Review, 79*(3), 457-484. doi:10.1177/0003122414528936

Chabra, S., Rai, D., Hegde, A., V, M., & Devan, A. (2015). The Neurobiological, Social and Evolutionary Aspects of Inter Personal Attraction. *Journal of Evolution of Medical and Dental Sciences, 4*(27), 4612-4621. doi:10.14260/jemds/2015/668

Chappell, T. (2016). When do kids start losing baby teeth? Retrieved from http://www.todaysparent.com/kids/baby-teeth-when-do-kids-start-losing-them/

Children, S. H. f. (2018). Shriners Hospitals for Children. Retrieved from http://www.shrinershospitalsforchildren.org/

Chorale, G. S. (2017). Garden State Chorale, Inc. Retrieved from http://www.gschorale.org/

Circle Sanctuary, I. (2018). Pagan Spirit Gathering. Retrieved from https://www.circlesanctuary.org/index.php/pagan-spirit-gathering/pagan-spirit-gathering

College, J. (2018). Non-Discrimination Policy. Retrieved from https://www.jeffco.edu/non-discrimination-policy#.WkbZiTdG1PY

Collins. (2019). Definition of 'sexual services'.

Committee, H.-J. E. a. C. (2018). H.R.1865 - Allow States and Victims to Fight Online Sex Trafficking Act of 2017. Retrieved from https://www.congress.gov/bill/115th-congress/house-bill/1865/text

Company, T. U. S. P. C. (2018). War. Retrieved from https://www.bicyclecards.com/how-to-play/war/

Conferences, T. (Unknown). TEDx Program. Retrieved from https://www.ted.com/about/programs-initiatives/tedx-program

Cosmetics, M.-U. A. (2018). MAC. Retrieved from http://www.maccosmetics.com/

Council, P. C. (2013). An Ordinance. Retrieved from https://phila.legistar.com/LegislationDetail.aspx?ID=1323523&GUID=1A208E09-EA46-4856-A4FB-7FF9687E5094

Cowling, M., & Reynolds, P. (2004). *Making Sense of Sexual Consent.* New York, NY: Routledge.

Coy, M., Kelly, L., Vera-Gray, F., Garner, M., & Kanyeredzi, A. (2016). From 'no means no' to 'an enthusiastic yes': Changing the Discourse on Sexual Consent Through Sex and Relationships Education. In V. Sundaram & H. Sauntson (Eds.), *Global Perspectives and Key Debates in Sex and Relationships Education: Addressing Issues of Gender, Sexuality, Plurality and Power* (pp. 84-99). London: Palgrave Macmillan UK.

Craven, S., Brown, S., & Gilchrist, E. (2006). Sexual grooming of children: Review of literature and theoretical considerations. *Journal of Sexual Aggression, 12*(3), 287-299. doi:10.1080/13552600601069414

Crenshaw, K. (1989). Demarginalizing the Intersection of Race and Sex: A Black Feminist Critique of Antidiscrimination Doctrine, Feminist Theory and Antiracist Politics *U. Chi. Legal F., 139*(1).

Cubilla, A., & Chaux, A. (2018). Scrotum - normal. Retrieved from http://www.pathologyoutlines.com/topic/penscrotumscrotumnormal.html

Davis, E. (2012). *Heart and Hands, Fifth Edition: A Midwife's Guide to Pregnancy and Birth* (5 ed.): Ten Speed Press.

Davis, H. F. (2018). *Beyond Trans: Does Gender Matter?* : NYU Press.

Davis, M. (N.D.). Gerald Brosseau Gardner (1884-1964). Retrieved from http://www.geraldgardner.com/

Day, M. (2011). Song of the Sacred Whore. Retrieved from https://www.facebook.com/The-Sensual-Life-201136597700/photos/?tab=album&album_id=10150194873772701

Day, M. (2014). The Essensual Experience. Retrieved from http://www.thesensuallife.com/wp-content/uploads/2012/05/Intro-to-the-Essensual-Experience-Monica-Day.pdf

de Jong, R., Alink, L., Bijleveld, C., Finkenauer, C., & Hendriks, J. (2015). Transition to adulthood of child sexual abuse victims. *Aggression and Violent Behavior, 24*, 175–187.

Deutsch, M. (2015). Information on Estrogen Hormone Therapy Retrieved from https://transcare.ucsf.edu/article/information-estrogen-hormone-therapy

Deutsch, M. B. (2018). Screening for breast cancer in transgender women. Retrieved from http://transhealth.ucsf.edu/trans?page=guidelines-breast-cancer-women

Diamond, J. (1989). *Your Body Doesn't Lie: Unlock the Power of Your Natural Energy!* : Grand Central Publishing

Dictiionary, U. (2019). mooning. Retrieved from https://www.urbandictionary.com/define.php?term=mooning

Dictionary, U. (2011). LGBTQIA Retrieved from https://www.urbandictionary.com/define.php?term=LGBTQIA

Dictionary, U. (2018a). deadnaming. Retrieved from https://www.urbandictionary.com/define.php?term=deadnaming

Dictionary, U. (2018b). trans*. Retrieved from https://www.urbandictionary.com/define.php?term=trans%2A

Dictionary, U. (2019a). Hijra Retrieved from https://www.urbandictionary.com/define.php?term=Hijra

Dictionary, U. (2019b). sexual service.

Dictionary.com. (2002). sexual preference. Retrieved from http://www.dictionary.com/browse/sexual-preference

Dictionary.com. (2018). hedonist. Retrieved from http://www.dictionary.com/browse/hedonist

Distillers, D. K. R. (2018). Sour Apple Pucker. Retrieved from https://www.dekuyper.com/liqueurs-spirits/puckers-schnapps/pucker-sour-apple

Ditmore, M. H., Levy, A., & Alys, W. (2010). *Sex Work Matters*: Zed Books

Doorley, K., & Sierminska, E. (2012). *Myth or Fact? The Beauty Premium across the Wage Distribution* Retrieved from Bonn: http://hdl.handle.net/10419/62417

Doucette, T. (2012). Secret Strong Enough for a Man (80's). Retrieved from https://www.youtube.com/watch?v=d7YYNaNy520

Drugs.com. (2018). Rohypnol. Retrieved from https://www.drugs.com/illicit/rohypnol.html

elanor1987. (2011). The sound of music - Do Re Mi. Retrieved from https://www.youtube.com/watch?v=1RW3nDRmu6k

Ellis, C., Adams, T. E., & Bochner, A. P. (2010). Autoethnography: An Overview. *Forum: Qualitative Social Research, 12*(1).

Ellis, E. G. (2016). Guess How Much That Anti-LGBTQ Law Is Costing North Carolina. Retrieved from https://www.wired.com/2016/09/guess-much-anti-lgbtq-law-costing-north-carolina/

Ensler, E. (2018). The Vagina Monologues. Retrieved from https://www.eveensler.org/plays/the-vagina-monologues/

Erickson-Schroth, L. (2014). *Trans Bodies, Trans Selves: A Resource for the Transgender Community*: Oxford University Press.

Etscovitz, L. A. P. (2014). *An Inner Roadmap of Gender Transformation*: Unknown.

Eutsey, A. D. D. (2019). The Take it Easy Manifesto. Retrieved from https://dudeism.com/takeiteasymanifesto/

FAA. (2016). William J. Hughes Technical Center. Retrieved from http://www.faa.gov/about/office_org/headquarters_offices/ang/offices/tc/

Falcons, P. (2018). Philadelphia Falcons. Retrieved from http://falcons-soccer.org/

Farrell, B. S. (2013). *DOD Has Taken Steps to Meet the Health Needs of Deployed Servicewomen, but Actions Are Needed to Enhance Care for Sexual Assault Victims*. Retrieved from https://www.gao.gov/products/GAO-13-182

Fausto-Sterling, A. (2018). Books. Retrieved from http://www.annefaustosterling.com/book/

Fellowship/USA, I. C. (2018). InterVarsity Christian Fellowship/USA Retrieved from https://intervarsity.org/

FEMEN. (2018). FEMEN Official Blog. Retrieved from https://femen.org/about-us/

FindLaw. (2019). Strip Club Laws and the Regulation of Sexually Oriented Business. Retrieved from https://smallbusiness.findlaw.com/business-laws-and-regulations/adult-entertainment-law-zoning-and-other-regulations.html

Fine, C. (2017). *Testosterone Rex Myths of Sex, Science, and Society*. New York, NY: W. W. Norton.

Fitness, A. P. D. (2018). Awakenings Pole Dance Fitness. Retrieved from http://www.awakeningspolefitness.com/#

Foundation, W. (2017a). Androphilia and gynephilia. Retrieved from https://en.wikipedia.org/wiki/Androphilia_and_gynephilia

Foundation, W. (2017b). Drawing Down the Moon (book). Retrieved from https://en.wikipedia.org/wiki/Drawing_Down_the_Moon_(book)

Foundation, W. (2017c). Epiphysiodesis Retrieved from https://en.wikipedia.org/wiki/Epiphysiodesis

Foundation, W. (2017d). Gender identity. Retrieved from https://simple.wikipedia.org/wiki/Gender_identity

Foundation, W. (2017e). Keratin. Retrieved from https://en.wikipedia.org/wiki/Keratin

Foundation, W. (2018a). Back in Black. Retrieved from https://en.wikipedia.org/wiki/Back_in_Black

Foundation, W. (2018b). Boundary Waters Canoe Area Wilderness. Retrieved from https://en.wikipedia.org/wiki/Boundary_Waters_Canoe_Area_Wilderness

Foundation, W. (2018c). Fascinator. Retrieved from https://en.wikipedia.org/wiki/Fascinator

Foundation, W. (2018d). Passing (sociology). Retrieved from https://en.wikipedia.org/wiki/Passing_(sociology)

Foundation, W. F. (2019). Woodhull Freedom Foundation. Retrieved from https://www.woodhullfoundation.org/

Franklin, A. (2018). What is Handfasting? Retrieved from https://www.llewellyn.com/journal/article/1358

Fryer, D. R. (2011). *Thinking Queerly: Race, Sex, Gender, and the Ethics of Identity*: Routledge

Gaga, L. (2018). Lady Gaga. Retrieved from http://www.ladygaga.com/

GAO. (2004). *Defense of Marriage Act: Update to Prior Report*. Retrieved from https://www.gao.gov/products/GAO-04-353R

Gaskin, I. M. (2002). *Spiritual Midwifery*: Book Publishing Company

Geary, P. J., & Turner, H. A. (2018). Germany *Encyclopædia Britannica*: Encyclopædia Britannica, inc. .

GEMS. (2018). GEMS NEEDS YOUR HELP. Retrieved from https://www.gems-girls.org/

GLAAD. (2018a). 84 attacks ON LGBTQ PEOPLE in 698 Days. Retrieved from https://www.glaad.org/trump

GLAAD. (2018b). Transgender Day of Remembrance #TDOR - November 20. Retrieved from https://www.glaad.org/tdor

GLAAD. (2018c). What does transgender mean? Retrieved from http://www.glaad.org/transgender/transfaq

GlamourBoutique.com. (2018). Glamour Boutique. Retrieved from http://www.glamourboutique.com/

GoFundMe. (2018). How It Works. Retrieved from https://www.gofundme.com/tour

Gucci, G. (2016). Gucci Guilty EAU. Retrieved from https://www.gucci.com/us/en/pr/gifts/gifts-for-her/womens-beauty-fragrance/gucci-guilty-75ml-eau-de-toilette-p-423998999990099?position=6&listName=SearchResultGridComponent

HANSSEN, S. (2017). *Beyond Male or Female: Using Nonbinary Gender Identity to Confront Outdated Notions of Sex and Gender in the Law* (J.D.), University of Oregon 96 Or. L. Rev.

Harbach, M. J. (2016). Sexualization, Sex Discrimination, and Public School Dress Codes. *U. Rich. L. Rev, 50*, 1039.

Hay, S. K. (2018). Ecstatic Birth ...riding the waves of life, love, pleasure, & birth! Retrieved from http://ecstatic-birth.com/

Heguy, A. (2016). The Unpredictable Genetics Of Male-Pattern Baldness. Retrieved from http://www.forbes.com/sites/

quora/2016/04/29/the-unpredictable-genetics-of-male-pattern-baldness/#65a530c5345e

Henderson, B. (2006). *The Gospel of the Flying Spaghetti Monster* Villard.

Henderson, B. (2019). Church of the Flying Spaghetti Monster. Retrieved from https://www.venganza.org/

HerRoom. (2018). HerRoom. Retrieved from http://www.herroom.com/

Heyman, G. D., & Giles, J. W. (2006). Gender and Psychological Essentialism. *Enfance, 58*(3), 293–310.

Hightower, E. (2017). *An Exploratory Study of Personality Factors Related to Psychological Abuse and Gaslighting.* (Ph.D.), William James College, ProQuest Dissertations Publishing. Retrieved from https://search.proquest.com/openview/0c6d2066bc1732bdd632be2194fad496/1?pq-origsite=gscholar&cbl=18750&diss=y

hobbitsaarebas. (Unknown). lizziethelezzie. Retrieved from http://lizzyduck1022.tumblr.com/post/153583146098/hobbitsaarebas-gothiccharmschool

Hodges, M. J., & Budi, M. J. (2010). Who Gets the Daddy Bonus? : Organizational Hegemonic Masculinity and the Impact of Fatherhood on Earnings. *Gender & Society, 24*(6), 717-745. doi:10.1177/0891243210386729

Holter, L. (2017). The Murder Rate Of Transgender Women In The U.S. Isn't Declining. Retrieved from https://www.refinery29.com/en-us/2017/04/151401/transgender-women-murder-rate-us-2017

hooks, b. (2018). bell hooks > Quotes Retrieved from https://www.goodreads.com/author/quotes/10697.bell_hooks?page=2

House, P. R. (2018). Stranger in a Strange Land. Retrieved from http://www.penguinrandomhouse.com/books/538963/stranger-in-a-strange-land-by-robert-a-heinlein/9780143111627

HRC. (2018a). Finding Insurance for Transgender-Related Healthcare. Retrieved from https://www.hrc.org/resources/finding-insurance-for-transgender-related-healthcare

HRC. (2018b). Violence Against the Transgender Community in 2017. Retrieved from https://www.hrc.org/resources/violence-against-the-transgender-community-in-2017

Hulshoff Pol, H. E., Cohen-Kettenis, P. T., Van Haren, N. E. M., Peper, J. S., Brans, R. G. H., Cahn, W., . . . Kahn, R. S. (2006). Changing your sex changes your brain: influences of testosterone and estrogen on adult human brain structure. *155*(suppl_1), S107. doi:10.1530/eje.1.02248

Humber, N. (2016). *Heal Your Inner Good Girl. A guide to living an unbound life*: CompletelyNovel.

Humber, N. (2018a). *Unbound*: That Guy's House

Humber, N. (2018b). The Unbound Press: Women with a Story. Retrieved from https://www.theunboundpress.com/

Hyde, J. S., Bigler, R. S., Joel, D., Tate, C. C., & van Anders, S. M. (2018). The Future of Sex and Gender in Psychology:

Five Challenges to the Gender Binary. *American Psychologist*. doi:http://dx.doi.org/10.1037/amp0000307

Iannitti, T., Morales-Medina, J. C., Bellavite, P., Rottigni, V., & Palmieri, B. (2016). Effectiveness and Safety of *Arnica montana* in Post-Surgical Setting, Pain and Inflammation. *American Journal of Therapeutics, 23*(1), e184–e197. doi:10.1097/MJT.0000000000000036

IMDb.com. (2018a). The Danish Girl (2015). Retrieved from http://www.imdb.com/title/tt0810819/?ref_=kw_li_tt

IMDb.com. (2018b). Dexter. Retrieved from http://www.imdb.com/title/tt0773262/?ref_=nv_sr_1

IMDb.com. (2018c). Father Knows Best. Retrieved from https://www.imdb.com/title/tt0046600/?ref_=nv_sr_1

IMDb.com. (2018d). Glenn Close. Retrieved from http://www.imdb.com/name/nm0000335/?ref_=fn_al_nm_1

IMDb.com. (2018e). Into The Woods. Retrieved from http://www.imdb.com/title/tt2180411/?ref_=nv_sr_1

IMDb.com. (2018f). Law & Order. Retrieved from http://www.imdb.com/title/tt0098844/?ref_=fn_al_tt_1

IMDb.com. (2018g). Michael Learned. Retrieved from http://www.imdb.com/name/nm0495229/?ref_=fn_al_nm_1

IMDb.com. (2018h). Pay It Forward. Retrieved from http://www.imdb.com/title/tt0223897/?ref_=nv_sr_1

IMDb.com. (2018i). Project Runway. Retrieved from https://www.imdb.com/title/tt0437741/?ref_=nm_flmg_prd_1

IMDb.com. (2018j). The Rocky Horror Picture Show (1975). Retrieved from https://www.imdb.com/title/tt0073629/?ref_=nv_sr_1

IMDb.com. (2019). The Big Lebowski (1998). Retrieved from https://www.imdb.com/title/tt0118715/?ref_=fn_al_tt_1

Information, S. o. C. a. (2018). Gender and Technology. Retrieved from https://comminfo.rutgers.edu/academics/courses/27?courses=340&program=All

Institute, A. P. (Unknown). The Equal Rights Amendment. Retrieved from http://www.equalrightsamendment.org/

interACT. (2016). interACT Advocates for Intersex Youth. Retrieved from https://interactadvocates.org/

Jaliman, D. (2017). Electrolysis for Hair Removal. Retrieved from https://www.webmd.com/beauty/cosmetic-procedures-electrolysis#1

Decree, 1031 C.F.R. (2015).

Jill. (N.D.). What Does a Life Coach Do? Retrieved from http://www.nationalcoachacademy.com/what-does-a-life-coach-do

Jindra, A. (2018). *Woman and Me: Becoming the Goddess*: Independently published

Johnson, L. E., & Kelley, H. M. (2011). *Permissive Parenting Style*. Boston, MA: Springer.

Jones, Z., McNamara, H., & Robo, P. (2018). Gender Analysis Studies on trans women's breast development.

Retrieved from https://genderanalysis.net/resources/studies-on-trans-womens-breast-development/

Jorgensen, C., & Stryker, S. (2000). *Christine Jorgensen: A Personal Autobiography*: Cleis Press.

Justice, D. o. (2014). Prostitution Criminal Law Reform: Bill C-36, the Protection of Communities and Exploited Persons Act. Retrieved from https://www.justice.gc.ca/eng/rp-pr/other-autre/c36faq/

JUSTICE, R. H. A. (2018). What do SESTA and FOSTA say? Retrieved from https://www.woodhullfoundation.org/wp-content/uploads/2018/02/SESTAFOSTA_1p.pdf

Justice, U. D. o. (2018). Information and Technical Assistance on the Americans with Disabilities Act. Retrieved from https://www.ada.gov/

Kahn, J. R., García-Manglano, J., & Bianchi, S. M. (2014). The Motherhood Penalty at Midlife: Long-Term Effects of Children on Women's Careers. *Journal of marriage and the family, 76*(1), 56-72. doi:10.1111/jomf.12086

Keys, S. C. (2016). Skydive Cross Keys. Retrieved from https://scontent-lga3-1.xx.fbcdn.net/v/t1.0-9/13567251_10153683132392747_6423537854161496073_njpg?oh=5bc715e367aa60a0b6d68ac3dc13b1e4&oe=59306390

Killermann, S. (2013). Comprehensive* List of LGBTQ+ Vocabulary Definitions. Retrieved from http://itspronouncedmetrosexual.com/2013/01/a-comprehensive-list-of-lgbtq-term-definitions/#sthash.ppe32RjV.dpbs

Kosciw, J. G., Greytak, E. A., Giga, N. M., Villenas, C., & Danischewski, D. J. (2016). *The 2015 National School Climate Survey: The Experiences of Lesbian, Gay, Bisexual, Transgender, and Queer Youth in Our Nation's Schools.* Retrieved from http://files.eric.ed.gov/fulltext/ED574780.pdf

Law, A. A. a. (2016). Stephanie J. Zane. Retrieved from http://www.archerlaw.com/attorneys/stephanie-j-zane/

Lawyer, R. B. J., & Lubbers, L. M. (1980). Use of the Hoffmann apparatus in the treatment of unstable tibial fractures. *J Bone Joint Surg Am., 62*(8), 1264-1273.

Lee, S., Pitesa, M., Pillutla, M., & Thaud, S. (2015). When beauty helps and when it hurts: An organizational context model of attractiveness discrimination in selection decisions. *Organizational Behavior and Human Decision Processes, 128*, 15-28. doi:https://doi.org/10.1016/j.obhdp.2015.02.003

LegalZoom. (2018). Restrictions on a Name Change. Retrieved from https://www.legalzoom.com/knowledge/name-change/topic/name-change-restrictions

Levitt, H. M., & Ippolito, M. R. (2014). Being Transgender: The Experience of Transgender Identity Development. *Journal of Homosexuality, 61*(12), 1727-1758. doi:10.1080/00918369.2014.951262

Lieberman, M. D. (2012). The Mind-Body Illusion. Retrieved from https://www.psychologytoday.com/blog/social-brain-social-mind/201205/the-mind-body-illusion

Living., W. (2019). Maiden, Mother, and Crone: The Wiccan Triple Goddess. Retrieved from http://wiccaliving.com/wiccan-triple-goddess/

LLC, W. o. t. C. (2017). Dungeons & Dragons. Retrieved from http://dnd.wizards.com/

Lloyd, R. (2012). *Girls Like Us: Fighting for a World Where Girls Are Not for Sale: A Memoir*: Harper Perennial.

Luders, E., Sanchez, F. J., Gaser, C., Toga, A. W., Narr, K. L., Hamilton, L. S., & Vilain, E. (2009). Regional gray matter variation in male-to-female transsexualism. *Neuroimage, 46*(4), 904-907. doi:10.1016/j.neuroimage.2009.03.048

MA-Shops. (2018). Halb-Batzen (2 Kreuzer) 1624 Bayern bavaria silver coin, 2 kreuzer, like scan VF-EF. Retrieved from https://www.ma-shops.com/fuerth/item.php?id=22850&lang=en

MacArthur, D. G., & North, K. N. (2005). Genes and human elite athletic performance. *Human Genetics, 116*(5), 331–339.

Magazine, s. C. B. (2016). Burlesque Performer: You Are Not A Sex Worker. Retrieved from http://21stcenturyburlesque.com/burlesque-performer-you-are-not-a-sex-worker/

Maldoven. (2004). Sambo. Retrieved from https://www.urbandictionary.com/define.php?term=Sambo

Marnach, K. J. W. (2018). *My Body's Mine: A Book on Body Boundaries and Sexual Abuse Prevention*: CreateSpace Independent Publishing Platform.

Marsden, A. L., & Esmaily-Moghadam, M. (2015). Multiscale Modeling of Cardiovascular Flows for Clinical Decision Support. *Applied Mechanics Reviews, 67.*

Martini, F. H., Nath, J. L., & Bartholomew, E. F. (2017). *Fundamentals of Anatomy & Physiology* (11 ed.): Pearson.

Mayer, S. (2018). The Erotic Literary Salon. Retrieved from http://theeroticsalon.com/

McCall, L. (2005). The Complexity of Intersectionality. *Signs, 30*(3), 1771-1800.

Media, H. (2018). Macrocephaly Retrieved from http://www.healthline.com/health/macrocephaly

Media, L. B. (2017). Classical Music in Cartoons | Looney Tunes, Bugs Bunny, Disney, Mickey Mouse, Fantasia, Tom & Jerry. Retrieved from https://www.youtube.com/watch?v=F5-fP4QpL0A

MedlinePlus. (2017a). Androgen insensitivity syndrome. Retrieved from https://medlineplus.gov/ency/article/001180.htm

MedlinePlus. (2017b). Congenital adrenal hyperplasia. Retrieved from https://medlineplus.gov/ency/article/000411.htm

MedlinePlus. (2017c). Hypogonadism. Retrieved from https://medlineplus.gov/ency/article/001195.htm

Mehta, N. (2011). Mind-body Dualism: A critique from a Health Perspective. *Mens Sana Monogr., 9*(1), 202–209.

Melinda, C. (2015). *Sex Workers Unite: A History of the Movement from Stonewall to SlutWalk*: Beacon Press

Mendes, K. (2015). *SlutWalk: Feminism, Activism and Media*: Palgrave Macmillan.

Merriam-Webster. (2017). polyamory. Retrieved from https://www.merriam-webster.com/dictionary/polyamory

Merriam-Webster. (2018a). social construct noun. Retrieved from https://www.merriam-webster.com/dictionary/social%20construct

Merriam-Webster. (2018b). transphobia. Retrieved from https://www.merriam-webster.com/dictionary/transphobia

Merriam-Webster. (2018c). Word We're Watching: Intersectionality. Retrieved from https://www.merriam-webster.com/words-at-play/intersectionality-meaning

Merriam-Webster. (2019). gratification noun. Retrieved from https://www.merriam-webster.com/dictionary/gratification

Midwives, C. A. o. (Unknown). California Association of Midwives. Retrieved from http://www.californiamidwives.org/

Miller, T., & Boulton, M. (2007). Changing constructions of informed consent: Qualitative research and complex social worlds. *Social Science & Medicine, 65*(11), 2199-2211.

Montemurro, B., & Gillen, M. M. (2013). How Clothes Make the Woman Immoral: Impressions Given Off by Sexualized Clothing. *Clothing and Textiles Research Journal, 31*(3), 167-181. doi:10.1177/0887302X13493128

Morehouse, L. (2018). SUGAR'S TOP 10 REASONS TO GO TO A MARK GROUP. Retrieved from http://www.lafayettemorehouse.com/markgroup.html

Morgan, K., Buller, A. M., Evans, M., Trevillion, K., Williamson, E., & Malpass, A. (2016). The role of gender, sexuality and context upon help-seeking for intimate partner violence: A synthesis of data across five studies. *Aggression and Violent Behavior, 31*, 136–146.

Morrison, K. (2017). Male to female gender reassignment surgery. Retrieved from https://www.youtube.com/watch?v=d90SaW1ODlQ

Mottet, L. (2013). Modernizing State Vital Statistics Statutes and Policies to Ensure Accurate Gender Markers on Birth Certificates: A Good Government Approach to Recognizing the Lives of Transgender People. *Michigan Journal of Gender and Law, 19*(2).

Mullone, L. (2013). Burlesque is not as bad as stripping. It's far worse. Retrieved from https://www.spectator.co.uk/2013/07/why-burlesque-is-morally-worse-than-stripping/

Nazaruk, M. (2011). Reflexivity in anthropological discourse analysis. *ANTHROPOLOGICAL NOTEBOOKS, 17*(1), 73-83.

NCTE. (2009). National Transgender Discrimination Survey. Retrieved from http://www.thetaskforce.org/static_html/downloads/reports/fact_sheets/transsurvey_prelim_findings.pdf

NIMH. (Unknown). Borderline Personality Disorder. Retrieved from http://www.nimh.nih.gov/health/topics/borderline-personality-disorder/index.shtml

Nurses, F. (2017). Sexual Assault Nurse Examiners. Retrieved from https://www.forensicnurses.org/page/AboutSANE

O'Hara, M. E. (2018). Trans Women Say the State Department Is Retroactively Revoking Their Passports. Retrieved from https://www.them.us/story/trans-women-state-department-passports

Office, H. B. (2018). HBO. Retrieved from http://www.hbo.com/

Orenstein, A. R. (2017). (Trumps A) Total Jerk - Katy Perry 'Firework' Parody. Retrieved from https://www.youtube.com/watch?v=0IhsTsZqTj4

Palmer, J. (2015). Welcome to Jerner & Palmer, P.C. Retrieved from www.jplaw.com

Parekh, R. (2016). Help With Gender Dysphoria. Retrieved from https://www.psychiatry.org/patients-families/gender-dysphoria

Parekh, R. (2017). What Is Posttraumatic Stress Disorder? Retrieved from https://www.psychiatry.org/patients-families/ptsd/what-is-ptsd

Paris, L. d. (2018). Lido de Paris. Retrieved from https://www.lido.fr/en

Party, T. G. (2016). Ten Key Values. Retrieved from http://www.gp.org/ten_key_values_2016

Pennsylvania, C. o. (2018). Change your Name or Address. Retrieved from http://www.dmv.pa.gov/Driver-Services/Driver-Licensing/Pages/Change-Your-Name-or-Address.aspx

Pernick, N. (2017). Vagina General Normal anatomy. Retrieved from http://www.pathologyoutlines.com/topic/vaginaanatomy.html

Perry, T. (2017). How Gender Confirmation Surgery Actually Works. Retrieved from https://www.good.is/articles/gender-reassignment-animation

Peterson, J. (2018). True Freedom Life Coaching with Jennifer. Retrieved from https://truefreedomlifecoaching.com/

Philadelphia, S. (2019). Slutwalk Philly. Retrieved from https://www.slutwalkphiladelphia.com/

PhillyRUA. (2019). Philly Red Umbrella Alliance. Retrieved from https://www.facebook.com/PhillyRUA/

Place, A. W. s. (2018). A Woman's Place. Retrieved from http://awomansplace.org/

PNBR. (2018). Philly Naked Bike Ride. Retrieved from https://philadelphianakedbikeride.wordpress.com/

Project, R. O. D. (2018). Transgender Day of Remembrance Retrieved from https://tdor.info/

Provost, M. P., Kormos, C., Kosakoski, G., & Quinsey, V. L. (2006). Sociosexuality in Women and Preference for Facial Masculinization and Somatotype in Men. *Archives of Sexual Behavior, 35*(3), 305–312.

Quinet, K. (2011). Prostitutes as Victims of Serial Homicide: Trends and Case Characteristics, 1970-2009. *Homicide Studies, 15*(1), 74-100. doi:0.1177/1088767910397276

ragefc. (2006). Sarah McLachlan Animal Cruelty Video. Retrieved from https://www.youtube.com/watch?v=9gspElv1yvc

Rametti, G., Carrillo, B., Gomez-Gil, E., Junque, C., Segovia, S., Gomez, A., & Guillamon, A. (2011). White matter microstructure in female to male transsexuals before cross-sex hormonal treatment. A diffusion tensor imaging study. *J Psychiatr Res, 45*(2), 199-204. doi:10.1016/j.jpsychires.2010.05.006

Records, G. W. (2018). Guinness World Records Retrieved from http://www.guinnessworldrecords.com/

Reisner, S. L., White, J. M., Bradford, J. B., & Mimiaga, M. J. (2014). Transgender Health Disparities: Comparing Full Cohort and Nested Matched-Pair Study Designs in a Community Health Center. *LGBT Health, 1*(3), 177-184. doi:10.1089/lgbt.2014.0009

Reiss, J., & Sprenger, J. (2014). Scientific Objectivity. Retrieved from https://plato.stanford.edu/entries/scientific-objectivity/

Research, M. F. f. M. E. a. (2018a). Preeclampsia Retrieved from http://www.mayoclinic.org/diseases-conditions/preeclampsia/basics/definition/con-20031644

Research, M. F. f. M. E. a. (2018b). Seasonal affective disorder (SAD). Retrieved from http://www.mayoclinic.org/

diseases-conditions/seasonal-affective-disorder/basics/definition/con-20021047

Rode, J. A., Weibert, A., Marshall, A., Aal, K., von Rekowski, T., el Mimoni, H., & Booker, J. (2015). *From Computational Thinking to Computational Making*. Paper presented at the UbiComp '15, Osaka, Japan.

Romano, A. (2018). A new law intended to curb sex trafficking threatens the future of the internet as we know it. Retrieved from https://www.vox.com/culture/2018/4/13/17172762/fosta-sesta-backpage-230-internet-freedom

Romei, A., & Ruggieri, S. (2013). Discrimination Data Analysis: A Multi-disciplinary Bibliography. In B. Custers, T. Calders, B. Schermer, & T. Zarsky (Eds.), *Discrimination and Privacy in the Information Society* (Vol. 3). Berlin, Heidelberg: Springer.

Ruiz, d. M., & Mills, J. (2018). The Four Agreements (Trade Paperback). Retrieved from http://www.amberallen.com/product/books/the-four-agreements-trade-paperback/

Russell, S. T., Pollitt, A. M., Li, G., & Grossman, A. H. (2018). Chosen Name Use Is Linked to Reduced Depressive Symptoms, Suicidal Ideation, and Suicidal Behavior Among Transgender Youth. *Journal of Adolescent Health, 63*(4), 503-505.

Rutan, B. (2015). Burt Rutan. Retrieved from http://www.burtrutan.com/

safephila. (2019). Project SAFE. Retrieved from https://www.facebook.com/safephila/

Sanders, C. K. (2015). Economic Abuse in the Lives of Women Abused by an Intimate Partner:A Qualitative Study. *Violence Against Women, 21*(1), 3-29. doi:10.1177/1077801214564167

SCA. (2018). SCA The Society for Creative Anachronism, Inc. Retrieved from http://www.sca.org/

Schools, N. P. (2018). How to Become a Certified Nurse-Midwife (CNM). Retrieved from https://www.nursepractitionerschools.com/faq/how-to-become-nurse-midwife

Schrock, D., & Schwalbe, M. (2009). Men, Masculinity, and Manhood Acts. *Annu. Rev. Sociol., 35*(2), 77–95.

Senate - Commerce, S., and Transportation Committee. (2018). S.1693 - Stop Enabling Sex Traffickers Act of 2017. Retrieved from https://www.congress.gov/bill/115th-congress/senate-bill/1693?q=%7B%22search%22%3A%5B%22Stop+Enabling+Sex+Traffickers+Act%22%5D%7D&r=3&s=3

Serrano, J. (2013). *EXCLUDED Making Feminist and Queer Movements More Inclusive*: Seal Press.

Services, C. s. D. (2018). Chico's. Retrieved from https://www.chicos.com/store/

SexInfo, U. (2018). Anatomy Diagrams. Retrieved from http://www.soc.ucsb.edu/sexinfo/article/anatomy-diagrams

Smith, D. W. (2013). Phenomenology. Retrieved from https://plato.stanford.edu/entries/phenomenology/

Smith, M., & Segal, J. (2017). Domestic Violence and Abuse. Retrieved from https://helpguide.org/articles/abuse/domestic-violence-and-abuse.htm?pdf=true

Smith, M. W. (2017). Hair Transplants: What to Expect. Retrieved from https://www.webmd.com/skin-problems-and-treatments/hair-loss/men-hair-loss-17/hair-transplants

Snodgrass, B. (2018). Large breasts causing back pain? Breast reduction surgery offers relief. Retrieved from https://www.plasticsurgery.org/news/blog/large-breasts-causing-back-pain-breast-reduction-surgery-offers-relief

Sorella, L. (2018). 5 Feminine Body Language Dos and Don'ts (MTF Transgender / Crossdressing Tips). Retrieved from http://feminizationsecrets.com/transgender-crossdressing-body-language-do-dont/

Staff, N. (2017). How the Kennedy-Nixon debate changed the world of politics. Retrieved from https://constitutioncenter.org/blog/the-debate-that-changed-the-world-of-politics

Starhawk. (2018). The Spiral Dance. Retrieved from http://starhawk.org/writing/books/the-spiral-dance/

Stars, S. (2017). Dudley Do-Right Emporium Retrieved from http://www.seeing-stars.com/Shop2/DudleyDoRight.shtml

STATES, S. C. O. T. U. (2015). OBERGEFELL ET AL v .HODGES, DIRECTOR, OHIO DEPARTMENT OF HEALTH, ET AL. . Retrieved from https://www.supremecourt.gov/opinions/14pdf/14-556_3204.pdf

Statistics, N. C. f. H. (2016). Men, Women, Kids All Heavier, Not Much Taller Than 20 Years Ago. Retrieved from https://www.cdc.gov/nchs/pressroom/nchs_press_releases/2016/201608_Height_Weight.htm

Steinem, G. (Unknown). Gloria Steinem. Retrieved from http://www.gloriasteinem.com/

Steinmetz, K. (2014). Why It's Best to Avoid the Word 'Transgendered'. Retrieved from http://time.com/3630965/transgender-transgendered/

Supplements, O. o. D. (2018). Vitamin E Fact Sheet for Health Professionals. Retrieved from https://ods.od.nih.gov/factsheets/VitaminE-HealthProfessional/

Surgeons, A. S. o. P. (2018). Transfeminine bottom surgery candidates Retrieved from https://www.plasticsurgery.org/reconstructive-procedures/transfeminine-bottom-surgery/candidates

SWOP-USA. (2019). Sex Workers Outreach Project USA. Retrieved from http://swopusa.org/

Tarrant, S., & Jolles, M. (2012). *Fashion Talks: Undressing the Power of Style*: SUNY Press

Thomashauer, R. (2018). *Pussy: A Reclamation*: Hay House Inc.

Thomashauer, R. (2018). SISTERS, WELCOME. I'M REGENA. Retrieved from http://mamagenas.com/

Thorne, F. (2018). Farrah Thorne (Tara). Retrieved from https://www.facebook.com/robingravesentertainer

TNP. (2018). Transylvania Nipple Productions Retrieved from https://www.facebook.com/PhillyRockyHorror/

Trimarchi, M., & Edmonds, M. (2011). Stages of Gender Reassignment. Retrieved from https://health.howstuffworks.com/medicine/surgeries-procedures/stages-of-gender-reassignment4.htm

Turban, J. L., & Ehrensaft, D. (2018). Research Review: Gender identity in youth: treatment paradigms and controversies. *Journal of Child Psychology & Psychiatry, 59*(12), 1228-1243. doi:10.1111/jcpp.12833

tvtropes.org. (Unknown). None. Retrieved from http://static.tvtropes.org/pmwiki/pub/images/poindexter1_8833.jpg

Unger, C. A. (2016). Hormone therapy for transgender patients. *Transl Androl Urol., 5*(6), 877–884. doi:10.21037/tau.2016.09.04

University, D. (2017). Discrimination, Harassment, and Bias Incident Prevention Policy. Retrieved from http://drexel.edu/oed/policies/overview/OED-1/

Unknown. (2018). Bicycling. Retrieved from https://www.bicycling.com/

Unknown. (2019). Rest In Power: International Day to End Violence Against Sex Workers. Retrieved from http://www.december17.org/

Unknown. (Unknown-a). Fig. 1A: Anteriorposterior view with external-fixation device (Hoffman apparatus).

Unknown. (Unknown-b). None. Retrieved from http://www.fashiongonerogue.com/wp-content/uploads/2016/01/Jennifer-Lopez-Green-Versace-Dress-2000-Grammys.jpg

USA, S. (2018). Sephora. Retrieved from http://www.sephora.com/

User. (Unknown). None. Retrieved from https://www.pinterest.com/pin/422001427556099676/

USMA. (2017). West Point. Retrieved from http://www.westpoint.edu/SitePages/Home.aspx

USPA. (2018). *USPA A License Proficiency Card and Application*. Retrieved from https://uspa.org/Portals/0/files/Form_ALicenseProfandApp.pdf

UXID. (2010). Where Do I Go? from the motion picture HAIR. Retrieved from https://www.youtube.com/watch?v=SLz_ykBGGUY

Van Pelt, J. (2009). Eating Disorders on the Web — The Pro-Ana/Pro-Mia Movement. *Social Work Today, 9*(5).

Various. (2009). Proanorexia. Retrieved from https://proanorexia.livejournal.com/

Vera, M. (2018). Miss Vera's Finishing School For Boys Who Want To Be Girls. Retrieved from http://www.missvera.com/

Vera, M. (Unknown). Course Descriptions. Retrieved from http://www.missvera.com/courses.html

Viera, G. (2018). Gisela Viera Style. Retrieved from https://www.facebook.com/giselavierastyle/?fref=ts

Viking, H. (2018). Husqvarna VIKING. Retrieved from http://www.husqvarnaviking.com/en-US/

Watch, H. R. (2017). World Report 2017. Retrieved from https://www.hrw.org/sites/default/files/world_report_download/wr2017-web.pdf

Webmaster. (Unknown). The 1734 Witch 'Laws' Retrieved from http://www.1734.us/

WebMD. (2017). Hair Transplants: What to Expect. Retrieved from http://www.webmd.com/skin-problems-and-treatments/hair-loss/men-hair-loss-16/hair-transplants?page=2

WebMD. (2018a). Breast Implants. Retrieved from http://www.webmd.com/beauty/cosmetic-procedures-breast-augmentation#1

WebMD. (2018b). Delestrogen Vial. Retrieved from http://www.webmd.com/drugs/2/drug-5930/delestrogen-intramuscular/details

WebMD. (2018c). Spironolactone. Retrieved from http://www.webmd.com/drugs/2/drug-6288/spironolactone-oral/details

WebMD.com. (2018). Hysterectomy. Retrieved from https://www.webmd.com/women/guide/hysterectomy#1

Weinand, J. D., & Safer, J. D. (2015). Hormone therapy in transgender adults is safe with provider supervision; A review of hormone therapy sequelae for transgender individuals *Journal of Clinical & Translational Endocrinology*. doi:10.1016/j.jcte.2015.02.003

Westmoreland, P., Krantz, M. J., & Mehler, P. S. (2016). Medical Complications of Anorexia Nervosa and Bulimia. *The American Journal of Medicine, 129*, 30-37.

White Hughto, J. M., & Reisner, S. L. (2016). A Systematic Review of the Effects of Hormone Therapy on Psychological Functioning and Quality of Life in Transgender Individuals. *Transgender Health, 1*(1). doi:10.1089/trgh.2015.0008

WHO. (2002). Sex work and HIV/AIDS. Retrieved from https://www.who.int/hiv/topics/vct/sw_toolkit/sex_work_hiv_aids.pdf

Widom, C. S., Czaja, S. J., & DuMont, K. A. (2015). Intergenerational transmission of child abuse and neglect: Real or detection bias? *Science, 347*(6229), 1480-1485. doi:10.1126/science.1259917

Wierckx, K., Elaut, E., Van Hoorde, B., Heylens, G., De Cuypere, G., Monstrey, S., . . . T'Sjoen, G. (2014). Sexual Desire in Trans Persons: Associations with Sex Reassignment Treatment. *J Sex Med, 11*, 107-118. doi:10.1111/jsm.12365

Wierckx, K., Gooren, L., & T'Sjoen, G. (2014). Clinical review: Breast development in trans women receiving cross-sex hormones. *J Sex Med, 11*, 1240–1247. doi:https://doi.org/10.1111/jsm.12487

Wiki, G. (Unknown). Gender Fluid. Retrieved from http://gender.wikia.com/wiki/Gender_Fluid

Wiki, G. F. (Unknown). Toxic Masculinity. Retrieved from http://geekfeminism.wikia.com/wiki/Toxic_masculinity

wikiHow. (2018). How to "Pass" As a Woman. Retrieved from https://www.wikihow.com/%22Pass%22-As-a-Woman

Wikipedia. (2018). Otto von Bismarck. Retrieved from https://en.wikipedia.org/wiki/Otto_von_Bismarck

Williams, L. R., Degnan, K. A., Perez-Edgar, K. E., Henderson, H. A., Rubin, K. H., Pine, D. S., . . . Fox, N. A. (2009). Impact of Behavioral Inhibition and Parenting Style on Internalizing and Externalizing Problems from Early Childhood through Adolescence. *Journal of Abnormal Child Psychology, 37*(8), 1063–1075.

Wilson, J. (2015). Caitlyn Jenner "spent $4MILLION" on transformation into a woman from surgery to clothes. Retrieved from http://www.mirror.co.uk/3am/celebrity-news/caitlyn-jenner-spent-4million-transformation-5824012

Women, N. O. f. (2018). National Organization for Women. Retrieved from https://now.org/

Wong, J. S., & Gravel, J. (2018). Do Sex Offenders Have Higher Levels of Testosterone? Results From a Meta-Analysis. *Sexual Abuse, 30*(2), 147-168. doi:10.1177/1079063216637857

Woodward, S. (2007). Why Women Wear What They Wear. Retrieved from http://www.bloomsbury.com/us/why-women-wear-what-they-wear-9781845206994/

WPATH. (2018a). *Standards of Care for the Health of Transsexual, Transgender, and Gender Nonconforming People*. Retrieved from https://s3.amazonaws.com/amo_hub_content/Association140/files/Standards%20of%20Care%20V7%20-%202011%20WPATH%20(2)(1).pdf

WPATH. (2018b). World Professional Association for Transgender Health Retrieved from http://www.wpath.org/

Younger, M. (2018). Michele Younger. Retrieved from https://www.facebook.com/michele.younger.3

Younger, M. t., & Ravenhurst, O. K. (2011). *Principia Discordia*: CreateSpace Independent Publishing Platform

Appendix C: 12 Minutes

This describes an event which occurred early in my adulthood and was documented and published formally a couple of years later. (G. Booker, 1989) Shortly after starting formal study of Wicca, I semi-accidentally invoked the Egyptian Goddess Isis. This is what she taught me in 12 minutes.

The following is an attempt to describe a special encounter with the Great Lady that I experienced. I realize that much of what I experienced cannot be described adequately in words, but I hope the images I saw and felt may be helpful to others; either by way of recognizing similar events you have seen, or to inspire you to seek Her out.

> I had started studying with a San Diego-based pseudo-Gardnerian coven six weeks before this event. My studies had already included learning a technique to open one's aura (which I am afraid I can't share – you know Gardnerians...), and the daily use of morning and evening "prayers," dedicated to the Lord and Lady, respectively, to help build a close relationship with them. I also had used the evening prayer time occasionally to work on memorizing some of the blessings used for the Full Moon and Great Rite rituals.

I was living in a run-down 28-year-old, 40-foot-long travel trailer, which I had recently moved with a great deal of tribulation, since the pickup I was using could barely move such a beast. I was an aerospace engineer in the Mojave Desert, single, and age 23. My religious upbringing was generic Protestant (Lutheran,

Baptist, Methodist, whatever's handy). Before this event, I was intrigued by, but still unsure of, the existence of a Goddess.

The day of October 30 was a good one for me. I had accomplished a lot of little tasks that I had been meaning to get out of the way; tidying up my home, getting letters written, and so on. And just for the record, I was under the influence of no drugs stronger than caffeine. Though it was slightly after midnight before I started getting ready for bed, I felt good and my mind was free from immediate concern. I sat nude on my bed, facing West, my left leg folded under the right. I paused for a moment to gather my thoughts and center myself. I opened my aura slowly, making sure I felt each part of me respond to the ritual before moving on. Then I started the evening prayer, which goes like this:

Glory be to Thee, Goddess of Light

Let Thy Light shine forth

To Illuminate my Darkness

(already I started to feel a wave of presence flow down my body. I knew something unusual was happening, and recognized the wave as being similar to that I had felt second-hand when someone nearby was doing an Invocation. I decided to flow with it and keep going uninterrupted.)

Grant unto me the Aid of my Higher Self,

That I may Realize the Throne of Thy glory

The Center of the Universe

Of Light, and Life

I paused, noting that my breathing had slowed to a deep, methodical pace. My heart pounded in a slow rhythm, reverently staying out of the way of what was going on so my attention could be elsewhere. I was clearly in a light trance.

I was drawn, almost forced, by the Presence into reciting the Great Rite blessing for the wine. With a shift of emphasis on "this cup," the relevance of the blessing becomes obvious. It goes like this:

Isis, Isis, Holiest of the Holy

Perpetual Comfort of Mankind

Isis Athene, Isis Hathor, Isis Nut

Isis Sothis, Isis Sati

Natural Mother of all things

Mistress of all the Elements

Great Lady, God Mother

Accept this Self I offer thee

Fill this Cup with thy manifested Love !

My trance state had intensified all through the wine blessing; I breathed partially through my mouth to keep enough oxygen supply coming in. I felt my degree of concentration increasing to levels I had never experienced before. My body seemed rigid because any voluntary movement would have required far more energy than I could spare. I was briefly terrified to realize that I had completely lost control of the situation, and utterly vulnerable to Someone I never (?) met before. I was focused on the Presence, waiting to see what She would do. (I deduced it must be Her, in light of the blessing prayer as well as the tone of the whole evening.)

I looked upward a little bit and saw an intense white light flooding around me. As I got accustomed to its strength, I first realized that the amount of energy I was being mentally exposed to was just as much as I could handle. Any more would have been painful or simply overwhelming. I saw eventually that the light seemed to come from a point source, not very far away. Then the purpose of this demonstration hit me: what better way to demonstrate extraordinary power than to show someone exactly as much as they can comprehend, then point out that it only required a tiny fraction of what you can do!

I pondered this a few seconds, then the demonstration continued.

My eyes wandered around the room, with me still in the trance state as before. I focused on a small section of wall, which I knew to consist of a thin layer of plywood covered by many old layers of wallpaper. My eyes (point of view) started to dispassionately look through the wallpaper to the plywood, which I pictured to be full of decade-old dust. Not a pretty sight by most standards. Then it was as if a nonverbal voice was starting to argue with me; she was insisting that the wall was a delightful and dear object. I looked through her eyes and saw the same wall but felt child-like joy at the pretty patterns in the wood grain. She was proud of the wall for the humble task it had done so well. I returned to my engineer self and argued that it was just a musty piece of of plywood, with certain mechanical properties and so on. She returned and repeated her points, looking on the wall with pride and affection. I felt silly trying to argue with her, since much of her argument came from her heart; mine came from Mechanics of Composite Materials. I soon concluded that it was pointless to continue, but thanked her for her perspective.

After a brief rest, my point of view shifted to as if I were sitting in the living room, facing West and a little South, out of the trailer. Outside it looked like daytime, and I looked around the trailer park. A small bird (a sparrow, perhaps) flew by slowly, almost in slow motion. I suddenly felt boundaries between things start dissolving; that is to say, everything still had its own distinct physical boundaries but they seemed to become less important, more receptive to interaction between them. My heartbeat became more intense, and the air around me seemed to become more in tune with my pulse; I could feel the air respond to my heart. And the walls of the trailer started beating in tune with my heart, too. The flapping of the bird's wings left ripples that flowed through the air, through the walls, to my heart. And my pulsing heart responded with its own rhythm being transmitted through the air and wall to the bird, a tiny movement of the bird could be seen with each beat of my heart. A young tree, not too far away, seemed now to have its own very slow but brave beat; and its beat added to the chorus. The air, the walls, the bird, the tree, and me formed a continuous symphony as we all communicated to each other though the patterns of our respective lives. Then I realized that we really are All One, even if we don't recognize it all the time. This interaction goes on all the time, and this was the first time I could experience it in a meaningful way.

And within this symphony I saw through Her eyes. I felt Her quietly savoring the interaction before Her. She looked in turn at the cast of this play with genuine Love and affection. I felt Her own rhythm quietly supporting each of them, without bias or preference. I felt Her Love expressed as tension, for She saw each going its own way, choosing its own path; She did not want harm to come to any of them, yet realized the importance of allowing each its own path. The Love She felt had to be tempered by allowing free will, and this produced the tension. A knot formed in my stomach as I felt the interplay between these forces. I realized that the intensity of the experience was because each of us in the cast of the play is Her child. She and the One are the same. All fear of death melted away as I realized that I am always in the arms of the Mother.

I "returned" to my body again for a brief respite. Soon I noticed the temp-erature in the room seemed to rise a fair bit (10 or 20 degrees). The air around me started to become thicker and almost sticky in consistency, like I was trying to breath a fluid. Surprisingly, I felt no panic at all, as though this were normal. The warm air started to press against my body evenly and lightly from all sides. I looked down a my left arm, half expecting to be covered in warm goo. There was none. I felt a new pulsing sensation in the background, slower than my pulse, deep and very comforting. My mind raced, trying to put together the pieces of this experience, when my head lowered and it finally hit me. I was in a womb !!! Soon, sadly, the sensations left me.

This seemed to be becoming a tour of the Goddess! I wondered briefly if what I was experiencing was related to an Aspect. (An Aspect in the sense I am using it is the ritual invocation of a Deity, generally for oracular purposes in the case of a Full Moon ritual.) Accordingly, I tried to move my lips to see if She had anything to say verbally. I could barely nudge any movement at all, not to mention speak. I dismissed this as a futile effort, especially since there was noone around to hear me if I spoke, anyway.

I thought over my 15-year involvement with Christianity, and felt profusely apologetic for not acknowledging Her before! I kept waiting for Her to chastize me or curse at me for ignoring Her for so long. She never did. As far as I could tell, She was just extremely glad that I had called Her again, and was having a great time giving me this "tour." Her main message seemed to be "Welcome Back!"

I wondered briefly why She was doing this for me. I soon realized that She was just answering my prayer ! (Be careful what you ask for...)

My perspective shifted to as if I were suspended in the middle of the air, several feet off the ground and a hundred feet or so from the trailer, looking at it. Soon my trailer and pickup (parked in front of the trailer) and a huge hemisphere of earth under both of them – at least 50 feet across – seemed to be marked off with a thin line of white light. Then the hemisphere of earth and my home underwent a subtle change. It seemed that they were lifted up a tiny bit to mark them off, and then were left teetering on the head of a pin. A shiver went very slowly down my back as I realized that they were on the brink of being spun around like a top. Or of being tossed in the air. Or of being flipped over like a pancake. Or disappearing entirely. I saw everything I had worked for and taken to be so hard to handle being treated like it could be a toy. At first I was rather surprized by this attitude in light of the previous experience. Then I realized that this was to show a shift in perspective. The message was that there is immense power available to transform things – even things that we may consider insurmountable by our modest standards. Anything is possible.

I returned to my body again. My body started feeling stuffed in the sense of another being taking up part of every cell of my being. It was as if someone slowy "beamed" into the same space as my body. My arms felt full and heavy as this sensation finished filling me up. Oddly enough, when the process was complete, I started feeling very light. As though I were made of air. I looked around me in the bedroom, and felt the boundaries between me and the air become less important again. I thought about this in contrast to my schooling in engineering, which broke things down into distinct catagories so it can be analyzed properly. This beam is loaded elastically. This air flow is inviscid, subsonic, and 2-dimensional. This computer is digital – absence or presence of a signal is all that matters to it. Again I felt the Oneness from before; me and the air and the trailer and the earth are one, breathing together.

And with that thought, She slowly left.

I realized that She had gone. My mind was still racing to try making sense of what had happened and to remember it all. I slowly laid back on the bed. I summoned the strength to lift my head and look at the clock on my nightstand. The entire experience had taken twelve minutes.

Appendix D: Coming out letter to my family

This is the complete text of the letter I sent to my family upon coming out. Vati is my father's nickname (a German affectionate form of 'father'), Paulette is my stepmother, Michael and Anne are my brother and sister-in-law.

Dear Vati, Mom, Paulette, Michael, and Anne,

There have been some big and very surprising changes in my life over the last year or so, and it's time for me to share them with you. I was waiting to see if they were a passing phase, but at this point they are likely to be permanent (that sounds harsh, but I can't find a better word).

To alleviate tension in the universe, I'll get to the big reveal now. This is my coming out letter, but ***not*** *in the sense you probably just thought. Last April I realized I'm transgender.*

I'll try to answer your most likely questions and maybe a few more. I'm putting this in a letter so you have time to digest it before we talk. I assume that Michael and Anne will figure out how and when to tell Jonathan and Timmy, though I realize the former is certainly an adult now.

What does transgender mean? I'm going to summarize some terms because they have been coined fairly recently. Transgender is an umbrella term for people whose gender identity differs from what is typically associated with the sex they were assigned at birth.19 Gender identity is in your head,

---

[19] Yes, I'm enough of an academic to cite sources, even for my family! http://www.glaad.org/transgender/trans101

namely the sex you identify with, in contrast with gender presentation, which is how you present yourself to the outside world as masculine or feminine or androgynous. In this context, 'sex' refers to male, female, or intersexed (somewhere between M and F).

Have I seen a shrink about this? Yes, I'm under medical and psychological care through the Mazzoni Center, a local clinic for LGBT (lesbian/gay/bisexual/transgender) people.

Am I crazy? Yes, but only a little. The diagnostic manuals (DSM IV and V) talk about gender dysphoria or gender identity disorder, and apparently I've been diagnosed with something like that. The good part is that means my ongoing treatment is covered by health insurance. More on treatment later.

How did this come about? I was getting help with dating and developing social skills, in particular focusing on being genuinely myself instead of trying to project the right illusion for my audience. A little light bulb went off that I have a very strong feminine side that desperately wanted to be let out, and incidentally was messing up my social life. At first my mind was reeling and firmly in denial, because I literally never considered this to be possible for me.

Then I checked in with my body, and noticed that it had relaxed enormously and let out a huge sigh of relief. I learned a long time ago from massage therapy classes that the body can't tell a lie; and here my body was clearly telling me that this shocking revelation was true. Later when I had time to reflect, I traced some early signs to as far back as junior high.

What caused this? Nothing, it's just me coming to terms with a persistent feeling of not fitting in with the roles I'm supposed to fulfill. It isn't related to my abuse history, or the diagnosis a while ago of being somewhat intersexed (which was refuted by several doctors), or my birth defect history. I specifically asked my doctor about the first two, and he assured me they weren't relevant. And no, Mom and Vati, it has nothing to do with anything you did or didn't do as parents.

What does this mean? Well my wardrobe has gotten a lot more diverse. Almost all of it is now either unisex or came from the misses' section instead of the men's. But me the person hasn't particularly changed. I just found the right way to express who I am, and our society calls that feminine.

Does that mean I'm cross-dressing? Technically no. No because I identify as a transgender woman now, and therefore wearing women's clothing is only appropriate. But since the outside world can't see inside my head, they see a 50-year-old man in a knit top and probably think that means I'm cross-dressing. It's a matter of perspective.

Is my job in danger? Probably not. Drexel and the City of Philadelphia both have very clear and progressive anti-discrimination policies that include protection for transgender people. I've gotten some amused looks from co-workers, especially several women, but no one has said anything. Gender isn't relevant to my job, and frankly this is a very personal matter which isn't really their business.

Does this mean I'm gay? I still prefer to date women, so the literal answer is 'no,' but since I'm trans that means I'm a transgender lesbian, if you have to put a label on it.

Am I going to get surgery 'down there?' I don't know, that's a huge and very personal decision.

Am I changing my name? Sort of. In a couple of contexts I have started using Jennifer. Why Jennifer? It's always been my favorite girl name. Unfortunately it's also the most common girl name for the 80's and half of the 90's, so it's not a very original choice. Most of the time (including professionally) I still use Glenn.

What do I hope for from you? Love. Acceptance. I know this might take a little while to process (it did for me!) but I know that you want me to be happy, and this is part of that journey. That's the important thing to remember.

Okay, so much for Q&A.

Last November I started hormone therapy. I figured as long as I was identifying and dressing more femininely, I might as well look the part a little better. It felt awkward to look masculine and not identify with it. Hormone therapy means I'm taking one drug to suppress testosterone (T) to the low level typical of women, and periodically giving myself injections of estrogen.

Over the next two years or so, this will result in some feminizing of my body (softer skin, reduced body hair, fat redistribution (away from shoulders and waist, toward boobs and butt), and many others) and reduced strength due to the lack of T. When I cautiously started, I figured I'd watch carefully for negative signs physically or psychologically, and stop right away if there were any. There haven't been. My body has been almost bored in spite of the major change in fundamental hormones, so I'm taking this as a sign that it's something my body wants too.

That's enough for now. I've done a lot of writing both before and since this transition started, and I'm more than happy to share more if you're interested. Just ask.

Love and hugs and stuff,

Glenn

Appendix E: Coming out rebuttals

This Appendix contains the letters I received from two cousins and my brother after coming out. The parts written by them have been paraphrased to avoid intellectual property issues. My responses to them, paragraph by paragraph, are in red. Kathy and Dave are my cousins, both of whom I've barely seen in person in the last 30 years. Michael is my brother.

Dear family,

My transgender 'coming out' letter has certainly evoked a lot of response, and I want to respond to all of you as well as I can. Today is the one year anniversary of coming out to myself, so it's an apt time to pause and reflect on your concerns. I'll also attach the original letter, since I'm not sure if all of you saw it already.

I have received large emails or messages from David, Michael, and Kathy, so I'll address them in chronological order. I'm sharing all of them with everyone to avoid repeating myself too much. I'll just insert my comments in red in the middle of the missives.

I love you all, and truly appreciate your concern for my wellbeing.

Love,

Glenn

[Email from Dave]

Glenn,

We haven't crossed paths in many years, but I had to write you after finding out about the new direction in your life. Please don't consider it condemnation or judgmental.

Hi Dave, thank you for taking the time to compose this, and I appreciate your lack of judgment.

We have both been alive over 50 years. I often wonder how different my life would be if I made other choices. What if I didn't make the mistakes I made? How have they affected my life, education, income, family, or hopes and dreams? Even if I had a crystal ball I probably would have just traded one set of circumstances for another.

It's easy to try to second-guess our choices, and certainly some of them would have resulted in very different life outcomes. Even very poor choices at the time (like my marriage) still had very good consequences in some respects, so too much speculating on what we should have done is akin to guessing how many angels can dance on the head of a pin.

Age has taught me how fleeting life is and how poorly I understand it. Sometimes life is peaceful, and other times are stormy. My wife of 25 years nearly died a few years ago, and the life-altering scars it left still keep her from enjoying daily life. She questions whether the experience was worth the effort.

As we approach (?) middle age we've had a lot of time to go through the good the bad and the ugly. I certainly know that some scars stay with us longer than others, but we don't have to let them define us either.

Years ago I chose to have a family and have raised two boys to value education and become productive and fruitful. Staying in a position of strength in spite of being surrounded by a society full of alcohol, drugs, sex, and depravity. The fast pace of society and liberal media have removed the taboo from many limits and boundaries. Just because something is possible, should you?

Always a good question. In some ways our society is becoming more tolerant of minority views, and that's causing a backlash from those who don't want to believe that those perspectives are right or worthy of respect. We still have a lot of limits and boundaries, however; compared to some cultures we are very regimented. Imagine trying to explain to someone from the middle of Africa what our rules are for what clothes you're allowed to wear or what kinds of humor are allowed in different circumstances.

If I won the lottery , I'd love to enjoy the wild life, but I know it's only a dream. Just because you can try to reach your desires, it can't be achieved. You lack the genes and life experience of being raised a woman. Women are sensual, sexual beings that are desired and revered. They are wired differently than we are. You may want this and imitate their behavior, being born male you can't.

Agreed, having been raised male, there is a wealth of female experiences I will never know.

Women's experiences, expectations, and social norms are very different from men's. Their dreams and world view have been shaped from birth. They nurture, help, and mother. Men under stress will weep for their mother. An adopted child will long for their birth mother, no matter how good their adopted mother is. You will never understand what it is to be a woman. No amount of money can change that.

I'm not sure that you're any more qualified than I am to speculate on what "being a woman is truly about." I'd bet there's more than one answer.

Your path has had many challenges that mine hasn't, and I don't pretend to understand what you've been through. You think this is the answer, but it isn't, it will only cause more heartache. Doing this will isolate you from the women you wish to be your peers, and from friends, family, and colleagues. People who approve of what you're doing also have deep scars, because they were damaged by those who were supposed to love them.

It sounds like you're trying to connect this to my tumultuous past. I don't think there's a connection between them. I have spent years healing the scars of the past, and refuse to let them define me as a person. That took a major shift in perspective, to see myself as a whole person and not as a cripple.

I don't think this will isolate me from the people I want to associate with. I've already seen a couple of examples of transgender people within my circle of friends who lead perfectly happy lives and have found wonderful partners. My hope is that by being strong enough to express myself honestly, I'll attract someone who finds that person fantastic.

I think most people have had some challenges in their lives, and we're naturally drawn to people who understand our history and maybe have had some common elements in their lives. Our friends understand us. That doesn't mean we were all horribly damaged in some way, it just means that stuff happened and we dealt with it.

What you do privately is your business, but when your public life is affected your behavior is unhealthy and destructive. What is loose in your mind to bring about this decision? Many people have obsessions and demons, but this choice is not your birthright. That was decided at conception. This will only lead you to a bitter harvest.

I disagree, this isn't destructive, although it appears to be wreaking havoc with some people's worldviews.

Am I crazy? I'm guessing you didn't see the actual coming out letter, but yes, technically that could be true. The American Psychiatric Association recognizes Gender Identity Disorder. With regard to putting it "back in check," there is no cure for it. As much as it would appease some people, the only 'fix' would be to pretend that there isn't a pink elephant in the middle of the room, but that won't make the pink elephant go away.

Your birthright and conception points hint at biological determinism, the belief that biology determines sex (male/female/other) and gender (what defines masculine or feminine). That simply isn't true; gender is completely based on culture, and hence changes as our society changes. Sex is somewhat determined biologically, but the categories used and what constitutes them are still cultural. You want there to be absolutes where they don't exist.

Because of this you will be shunned by conservatives and even liberals because it violates natural order. You will probably lose what you have worked a lifetime to achieve. You will be considered a sexual deviant and may be prosecuted as a sexual predator. Your status among peers and professionally will be lose. Whoever has been your counselor has been ineffective and you should find someone else. Altering yourself for a lover is one thing, but altering your appearance to a women is out of bounds. It is not the master plan for your life regardless of how you feel. Consider moving closer to your family for support. Reconsider what direction and behavior led you to this.

I've been shunned by conservatives my whole life, that isn't new! And yes, even among liberals there are some who will judge me harshly. I'm not responsible for educating or enlightening those who don't understand. That's not my problem, that's theirs.

Sexual predator, offender, or deviant? I'm none of those. Okay, maybe deviant depending on one's definition of it. Some pretty tame things by my standards could be horribly deviant by yours. But more to the point, sexual preference is a completely separate issue from gender and sex, even though some people might think otherwise.

My position at Drexel should be safe – both Drexel and the City of Philadelphia have very strict laws protecting diversity, and explicitly protect transgender people from discrimination. That's one of the advantages of being in a city that's 95% Democrat. J

Yes, it's possible I could be assaulted for my fashion choices. Transgender women in particular have an even higher rate of assault and murder than homosexuals. I've already been the target of street harassment on several occasions, and I just hold my head high and keep walking. Even in this hotbed of rampant liberalism, there is still a lot of ignorance and bigotry. I can't fix that, just be prepared in case I need to defend myself.

> Which brings me to a key point. I knew the risks of what I'm doing before I started. I knew it's at least theoretically possible lose my family, my friends, my job, and maybe even my life. Since I'm not exactly the village idiot, doesn't that tell you something about how incredibly important this has to be to me?

I don't have any answers, and have tried to be more tolerant of other lifestyle choices. Please reconsider this decision before it ruins your life's work by chasing a dream that is outside your birthright. What you feel can't be attained. At our age, this decision seems creepy and disturbing. You told Kathy you don't want to live a lie, but now you are telling a new lie, even if you feel it's the truth.

Thank you Dave, I appreciate your deep concern for my wellbeing. Believe me, I've considered and reconsidered this dozens of times. My life's work is unaffected – I still have three engineering degrees and a solid history of work in the aerospace industry and academia. This doesn't take anything away from that.

I know that you and Kathy (I still want to call her Kathleen!) and others disagree emphatically with this decision, but I have to make the best choices I can in the moment. Right or wrong, brave or foolish, I have to make the call and live with the consequences just like everyone else.

Your cousin,

dave

[Letter from Michael]

Glenn,

I know you want unconditional love and support, but your family's love is conflicted when you're making a bad decision. When you got married, it was clear your wife was a screaming mess and I nearly walked out, but I stayed out of respect for your wishes. Not sure if that was the right choice.

Probably a good call from my point of view; I was already fairly stressed at that point, and might have melted into a puddle.)

I understand that most of my family thinks I'm making a horrible decision. I'm not sure if that's due to horror at the thought of a transsexual in the family tree, or because I have such a weak history for major decisions (as you noted and I certainly won't argue that point), or both.

You posted the following on Facebook: *"My mom took it well, my brother didn't say much, but my dad is having a rough time. I can see how it could be surprising, to say the least. But he's strong and loves me, so he'll come around before long."*

Point by point:

- Mom is trying to be supportive, but is freaking out. We spoke at length a couple of days ago, and she's quite clear she disagrees with this decision.
- I wanted to do research before saying anything. I've been a little surprised by your very academic approach to this. While most of it seems to revolve around indirect concern for my safety, it feels very distant.

- Our father is having a hard time. I was surprised he came out there to visit. He's getting a lot of support from Paulette. He's not likely to ever come around. No, I don't think he'll ever change his view, and I wouldn't expect him to. His visit went really well I though, and I believe that by seeing me he realizes that I'm still 99% the same person he's always loved.

I want to help you understand our parents' view. Per Jonathan Haidt, liberals don't understand conservatives when it comes to morality. See also his book The Righteous Mind.

Hmm, interesting. Now I'm worried how many 'immoral psychologists' are out there.

Per Charles Krauthammer, conservatives view liberals as wrong, whereas liberals view conservatives as bad. Framing this as 'you must agree with me if you love me' will create a dichotomy that will throw away your family as morally defective bigots. I don't want to do that.

Agreed, I'm not trying to force anyone into a binary decision; that would be horribly ironic and terribly ineffective.

Our parents think gender is determined at birth by genetics and genitals. Intersex conditions are a corruption, but not meaningful. Both genders have masculine and feminine traits but still match social stereotypes. A man can't become a woman, and vice versa. To think otherwise is as crazy as a human becoming a dolphin.

[Do you really think that men and women are THAT different?]

[Illustration from the right-wing social conservatives at South Park.]

Changing fundamental beliefs is difficult.

[Agreed.]

I want to explain our disagreement with a similar example, but don't think I'm equating transsexuality with homosexuality.

> Illustrative aside: Conversion Therapy
>
> Imagine a man is attracted to other men. He doesn't want to feel that way, and seeks out a therapist to fix him and make him straight. He finds the APA abhors such therapies and it's illegal to do so in California. He is confused because he would be happier as a straight man, but can't get the therapy he desires.

The main argument against Conversion Therapy is that one's sexual preference can't be changed. If you try to force an unnatural change, you'll just get a miserable pretend heterosexual. The therapist should instead help them accept their same-sex attraction.

The analogy to transsexuals is that transitioning won't make someone a different gender, just living a lie like the pretend heterosexual.

Another view of this analogy is that pretending to be cisgendered when one isn't is just as flawed as pretending you're straight when you're gay.

You want your family to accept who you are, but our father will always see you as Glenn, and I think our mom feels the same way.

I want to explain why I'm doing this so they're prepared when they see changes in my wardrobe, or posts on Facebook that otherwise would make no sense. No, I don't expect our parents to change their views or ever call me anything other than Glenn (or Grub or my #2 son).

As for my own opinion, I've taught trans issues for medical ethics, and one of my students came out as FTM. Most research studies have small sample sizes and few people complete them. Anecdotal evidence supports whichever view you support. The long-term data seems poor.

Transsexuals are quite rare (something like one person in 10,000 to 20,000), so collecting a meaningful amount of data isn't easy, especially with the social stigma many attach to it.

The suicide rate for the military was close to the civilian rate, and is now about double that. For transsexuals, estimates are in the 30-60% range, far higher than the general population.

The numbers I've seen for suicide rate are more like 2%; still far higher than the general population, but nowhere near your range. For the record, I have no plans of adding myself to that statistic.

If a military recruiter said joining the military made you happier, the higher suicide rate might make you question their logic. Similarly the transgender suicide rate might imply it doesn't make you happier. Though the real problem could be bigotry and social cruelty.

[Yes, I was about to go there.]

Someone transitioning MTF late in life will face cruelty, just like someone dressing as a dolphin will be treated badly.

[Now the next time I see you I'll expect you to throw raw mackerel at me.]

That's how things are now. We can't choose between reality and a utopia which doesn't exist.

True, but we can choose to live in a part of the world where we're more likely to be accepted, one that's closer to our ideal.

The bottom line is: why do you think you'll be more successful at being female than male?

That depends on how you measure success, doesn't it? I think of it in terms of being happy with who I am, how open and relaxed I can be among my friends, how honestly I can do things that make me happy, those things are successful for me, and yes, I think I'll be much happier as a female than I've been as a male.

I've wasted a lot of my life trying to fulfill expectations that are foreign to me. I've put on a lot of masks that I thought were what people wanted to see. All that got me was relationships with women who liked the masks, but not me.

I won't tell you to change your mind or what to do. I want to give you realistic expectations and hope you don't demonize people who believe in the gender binary. It's absurd to think people will support you in doing something they view as self-destructive.

I don't know what "something that's possible" means in concrete terms. I'm not trying to demonize anyone. "My" anthropology of gender isn't just mine, it's also shared by a lot of anthropologists and sociologists and various other social scientists. It's not something I just made up in my spare time.

As for "polite and civil" – well, I wouldn't call all of it that.

Well, anyhow, you're my brother and I love you.

I love you too.

Michael

[Email from Kathy]

Glenn,

This woman thinks you have never had female tendencies, unless you were putting on an act. You don't act or look like a woman, and you'd be a really ugly one. We all have male and female traits; I'm a bit of a tomboy and never liked dresses. But I've never considered becoming a man. I attribute my tomboy traits to my Viking heritage. My daughter is very girly; she can hunt and fish but it isn't a major focus of her life.

Hi Kathy!

Of course you're quite happy in your role as a woman, you're cisgendered (gender normal) just like the vast majority of people. And Katee is much more girly and that's wonderful too. I love seeing bits of her life on Facebook; she seems to be a wonderful young lady.

We all have male and female traits. I am still completely a woman. You don't have female traits at any level. If you did, they would have emerged at puberty. If your marriage affected your understanding of what women are, you need counseling to work through that and move on. Trying to become a woman won't solve your problems, make you happy, or fix your sex life.

As I mentioned in Michael's letter, you saw what I was allowed to show. It took many years and a massive shitload of courage to set aside the masks.

No, my marriage had nothing to do with this. She believed very strongly in the gender binary, so she probably kept this from emerging for at least 15 years.

Your parents and the rest of your extended family will never accept this. Your boss will say it's okay because the Constitution requires it. If any student complains about you being a sexual deviant you will lose your job, and the real world won't touch you. Academia is more forgiving of thinking outside of the box.

As mentioned earlier, I don't expect my parents or anyone else to change their mind. I'm not trying to convert anyone here, just inform.

I think it was the relative safety of academia and being in a liberal town (nominally) that helped me finally feel safe enough to realize this. I'm counting on that forgiving nature of academia to keep my job.

Michael was on the money by pointing out you won't be more successful as a woman than as a man. You don't have what it takes to be a woman. Not just physically, but thoughts, analysis, and emotions. You can't think like a woman. If you think hormone therapy will fix that you are mistaken. You have missed the essence of being a woman.

Interesting point – how do you know how a man thinks? And how does a woman think, in your opinion? Is there only one answer for each of those questions? I bet you and Katee think a lot differently from each other in many ways.

You will be a freak of nature, which will lead to abuse. You can't leave academia, and will be discriminated against regardless of the laws. You haven't thought this through and should seek counseling to recover from your marriage.

I've always been perceived as a freak of nature, that's nothing new.

I don't have plans to leave academia; I like the flexibility of schedule and ever-changing technology. Could I still be discriminated against? Sure, it's possible. I've dealt with worse.

I've seen a couple of very well qualified counselors who specialize in abuse and gender issues. They agree that I'm over my ex-wife, and that I am transgender.

We won't stop loving and caring for you, but this is a mistake. Social media approval means nothing. Stop the self-pity and grow up.

Thank you, I love you too and I appreciate your concern.

While some of my friends on Fb are distant acquaintances, most of the four dozen signs of support were people from every facet of my life – sports friends, theater friends, dance friends, and several colleagues from my office. My support network is very real, not a fantasy.

kma

Appendix F: Drugs and Foods to Avoid Pre-surgery

Tables F-1 to F-6 show the drugs and foods to avoid before surgery. Just because it's not on this list does not mean that it is safe to take while preparing for surgery.

4-way cold tabs	Carisoprodol Compound	Kaodene	Phenaphen/ Codeine #3
5-Aminosalicylic Acid	Cataflam	Lanorinal	Pink Bismuth
Acetylsalicylic acid	Cheracol	Lodine	Piroxicam
Actron	Choline Magnesium	Lortab ASA	Propoxyphene Compound products
Adprin-B products	Choline Salicylate	Magan	Robaxisal
Aleve	Cope	Magnaprin products	Rowasa
Alka-Seltzer products	Coricidin	Magnesium Salicylate	Roxeprin
Amigesic Argesic-SA	Cortisone Medications	Magsal	Saleto products
Anacin products	Damason-P	Marnal	Salflex
Anexsia w/ Codeine	Darvon Compound-65	Marthritic	Salicylate products

(continued)			
Arthra-G	Darvon/ASA	Mefenamic Acid	Salsalate
Arthriten products	Diclofenac	Meprobamate	Salsitab
Arthritis Foundation products	Dipenturn	Mesalamine	Scot-Tussin Original 5-Action
Arthritis Pain Formula	Disalcid	Methocarbamol	Sine-off
Arthritis Strength BC Powder	Doan's products	Micrainin	Sinutab
Arthropan	Dolobid	Mobidin	Sodium Salicylate
ASA	Dristran	Mobigesic	Sodol Compound
Asacol	Duragesic	Momentum	Soma Compound
Asciptin products	Easprin	Mono-Gesic	St. Joseph Aspirin
Aspergum	Ecotrin products	Motrin products	Sulfasalazine
Asprimox products	Empirin products	Naprelan	Supac
Axotal	Equagesic	Naproxen	Suprax

(continued)			
Azdone	Etodolac	Night-Time Effervescent Cold	Synalgos-DC
Azulfidine products	Excedrin products	Norgesic products	Talwin
B-A-C	Florgen PF	Norwich products	Triaminicin
Backache Maximum Strength Relief	Fiorinal products	Olsalazine	Tricosal
Bayer products	Flurbiprofen	Orphengesic products	Trilisate
BC Powder	Gelpirin	Orudis products	Trisalicylate
Bismatrol products	Genprin	Oxycodonc	Tussanil DH
Buffered Aspirin	Gensan	Pabalate products	Tussirex products
Bufferin products	Goody's Extra Strength Headache Powders	P-A-C	Ursinus-Inlay
Buffetts 11	Halfprin products	Pain Reliever Tabs	Vanquish
Buffex	IBU	Panasal	Wesprin
Butalbital/ASA/ Caff	Ibuprohm	Pentasa	Willow Bark products

(continued)			
Butalbital Compound	Indomethacin products	Pepto-Bismol	Zorprin
Cama Arthritis Pain Reliever	Isollyl Improved	Percodan products	

Table F-1. Aspirin Medications to Avoid: Affect blood clotting

Acular (opthalmic)	Haltran	Nabumetone	Rhinocaps
Advil products	Ibuprin	Nalfon products	Sine-Aid products
Anaprox products	Ibuprofen	Naprosyn products	Sulindac
Ansaid	Indochron E-R	Naprox X	Suprofen
Clinoril	Indocin products	Nuprin	Tolectin products
Daypro	Ketoprofen	Ocufen (opthalmic)	Tolmetin
Dimetapp Sinus	Ketorolac	Oruvail	Toradol
Dristan Sinus	Meclofenamate	Oxaprozin	Voltaren
Feldene	Meclomen	Ponstel	
Fenoprofen	Menadol	Profenal	
Genpril	Midol products	Relafen	

Table F-2. Ibuprofen Medications to Avoid: Affect blood clotting

Amigesic (salsalate)	Pepto-Bismol (bismuth subsalicylate)	Blackberries	Grapes
Disalcid (salsalate)	Salflex (salsalate)	Boysenberries	Pickles
Doan's (magnesium salicylate)	Salsalate	Cherries	Prunes
Dolobid (diflunisal)	Salsitab (salsalate)	Chinese Black Beans	Raspberries
Magsal	Trilisate (choline salicylate + magnesium salicylate)	Cucumbers	Strawberries
Mobigesic	Almonds	Currants	Tomatoes
Pabalate	Apples	Garlic	Wine
Pamprin (Maximum Pain Relief)	Apricots	Ginger	

Table F-3. Salicylate medications, food and beverages to avoid: Affect blood clotting

Avoid ALL Diet Aids - Over-the-counter & Herbal: Intensify anesthesia, serious cardiovascular effects			
Tricyclic Antidepressants to Avoid: Intensify anesthesia, cardiovascular effects			
Adapin	Desipramine	Limbitrol products	Protriptyline
Amitriptyline	Doxepin	Ludiomil	Sinequan
Amoxapine	Elavil	Maprotiline	Surmontil
Anafranil	Endep	Norpramin	Tofranil
Asendin	Etrafon products	Nortriptyline	Triavil
Aventyl	Imipramine	Pamelor	Trimipramine
Clomipramine	Janimine	Pertofrane	Vivactil

Table F-4. Diet Aids and Tricyclic Antidepressants to Avoid

4-way w/ Codeine	Dicumerol	Miradon	Stelazine
A.C.A.	Dipyridamole	Opasal	Sulfinpyrazone
A-A Compound	Doxycycline	Pan-PAC	Tenuate
Accutrim	Emagrin	Pentoxyfylline	Tenuate Dospan
Actifed	Enoxaparin injection	Persantine	Thorazine
Anexsia	Flagyl	Phenylpro-panolamine	Ticlid
Anisindione	Fragmin injection	Prednisone	Ticlopidine
Anturane	Furadantin	Protamine	Trental
Arthritis Bufferin	Garlic	Pyrroxate	Ursinus
BC Tablets	Heparin	Ru-Tuss	Virbamycin
Children's Advil	Hydrocortisone	Salatin	Vitamin E
Clinoril C	Isollyl	Sinex	Warfarin
Contac	Lovenox injection	Sofarin	
Coumadin	Macrodantin	Soltice	
Dalteparin Injection	Mellaril	Sparine	

Table F-5. Other medication to avoid: Affect blood clotting.

"The natural Viagra"	Dandelion root	Gmena	Melatonin
Ackee fruit	Devil's club	Goldenseal	Muwort
Alfalfa	Dong Quai root	Gotu Kola	Nem seed oil
Aloe	Echinacea	Grape seed	Onions
Argimony	Ephedra	Guarana	Papaya
Barley	Eucalyptus	Guayusa	Periwinkle
Bilberry	Fenugreek seeds	Hawthorn	Selenium
Bitter melon	Feverfew	Horse Chestnut	St. John's Wort
Burdock root	Fo-ti	Juniper	Valerian/ Valerian Root
Carrot oil	Garlic	Kava Kava	Vitamin E
Cayenne	Ginger	Lavender	Willow Bark
Chamomile	Gingko	Lemon verbena	Yellow root
Chromium	Gingko biloba	Licorice root	Yohimbe
Coriander	Ginseng	Ma Huang	

Table F-6. Vitamins and Herbs to Avoid: Affect blood clotting, blood sugar, increase or decrease the strength of anesthesia, rapid heartbeat, high blood pressure, liver damage.

Appendix G: The Federalist letter

This letter was published by The Federalist, written by my brother. (M. Booker, 2017)

Why I Don't Use Female Pronouns For My Transgender Brother

The demand that I refer to my sibling using a female pronoun is nothing less than thought policing. It is a demand that I assert what I do not believe.

By Michael Booker

September 11, 2017

Until I was in college, I went by *Mike*. When I found myself in a social circle that included two Mikes, I opted for *Michael* just to minimize confusion. Since then, the only person who still calls me *Mike* is my mother. (I did have a supervisor back in the '80s who called me *Mark* for a year, but she was otherwise quite kind to me, so I took it in stride.)

It's a simple matter of common courtesy to call someone by whatever name he or she chooses. Transgender activists have tried to latch on to this simple social courtesy to insist on the use of specific preferred pronouns, which they argue is no more than an extension of that common courtesy. The pushback on this has largely been on the profusion of novel potential identifiers: he/his, she/hers, they/theirs, xe/xirs, ze/hirs, ei/eirs...the list is really endless, with individuals generating new pronouns almost daily.

Some English Pronouns Convey Gender

But the complaints about the profusion of pronouns miss a far more important point of language that seems to have slipped under the radar, something that makes this far more than a matter of courtesy. It has to do with the nature of second-person and third-person pronouns in English.

When I talk to *you*, I can do so without a gendered pronoun. *You* is the same no matter who, or what, I'm talking to. I can call my misbehaving car "You old pile of garbage" without making my car a *he* or a *she*. Likewise, I can speak to a male, female, or non-binary individual with the same second-person pronoun.

It's the third-person pronoun in English that conveys gender (and here I'm so happy to be able to use the word *gender* in its appropriately technical and linguistic sense). I can use *he*, *she*, or *it* as singular pronouns, and each conveys information about the object I'm referring to. There are odd circumstances when I'd use a third-person pronoun in the presence of someone who is in the room with me, but it never feels polite. In the majority of cases, I am taking about a person or thing not present.

This is where preferred pronouns become critically intrusive. A courteous exchange about names might go like this: "Hi, my name is Richard, but I go by Dick." "Hi, Dick, pleased to meet you." What transgender activists are demanding manifests as follows: "Hi, I'm Scharr. I identify as gender non-conforming. When you talk about me to someone else, I want you to identify me as Xe, because that will indicate that you accept my identity as a non-binary individual."

This Is a Demand to Affirm a Falsehood

This isn't just an abstraction for me. At the age of 50, my brother informed our family that he identified as female. Where previously *Glenn*, he had his name legally changed to *Jennifer*. My father doesn't accept that his son is now his daughter, and still calls him *Glenn* and *he*. My mother tries to be more accommodating, but when we speak together about *Glenn*, she tries to say *Jennifer* and *she*. But she has trouble keeping that language, as it were, straight.

It's obvious from my use of language that I'm guilty of the two great sins of transphobia and deadnaming (deadnaming is the practice of calling a trans individual by his or her birth name). Or rather, I don't believe it to be factually correct that my brother is now female, despite his use of artificial hormones and a legal name change. To call my sibling *she* is to concede a reality that I do not believe to be the case.

I believe that the human animal has only two sexes because it has two kinds of gamete-producers. Give me a third human gamete, and I'll entertain the possibility of there being a third sex.

I understand that there are a variety of rare medical conditions that produce intersex individuals, and that fact has no bearing on the number of actual sexes. I do not believe that drugs or surgery can make a male into a female or a female into a male. Just a few years ago, that would have been simple science. Today it makes me a moral monster.

I do believe it's common that people feel uncomfortable in their own skins and that phenomenally few biological males adhere 100 percent to all male cultural stereotypes or biological females adhere 100 percent to all female cultural stereotypes. And that's okay. Back in the 1974 there was a surreal video called "Free to Be...You and Me," narrated by Marlo Thomas and Alan Alda, which argued the then-enlightened view that men could have traditionally female interests and that women didn't have to be all girl-girly if they didn't want to be.

A man who likes to cook is a man who likes to cook, not a woman. A woman who enjoys football is a woman who enjoys football, not a man. Now we're asking masculine girls and feminine boys if they aren't really trapped in the wrong bodies. Gender dysphoria has moved from being a mental illness to being a declaration of authenticity.

The demand that I refer to my sibling using a female pronoun is nothing less than thought policing. It is a demand that I assert what I do not believe, or at least a demand that I dare not evidence dissent from a particular pseudo-scientific understanding of human nature. Asking me to be polite is not the same thing as asking me to lie, or worse, to accept a lie as truth.

And that's no accident. That's the whole point of the pronoun games.

Michael Booker has a doctorate in philosophy and retired from the Army Reserve at the rank of lieutenant colonel. He has been married for 30 years, has two amazing sons, and is currently a low-level administrator in academia.

From http://thefederalist.com/2017/09/11/dont-use-female-pronouns-transgender-brother/

The 1677 comments (as of 12/19/2017) include:

Pinko of the Grange • 3 months ago

How cool Mike just came out as a pompous jerk.

Congratulations Mike.

Your parents must be so proud.

(of course we know your pops is.)

You are going to lose yous sibling over some words. Be honest you don't love them, you think you, and your words, are more important then they are and that is the height of hubris. Words are more important to you then family...that is just #FrickinSad

And

Marita • 3 months ago

I'd be surprised if Jennifer didn't cut off contact with Michael and most of her family besides her mom. No one needs that kind of abuse in their lives.

CPSIA information can be obtained
at www.ICGtesting.com
Printed in the USA
LVHW082323151219
640590LV00004B/16/P